Edith Wharton's
The House of Mirth

GW00692331

Edith Wharton's *The House of Mirth* (1905) is a sharp and satirical, but also sensitive and tragic analysis of a young, single woman trying to find her place in a materialistic and unforgiving society. *The House of Mirth* offers a fascinating insight into the culture of the time and, as suggested by the success of recent film adaptations, it is also an enduring tale of love, ambition and social pressures still relevant today.

Including a selection of illustrations from the original magazine publication, which offers a unique insight to what the contemporary reader would have seen, this volume also provides:

- an accessible introduction to the text and contexts of *The House of Mirth*
- a critical history, surveying the many interpretations of the text from publication to the present
- a selection of new critical essays on *The House of Mirth*, by Edith Thornton, Katherine Joslin, Janet Beer, Elizabeth Nolan, Kathy Fedorko and Pamela Knights, providing a range of perspectives on the novel and extending the coverage of key critical approaches identified in the survey section
- cross-references between sections of the guide, in order to suggest links between texts, contexts and criticism
- suggestions for further reading.

Part of the *Routledge Guides to Literature* series, this volume is essential reading for all those beginning detailed study of *The House of Mirth* and seeking not only a guide to the novel, but a way through the wealth of contextual and critical material that surrounds Wharton's text.

Janet Beer is Vice Chancellor of Oxford Brookes University. She has published widely on North American women's writing, especially Edith Wharton and Kate Chopin.

Pamela Knights is Senior Lecturer at the Department of English Studies, Durham University. She is interested in American fiction, especially Edith Wharton, women's literary culture and children's literature, and has published on all of these subjects.

Elizabeth Nolan is a lecturer at the Department of English, Manchester Metropolitan University. She has published in the area of nineteenth and twentieth century American literature and culture, and women's writing.

Routledge Guides to Literature

Editorial Advisory Board: Richard Bradford (University of Ulster at Coleraine), Shirley Chew (University of Leeds), Mick Gidley (University of Leeds), Jan Jedrzejewski (University of Ulster at Coleraine), Ed Larrissy (University of Leeds), Duncan Wu (St. Catherine's College, University of Oxford)

Routledge Guides to Literature offer clear introductions to the most widely studied authors and texts.

Each book engages with texts, contexts and criticism, highlighting the range of critical views and contextual factors that need to be taken into consideration in advanced studies of literary works. The series encourages informed but independent readings of texts by ranging as widely as possible across the contextual and critical issues relevant to the works examined, rather than presenting a single interpretation. Alongside general guides to texts and authors, the series includes 'Sourcebooks', which allow access to reprinted contextual and critical materials as well as annotated extracts of primary text.

Already available:*

Geoffrey Chaucer by Gillian Rudd
Ben Jonson by James Loxley
William Shakespeare's The Merchant of Venice: A Sourcebook edited by
   S. P. Cerasano
William Shakespeare's King Lear: A Sourcebook edited by Grace Ioppolo
William Shakespeare's Othello: A Sourcebook edited by Andrew Hadfield
William Shakespeare's Macbeth: A Sourcebook edited by Alexander Leggatt
William Shakespeare's Hamlet: A Sourcebook edited by Sean McEvoy
John Milton by Richard Bradford
John Milton's Paradise Lost: A Sourcebook edited by Margaret Kean
Alexander Pope by Paul Baines
Mary Wollstonecraft's A Vindication of the Rights of Woman: A Sourcebook
   edited by Adriana Craciun
Jonathan Swift's Gulliver's Travels: A Sourcebook edited by Roger D. Lund
Jane Austen by Robert P. Irvine
Jane Austen's Emma: A Sourcebook edited by Paula Byrne
Jane Austen's Pride and Prejudice: A Sourcebook edited by Robert Morrison
Byron, by Caroline Franklin
Mary Shelley's Frankenstein: A Sourcebook edited by Timothy Morton
The Poems of John Keats: A Sourcebook edited by John Strachan
The Poems of Gerard Manley Hopkins: A Sourcebook Edited by Alice Jenkins
Charles Dickens's David Copperfield: A Sourcebook edited by Richard J. Dunn
Charles Dickens's Bleak House: A Sourcebook edited by Janice M. Allan

---

* Some titles in this series were first published in the Routledge Literary Sourcebooks series, edited by Duncan Wu, or the Complete Critical Guide to Literature series, edited by Jan Jedrzejewski and Richard Bradford.

Edith Wharton's
The House of Mirth

*Janet Beer, Pamela Knights and
Elizabeth Nolan*

Routledge
Taylor & Francis Group

LONDON AND NEW YORK

First published 2007
by Routledge
2 Park Square, Milton Park, Abingdon, Oxon OX14 4RN

Simultaneously published in the USA and Canada
by Routledge
711 Third Ave, New York, NY 10017

Routledge is an imprint of the Taylor & Francis Group, an informa business

© 2007 Janet Beer, Pamela Knights and Elizabeth Nolan

Typeset in Sabon and Gill Sans by
RefineCatch Limited, Bungay, Suffolk

British Library Cataloguing in Publication Data
A catalogue record for this book is available from the British Library

Library of Congress Cataloging in Publication Data
A catalog record for this book has been requested

ISBN 13: 978–0–415–35009–9 (hbk)
ISBN 13: 978–0–415–35010–5 (pbk)
ISBN 13: 978–0–203–31164–6 (ebk)

Contents

Illustrations

Acknowledgements

We are grateful to the following.

Broadview Press for permission to quote from *The House of Mirth*, edited by Janet Beer and Elizabeth Nolan (Peterborough, Ontario: Broadview, 2005).

The Watkins Loomis Agency for permission to quote from Edith Wharton's manuscript notebook, held in the Edith Wharton Collection, Yale Collection of American Literature, Beinecke Rare Books and Manuscripts Library.

The British Library Newspaper Library, Collingdale and the Rare Books and Music Library, St Pancras; and the Literary and Philosophical Society of Newcastle-upon-Tyne.

Professor Julie Olin-Ammentorp, Marist College, Poughkeepsie, for enabling us to launch our essays at the centenary conference of *The House of Mirth* in June 2005.

Professor Kathy Fedorko, Middlesex County College; Professor Katherine Joslin, Western Michigan University; and Professor Edith Thornton, University of Wisconsin.

Our editor, Polly Dodson, and Christopher Gair, University of Birmingham, and our two other, anonymous, readers for their helpful comments on our draft manuscript.

Teresa Egan, for space and privacy.

Notes and references

Primary text

Unless otherwise stated, all references to the primary text are taken from *The House of Mirth*, Edith Wharton (Ontario: Broadview Press, 2005). The initial reference in each part will contain full bibliographic details and all subsequent references will be in parentheses in the body of the text, stating the book number, chapter number and page number, e.g., (I: ii, 70).

Secondary text

References to any secondary material can be found in the footnotes. The first reference will contain full bibliographic details, and each subsequent reference to the same text will contain the author's surname, title and page number.

Footnotes

All footnotes that are not by the author of this volume will identify the source in square brackets, e.g., [Baldwin's note].

Cross-referencing

Cross-referencing between sections is a feature of each volume in the Routledge Guides to Literature series. Cross-references appear in brackets and include section titles as well as the relevant page numbers in bold type, e.g., (see Texts and contexts, pp. 14–15).

Introduction

The House of Mirth tells the story of Lily Bart, glamorous, single, hanging on by her slender pink fingernails to New York high society, and desperate for a rich husband to secure her place in the Manhattan social elite. Lily has expensive tastes; she likes to buy clothes and jewellery and give generously to fashionable good causes, but she also likes to gamble – a dangerous pastime for an unmarried, impecunious twenty-nine year-old. Lily is fastidious in her habits; she not only wants a rich man, she wants one who is intellectually and physically her equal. Various suitors are rich enough, but they are too old, too unattractive or simply boring. In apparently playing fast and loose with their affections, however, Lily's image becomes tarnished, especially when she is seen to accept the attentions of the husband of her best friend. For a woman dependent upon her friends' favours, this proves fatal, and her consequent slide from the peak of society into the obscurity of the New York streets is charted by Wharton in a novel which caused a sensation. 'For the first time', the publisher proclaimed, 'the veil has been lifted from New York Society',[1] a description which Edith Wharton herself found crass, but which nevertheless summed up the way in which the novel was received by the American reading public. Readers had avidly followed Lily's progress in the popular *Scribner's Magazine*, which serialized the novel in monthly parts from January to November 1905. Published as a book on 14 October 1905, *The House of Mirth* broke all Scribner's previous records. Eclipsing such rival best-sellers as Thomas Dixon's racist polemic *The Clansman: A Historical Romance of the Ku Klux Klan* and Alice Hegan Rice's book for children, *Sandy*, Wharton's novel remained at the top of the lists well into 1906.

Edith Wharton herself was a member of New York's high society. She was born into an old New York family and her mother was reputed to be *the* Mrs Jones with whom all wanted to keep up. Unlike most of the members of aristocratic New York, Edith Wharton was a serious reader and intellectual. Her interests embraced European and American literary traditions; she spoke French, German and Italian fluently and made annotations in those languages in her books. She drew on her reading to frame her critique of twentieth-century America. In *The House of Mirth*, her subject matter is modernity: the fracturing of the self and of society.

---

1   R. W. B. Lewis, *Edith Wharton*, London: Constable, 1975, p. 151.

In her first novel, *The Valley of Decision*, Wharton had written of the Italian eighteenth century, a time and location distant from her own experience. The novel was well received by a select group of readers, among them the novelist, Henry James. In 1905, Henry James had enjoyed a long, productive and distinguished career, and it is not to overstate his importance to say that he had changed the face of American literature. Novels like *Washington Square* (1880), *The Portrait of a Lady* (1881), and *The Golden Bowl* (1904) featured characters from the American leisured classes. His narratives presented the detail of consciousness, perception and emotion as characters lived through intense experiences arising from clashes of culture or sensibility. Writing from his chosen home, England, he made the transatlantic theme his own but, on reading *The Valley of Decision*, he urged Edith Wharton in a letter of 17 August 1902:

> the *American Subject*. There it is round you. Don't pass it by – the immediate, the real, the ours, the yours, the novelist's that it waits for. Take hold of it & keep hold, & let it pull you where it will [. . .] What I would say in a word is: Profit, be warned by my awful example of exile & ignorance [. . .] DO NEW YORK! The 1ˢᵗ-hand account is precious.[2]

Edith Wharton took him at his word. Her New York book was an original take on contemporary high society. She imported into an aristocratic landscape some of the more brutal and sordid elements of naturalist fiction hitherto associated with vulgar, often violent, depictions of working-class city life. With her new canvas, Wharton came into her own as a cultural analyst. She read contemporary social scientists such as Herbert Spencer, ethnographers (anthropologists) of her day and Darwin's controversial works on human evolution (she kept in her library two copies of his *Origin of Species*, one dated 1895 and a revised edition of 1900, and she annotated these with her own commentary). Informed by such readings, *The House of Mirth* represents a remarkable study of social groups as competitive systems. Wharton's heroine Lily Bart is the victim of economic forces; and Darwinian readings of the text extend such suggestions to argue that she is a doomed specimen, unable to adapt to a more materialistic age. Beyond this, the novel is a psychological study. A number of individuals – from the attractive Lawrence Selden to the tedious Percy Gryce – come into sharp focus. However, the novel's central subject is the heroine Lily Bart, whose unconscious we glimpse as she sabotages her own chances of marriage. In these experimental and ambiguous passages, Wharton takes forward James's exploration of consciousness and presents Lily's blurred and contradictory motivations in ways that parallel those of the new psychology of her day. Critics have seen analogies with the work of the psychoanalyst, Sigmund Freud. Wharton's novel, like Freud's case studies of the troubled Viennese upper-classes, opened up the darker recesses of the individual psyche and hinted at the repressions of an entire society.

This guide presents a range of different approaches to *The House of Mirth*. It brings together many voices from 1905 to the present day, debating,

---

2   Henry James, letter written from Lamb House, Rye, England, 17 August 1904, from *Henry James and Edith Wharton: Letters: 1900–1915*, ed. Lyall H. Powers, New York: Scribner's, 1990, p. 36.

contextualising, questioning and offering fresh interpretations of the many dimensions of this fascinating, complex and infinitely varied novel. In Part 1, 'Text and contexts', Pamela Knights takes readers through *The House of Mirth*'s most distinctive features, setting the novel within its contemporary landscape. Moving between textual close-up and wider cultural perspectives, she suggests ways of understanding how even the smallest details might work within Wharton's larger narrative design. Her section on Wharton's own life and career offers another angle on her framing of Lily's story; and her final sections survey some of the most important literary and social contexts and present examples of other voices from the period. In extracts from now-forgotten commentators (held only in rare-book collections), Knights offers readers a chance to enter directly into the culture and to appreciate how Wharton drew on the opinions, observations and language of her day. Returning to the novel with such voices in mind opens up new avenues of inquiry – about women's lives, the city, rich and poor, the manners, fashions, and customs of Lily's New York tribe.

Since publication, *The House of Mirth* has inspired a vast body of criticism, and readers new to the text might well feel daunted. In Part 2, 'Critical history', Elizabeth Nolan introduces readers to the most significant stages and developments in this substantial, and ever-growing, scholarship. As a starting point, readers today can still find much to illuminate the text in the responses of the novel's earliest audiences; and so this section opens with an outline of the novel's first reviews and of Wharton's correspondence about her work. The rest of the chapter traces the novel's varied interpretations, clarifying different critical approaches and changing emphases. Nolan points readers to key contributions in the field, many of these available online, in libraries and in standard anthologies (see also the annotated bibliography in Further reading, **p. 157**). Her section, as a whole, offers help to readers in understanding the main critical issues and in beginning to find their own route through the debates.

The House of Mirth has passed its centenary year, and it continues to stimulate discussion. In Part 3, 'Critical readings', essays specially commissioned for this volume continue these debates, offering fresh readings of the novel in tune with the interests of today. It is all too easy to forget that this classic text first featured as a high-profile magazine story. In '*Beyond* the Page: Visual Literacy and the Interpretation of Lily Bart', Edith Thornton revives its initial impact by turning attention to *The House of Mirth*'s original illustrations. Placing Lily alongside popular representations of the fashionable 'American Beauty', she opens up some of the associations Wharton's first readers would have brought to the text. This new and exciting information adds further layers to modern encounters with Lily and her story. Lily's sexuality is given a different spin, as Katherine Joslin challenges the reader, with the question: 'Is Lily Gay?'. Her deliberately provocative essay problematises the grounds upon which Lily defines herself. Joslin here brings queer theory to bear on Wharton's novel, reading Wharton's own views on American women from the perspective of Judith Butler's contemporary feminist theories of gender and performance. Two essays take up Wharton's dialogue with different genres. The first seeks to reinvigorate the perennial discussion of Wharton's relationship with the tradition of nineteenth-century realism. To give readers a richer appreciation of Wharton as a changing and developing writer, Janet Beer and Elizabeth Nolan ('*The House of Mirth*: Genred Locations') read the novel in relation to Wharton's earlier fiction *The Valley of Decision* and her 1907 social-problem novel, *The Fruit of the Tree*. Configuring these three texts in a direct relationship, unexplored by previous scholars, gives a sense of the experimental nature of much of Wharton's writing.

Kathy Fedorko's ' "Seeing a Disfigurement": Reading the Gothic in *The House of Mirth*', explores genre from another angle, analysing how Wharton employs, and subverts, 'new Gothic' elements to uncover the unspoken in her text. Connecting this novel to the Gothic tradition, Fedorko uncovers many of the darkest aspects of the narrative, unnoticed in much of the earlier criticism. Finally, Pamela Knights' ' "Hypertexts" and the City: *The House of Mirth* at the Millennium' brings the novel right up to date. She examines new writers' reworkings of Wharton's narrative, and its heroine's emotions and desires, in the light of anxieties about the fate of the self in modern America. Glimpsed in an array of guises, from murder mysteries to chick lit, Lily Bart flits in and out of contemporary American literature; her reincarnations send us back to look again at the text itself, with new insights and emphases.

In addition to these reinterpretations of the life of Lily Bart, in criticism and in fiction, *The House of Mirth* has generated dramatic adaptations for stage and screen, including Wharton's own. In Part 4, 'Performance/adaptation', Pamela Knights and Janet Beer explore selected visual and textual reworkings of Wharton's novel, from 1906 to today. Again, this section guides readers to a wealth of representations: quotations from original newspaper interviews, descriptions of New York theatre and dance productions and analysis of *The House of Mirth* on film.

Finally, this guide points readers onwards: interpretations of the novel are underpinned by the critical and contextual resources, both online and in print form, enumerated in the closing section. With such resources, readers will be equipped to explore the novel in more detail and to develop independent lines of critical enquiry.

1

Text and contexts

The text

Reviewing *The House of Mirth* on 15 October 1905, the day after the book was published, the *New York Times* ranked it highly in two very different spheres: as a tragedy, worth its place in an illustrious Western tradition (a line of succession from the Bible, Greek drama and Shakespeare); and as a text tuned to its 'very hour' – 'the present era of vast wealth and ostentatious display':

> 'The House of Mirth' (Scribner) the title of which is derived from the Books of Ecclesiastes, vii., 4 ('The heart of the wise is in the house of mourning; but the heart of fools is in the house of mirth') is a tragedy of our modern life, in which the relentlessness of what men used to call Fate, and esteem, in their ignorance, a power beyond their control, is as vividly set forth as it ever was by Aeschylus or Shakespeare.
>
> The smallest details of the picture are recognizable as facts that are pulsing around us in this very hour, and the personages are so lifelike that, though it may be doubted if the living original of any one of them can be positively identified, yet there will surely be many plausible identifications by readers of the book who are proud of their familiarity with Society.[1]

As the review predicted, some readers treated the novel as an insider's gossip. *Vogue* asserted: 'Mrs. Wharton has only taken a few very notable incidents—there are three in the book which have become public property long ago—and with this background fitted in composite characters.'[2] Wharton's 'smallest details' substantiated the air of up-to-the-minute authenticity. But the more reflective of its audience realised that its topicality went deeper. *The House of Mirth* did not simply offer a snapshot of smart New York society, or a chance to spot-the-celebrity, but it uniquely captured that society in movement, at a crucial phase of transition. In its minutiae and its broadest narrative sweep, the text engages with

1   'New York Society Held up to Scorn', *New York Times*, Sunday issue, 15 October 1905, p. 6.
2   'As Seen by Him', *Vogue*, 30 November 1905, p. 715.

some of the most urgent discussions of its moment: What were the forces driving 'our modern life', the prospects for the self, the possible shape of the future? Wharton places her heroine, Lily Bart, at the centre of this inquiry.

Narrative design

In its subject matter, its pace, its structure and its restless narrative voice, *The House of Mirth* is uniquely 'modern' – a chart to new and confusing territory. Glimpses of the story appear in one of Wharton's early notebooks, which she dated 1900, the start of the twentieth century. There is a title, 'A Moment's Ornament', and jottings for names and character traits. Alongside a 'Gryce' and 'Mrs. Peniston' is a 'Selden' (who felt himself the 'unpremeditated' element in an otherwise 'disciplined' life); and a 'Lily', who had no place in the world that she loved more than any other; whose 'memories had no roots in the soil, her wandering impulses no hearth by which to rest'. There is also a key simile: 'She was like one of those bushes that are trained for flower-shows: all the buds had been pinched off but the one specimen-flower – the flower of her beauty.'[3] When Wharton later settled to work on the novel, she worked over and added to her book, in numerous manuscript revisions, keeping her alternative title almost to the end. Yet these early fragments hold, between them, some of the central ingredients fused so powerfully in the story of Lily's destiny.

The novel registers the shock of the new. Focusing on about eighteen months in the life of one young woman (from early September through a complete year, and on to late April), Wharton opens up her entire society, at the moment of writing. In endowing her individual figures with the 'lifelike' form so praised by the *New York Times* reviewer, she also captures the character of a larger cultural group. As critics since have emphasised, Wharton brings to the New York scene the analytical eye of a sociologist or anthropologist. *The House of Mirth* tracks the complex, criss-crossing paths of the social 'types' (to use the classificatory language of the period) who were at the forefront of contemporary comment – among them, the leisure-class lady, the new millionaire, and the parvenu wife (see Text and contexts, **pp. 40–1**). Unlike Wharton's first novel, *The Valley of Decision* (1902), located safely in a historical past, this story attempts to capture impressions as they unfold, in a swiftly changing world. Wharton sets the main action on the cusp of the new century – some ten years on from 1891, 'the spring of the year we went to Aix',[4] as Mrs Peniston helpfully dates it. The details of the text give a sense of time speeding up, as one century crowds out another. Lily stamps letters with an old-fashioned seal but is caught up in a world of instant communications (telephones and telegrams) and innovative technologies, where candles coexist with electricity. She cuts the pages of a book by hand, but this is

---

3   Edith Wharton Collection. Yale Collection of American Literature. Beinecke Rare Books and Manuscript Library. YCAL 42. Series No. I, Box No. 21. Folder 699 (Donnee Book), pp. 79, 111. A selection of *The House of Mirth*'s draft manuscript pages can be viewed at Library's web site (see Further reading and Web resources, **p. 160**).

4   Edith Wharton, *The House of Mirth*, ed. Janet Beer and Elizabeth Nolan, Peterborough, Ontario: Broadview Press, 2005, I: xv, 208. (All subsequent references to this novel are to this edition and are given in brackets in the text.)

also a society where early cinema broadcasts images of a society wedding, and where modes of transport range from Mrs Van Osburgh's traditional 'C-spring barouche' to Mrs Hatch's 'electric victoria' (II: xi, 336) or the Trenors' expensive motor. Nothing seems stable. Whole histories happen in a sentence: the rise and fall of Greiner, the millionaire, whose house is bought by Rosedale (I: xi, 157); Lily's expedition to Alaska (II: v, 274). Images of sudden transformations fill the narrative – of shifting scenes (whether produced on a conventional stage, or by the dissolving slides of an up-to-the-minute stereopticon); metaphors of hurtling transport, or of wilder, rushing tides, sweep characters along.[5]

Here, Lily, too, is at a critical point in her history. The novel positions her at the stage where a young woman was conventionally 'interesting', and, for the purposes of a traditional female plot, available for narrative: the brief period between being a girl and becoming a wife. However, this role of a 'girl' of marriageable years – a '*jeune fille à marier*' (I: vi, 105), as she was labelled – was one that, at twenty-nine, Lily, and her observers, know she is rather old to be playing. (Conduct books often referred to women unmarried at thirty as 'elderly girls'.) From the very start of the novel, then, there is a sense that Lily's course is precarious; her time running out. She is poised between worlds (a staid old society and an unknown new one), and between centuries. Wharton's early titles, 'A Moment's Ornament' and 'The Year of the Rose' catch at this sense of temporariness – the possibility that neither Lily, nor any of her cultural settings, will outlast the instant of observation.

Narration and structure are essential to Wharton's effects. Recalling writing the novel, she explained: 'My last page is always latent in my first; but the intervening windings of the way become clear only as I write.'[6] Her narrative displays this mixture of assurance and uncertainty. It gives a strong sense from the start that, as in traditions of literary realism (see Critical history, **pp. 74–5**), the narrator understands, through the accumulated details, the whole, larger, picture: the characters' choices and consciousness, key 'notes' which sum up the period, the directions of social movements. The predominantly linear movement of the narrative (disrupted only at times of Lily's severest distress) suggests a steady movement towards an inevitable climax. But other elements cut across. In these, Wharton's text seems on the cusp of Modernism – the forms that broke with the verisimilitude, plot and character focus and narrative stability of the past century. The modernist mode unsettles reading, breaking the illusion of reality and overturning the notion that the 'author' or narrative eye sees and understands the whole picture. Here, the narrative voice is always asking questions, trying to account for Lily, seemingly as unsure of what she is or might become as any of those who watch and speculate about her. Repeatedly, throughout the text, readers encounter an observer who is trying to find a frame of reference, or observers watching the observers. At the climax of the fatal Riviera trip, Selden, for example, notices the little gossip columnist, Dabham, with 'little eyes, like tentacles' trying to catch 'the floating intimations' in the air (II: iii, 254). Such moments almost become self-reflexive, indicating the difficulties faced by the novelist herself and anticipating the fragments and hesitations of Modernism.

---

5   For a fuller exploration of modernity, mobility and change in the novel, see Pamela Knights, Introduction, *The House of Mirth*, London: Everyman's Library, 1991, pp. v–xxix.
6   Edith Wharton, *A Backward Glance*, New York: D. Appleton-Century, 1934, p. 208.

In pursuing her inquiry, Wharton infuses the text with notes from other contemporary writings and inquiries (exemplified more fully in the contextual sections that follows, **pp. 21–6**). She keeps in play an extraordinary range of discourses from classical mythology to etiquette book, fairy tale to fashion feature. In this multistranded narrative, it becomes difficult to assign any single reason for Lily's fate, or even to assess her level of control or choice. In one strand of the narrative, the figure of Bertha features as a kind of malignant double to Lily, showing what she might become, how she might survive. But scientific and economic languages offer alternative frameworks for investigation. Wharton's extensive and serious reading in Charles Darwin and Herbert Spencer, and in contemporary ethnology and social science, enter the lexical and metaphorical structures of the narrative and its mode of speculation. In his seemingly wilful distance from Lily, Selden stands at times in the objective position of the naturalist writer or the new social scientist, trying to understand her as a specimen, within larger environmental systems. Overspecialised, trained for one world, she seems inevitably destined for extinction. Like George Eliot before her, in novels such as *The Mill on the Floss* (1860) or *Middlemarch* (1871–2), Wharton seems to concur that it is not always the finest species which flourish. But other strands complicate the view. Lily, too, in her detachment, strikes Gerty as 'like some cruel creature experimenting in a laboratory' (I: xiv, 200) – a simile which suggests that Lily, through whatever means, is capable of remaking herself. What subjectivity will become in the twentieth century remains unclear; whether a coherent 'self' will survive; and whether there is hope for rational choice, for any kind of agency.

Such doubleness seems inbuilt within the narrative's pace and structure. Although it is hard to imagine encountering the novel as a magazine serial in monthly instalments, some readers today might be interested in trying to reconstruct the effects. Beginning in *Scribner's Magazine* in the issue of January 1905, the novel was divided as follows (for convenience here, Arabic numerals are used for the chapters):

Book I: January–June 1905 (Chapters: January: 1–2; February: 3–4; March: 5–7; April: 8–10; May: 11–13; June: 14–15);
Book II: July–November 1905 (Chapters: July: 1–3; August: 4–5; September: 6–8; October: 9–11; November: 12–14).

Although the novel's cycles of the seasons did not match those in actual time, there were occasional parallels (for instance, the closing of the August number with the illustration, captioned, 'It was a good deal better than a broiling Sunday in town', see Figure 18, p. 95), and these perhaps added to the air of contemporaneity. To read in serial form must surely have highlighted the impression, strong enough in the complete book, of Lily's irreversible decline from first page to last and of the currents that momentarily cut across and retard the narrative. The gaps between issues may also have increased the effect of her spiralling and accelerated descent. After a slow start (in the expansive scenes at Bellomont), occupying January to March, the story enters the disturbed nightmarish sequence of Trenor's virtual rape (May and June), where Lily seems to split in two. After this, the second book seems to rush onwards (the entire Riviera episode is included in a single issue in July). Now the narrative turns into a strange reflection of its first book, as past episodes return, to destroy Lily. She passes into worlds 'behind the social tapestry' (II: ix, 315), in the unformed social scene of the Emporium and Mrs Hatch; and finds 'the fragmentary and distorted image of the world she had lived reflected in the mirror of the working-girls' minds' (II: x, 325).

Space and place

In her reflections on her craft in *The Writing of Fiction* (1924), Wharton emphasised that, for a novelist fully at home with the material, characters and scenic detail were part of one aspect. In *The House of Mirth*, local settings repeatedly press outwards towards wider significance. Wharton constructs the social spaces of the rich in terms of images of confinement: from 'the great gilt cage' where the rich 'were like flies in a bottle' (I: v, 90), to the bedroom where Lily paces up and down, and the 'last door of escape was closed' (I: xv, 211). Whether a Hudson Valley estate like Bellomont, or the steps of the Trenors' Fifth Avenue townhouse, any place seems part of a single sphere, a panopticon, where the eye of society is fixed on Lily. New York is both the hothouse, where she flourishes, and the casket which imprisons her. Suggestions of more nebulous vistas, or mythic territories, also enter the text to open up a view into other, bleaker, spaces: 'the long white road' (I: v, 91) of Lily's future; the arena of Greek tragedy, where she flees from the Furies; the deep 'abyss' of nameless threat; the precarious rockpool tossed by storms.

Wharton mapped out her social bounds early. In this anecdote, taken by many critics as a blueprint for her fiction, she described her first attempt at a novel (she was eleven):

> 'Oh, how do you do, Mrs. Brown?' said Mrs. Tompkins. 'If only I had known you were going to call I should have tidied up the drawing-room.' Timorously I submitted this to my mother, and never shall I forget the sudden drop of my creative frenzy when she returned it with the icy comment: 'Drawing-rooms are always tidy.' This was so crushing to a would-be novelist of manners that it shook me rudely out of my dream of writing fiction, and I took to poetry instead.[7]

Her vignette captures much about the configuration of an older New York still visible in the text and about the social territory Lily occupies. This society will be described more fully later in this chapter; but, even without any contextual information, the text powerfully conveys its nature, even in tiny incidents. Its routines and alliances produce a rule-bound, tidy space, where any variation can be monitored. To take another drawing room for an example – Mrs Peniston's: here, as Lily wonders what to do with the dirty newspaper containing Bertha's letters, her aunt notices the housemaid's negligence and pounces on the 'minute spot' of dust and the misaligned blind and crayon portrait (I: ix, 143–5). In what seems trivial fussiness, Wharton creates a ridiculous figure, but also an extremely

---

7 Wharton, *A Backward Glance*, p. 73.

authoritative and dangerous one. Like her room – in stiff, unchanging, dark, upholstered dress, with an imagination shrouded in dust sheets, Mrs Peniston embodies her society at its most rigid. Repeatedly associated with calendars, social rituals and surveillance, she sums up the wider obsessions with keeping the surfaces clean, with moral and social housekeeping. The moment, like many of the text's briefest episodes, is ominous, a warning about what she (and her circle) will not tolerate in Lily. Lily is already holding the contaminated letters; later, conspicuously out of line, with a spot on her name, she will be expelled from the drawing room.

Outside such narrow bounds, the geographical range of the text, charted in the characters' frequent travels, might seem to suggest a chance of mobility, even freedom. For Edith Wharton herself, travel was one of the most enriching of experiences; but in *The House of Mirth*, it represents another form of entrapment. Lily's memories of dismal European wanderings with her embittered mother, 'vegetating in cheap continental refuges' (I: iii, 68) add force to her later desolate reflections: 'the feeling of being something rootless and ephemeral, mere spin-drift of the whirling surface of existence' (II: xiii, 358–9). Throughout her story, place names convey glimpses of ignominious histories: Aix, Cannes, Cimiez, places of fashionable cures and recreation, all mark spots from which she has made an uneasy exit. More generally in the text, change of location, again, often in the briefest of allusions, contributes to the sense of frenetic and futile motion. Characters flee to settings we do not see, out beyond the edge of the narrative. Invitations (to the Adirondacks, Alaska, the Mediterranean) rescue Lily at uncomfortable moments. Other characters take off for refuges far from Lily's orbit (India for Dillworth, Cuba for Selden); Bertha whisks her yacht to Sicily to snuff out Lily's triumphs on the Riviera. But these are only further enclaves of the rich (the characters view the world from their private railcar or luxury vessel); and when a 'foreign' setting (Monte Carlo or Nice) is directly represented, it features largely as an extension of the New York social stage. For the Brys, as a prelude for a grander show in London; for the Dorsets as a backdrop for a marital charade.

Wharton parallels the text's sweeping geographies with attention to more domestic spaces. Given its emphasis in the novel's final title, the motif of the house and associated features – architecture, rooms, decorative features, lighting and the lived environment in general – represent one of the text's most pervasive sets of signification. As many critics have reminded readers, the house is a recurrent centre of meaning in American literature;[8] but its use in *The House of Mirth* merits particular attention.

Domestic descriptions offer key insights, for example, into matters of taste and form. In the realist register of the text, offences of taste often serve, in turn, to code gradations of status and breeding. Wharton's specialist interests give her detail unusual precision. Her first book, *The Decoration of Houses* (1897), co-authored with the architect, Ogden Codman Jr., had been a treatise on interior design. With chapters treating different rooms and structural features (such as

---

8   For extended discussions, see Judith Fryer, *Felicitous Space: The Imaginative Structures of Edith Wharton and Willa Cather*, Chapel Hill, NC: University of North Carolina Press, 1986; and Marilyn R. Chandler, *Dwelling in the Text: Houses in American Fiction*, Berkeley, Calif.: University of California Press, 1991.

'Windows', 'Doors', 'Hall and Stairs'), this book conducted an extended argument against architectural and decorative excess; and Wharton's practical knowledge underpins the figurations of such items in her fictional narratives.

In *The House of Mirth*, her eye for architectural abominations, for instance, sharpens Van Alstyne's supercilious commentary, as he reads the façades of Fifth Avenue (I: xiv, 197–8) to measure the social pretensions of their owners. Decorative detail invites readers, too, to make their own diagnoses: Selden's 'small library', for example, with its 'pleasantly faded Turkey rug' (I: i, 41) and 'warm background of old bindings' (I: i, 45) does much to suggest why he seems reluctant to disrupt his comforts; 'the complacent ugliness of Mrs Peniston's black walnut' (I: xi, 135) tells us much of what we need to know about the era whose solidity its mistress embodies; and Mrs Bry's recently built mansion, with its 'air of improvisation' (I: xii, 168) presents its opposite – an acquisition so new it resembles a 'rapidly-evoked' stage set. While giving Lily her own desire to 'do over' drawing rooms, Wharton frustrates her. Instead, sharing Lily's perspective, we view details of the rooms she inhabits, and track her exact social position, at each stage of her decline: from the 'softly-shaded lights' in Judy Trenor's quietly luxurious guest rooms (I: iii, 60), through the vulgar electric blaze of the Emporium Hotel, to the dimness of the dreary boarding house. As throughout Wharton's writing, gardens, too, feature as extensions of interior space, with the Bellomont balustrade or the Casino tropical plantings presenting new backdrops for the shifting social scene.

Such elements, however, can be more than social indicators. Interiors, in Wharton's writing, also offer insights into the individual self. During the 1890s, Wharton's contemporary, the Austrian psychoanalyst Sigmund Freud (1856–1939), was beginning to publish his first explorations of interior space, including *Studies in Hysteria* (1895) and *The Interpretation of Dreams* (1900). Wharton, too, discovered early that a room could tell an inner story. Here, in 'The Fullness of Life' (1893), one of her first short fictions, a woman muses on her less-than-satisfactory marriage:

> But I have sometimes thought that a woman's nature is like a great house full of rooms: there is the hall, through which everyone passes in going in and out; the drawing-room, where one receives formal visits; the sitting-room, where the members of the family come and go as they list; but beyond that, far beyond, are other rooms, the handles of whose doors perhaps are never turned; no one knows the way to them, no one knows whither they lead; and in the innermost room, the holy of holies, the soul sits alone and waits for a footstep that never comes.[9]

This extended simile hints at energies – spiritual, emotional, and erotic – prohibited expression in the tidy public surfaces of a drawing room, or in a polite realist novel. So, too, in moments throughout *The House of Mirth*, the realist, metonymic detail, turns, as we read, into a metaphoric mode, one which opens up

---

9   Edith Wharton, *Collected Stories 1891–1910*, selected Maureen Howard, New York: Library of America, 2001, p. 14.

other dimensions, taking readers inwards, into psychoanalytical interiors. Such moments add force to the novel as a psychological study as well as a social investigation. Enclosed spaces, dangerous thresholds, blinds and curtains, are, for instance, key to the kind of Gothic figuration of Lily explored by Kathy Fedorko (see Critical readings, **pp. 116–26**) and to other studies of character and consciousness.[10] So, Mrs Peniston's immoveable furniture, chilly grate and vault-like rooms fuse, for Lily and the reader, with 'the stifling limits' of the existence where her niece feels 'buried alive' (I: ix, 136). The shock of seeing herself in the shadowed mirror unlocks 'a whole train of association', as Lily, like a Freudian subject, 'lay in the darkness reconstructing the past out of which her present had grown' (I: iii, 63). Like Freud, Wharton is interested in motivation and choices that lie beneath consciousness, often buried in childhood. She suggests that both Lily and Selden, for example, are influenced by early experiences. She is sharply precise in unfolding some passages of thought – the triggering of Grace Stepney's 'dull resentment' into 'active animosity' (I: xi, 159), or Gerty's looming hatred (I: xiv, 200). But her mode of narration blurs for readers the level of awareness in many of Lily's decisions: she presents whole passages of thought in what is known as a 'free indirect discourse' – neither direct speech nor objective report. Lily's series of retreats from securing her capture of Gryce, for example, emerge almost despite her conscious convictions:

> If she did not marry Percy Gryce, the day might come when she would have to be civil to such men as Rosedale. *If she did not marry him?* But she meant to marry him—she was sure of him and sure of herself. She drew back with a shiver from the pleasant paths in which her thoughts had been swaying.
>
> (I: v, 92)

Wharton's repeated images of the drapes and closed doors in Lily's mind (I: vii, 118) further the impressions that she is swayed by deeper unconscious forces, prompting questions about what she screens off, or shuts out – what she represses.

The biblical resonances of the novel's title add yet another dimension. As the *New York Times* review suggested (see **p. 3**), the title phrase, taken from the Book of Ecclesiastes (subtitled 'or, The Preacher') (7:4), casts a pall over the narrative. Awaking echoes of this well-known Old Testament meditation on folly, ignorance and futile human activity (and of the rich, in particular), the novel condemns its own society. From the world where people 'lived like pigs' (I: iii, 65) to the brilliance of Bellomont, rooms in *The House of Mirth* are spiritually empty. At the novel's climax, in Lily's final evening, her inner vision awakes to a 'sense of deeper impoverishment' (II: xiii, 358). In this reflective narratorial passage, the text dwells explicitly on what is missing. It contemplates Lily's lack of relation to the 'slowly accumulated past' – 'whether in the concrete image of the old house stored with visual memories, or in the conception of the house not built with hands' (II: xiii, 359) – and so, at last, it intimates where meanings may be found.

---

10 For an in-depth discussion of the treatment of consciousness in the text, see Jill M. Kress, *The Figure of Consciousness: William James, Henry James, and Edith Wharton*, New York and London: Routledge, 2002, pp. 131–59.

Wharton's own life story (see Text and contexts, **pp. 13–19**) identifies her own sources of value, located deep in a European cultural tradition. She gives Lily some parallel encounters, but in diluted or ironic variations. Lily comes to despise her sense of Europe's 'immemorial tradition' as part of her 'futile and childish' romantic daydreams (I: iii, 70). She touches books throughout her story – 'fluttering the pages' (I: i, 45), cutting open a novel (I: ii, 52), borrowing a prayer book; or posing by bookshelves. But these are props for her flirtations: outer resources, not the way to inner strength. It is clear that she does not lack imaginative capability – her chance encounter with a piece of the Western canon, Aeschylus' tragic drama, the *Eumenides*, beats in her brain thereafter. But without reading, application, serious nurture, she remains outside a greater humane tradition.

A few scenes seem the exception. Examples that hint of transcendence might include Lily's drift from the formal terrace at Bellomont into the wood path beyond the gardens, and her talk on the open ledge with Selden on a glowing afternoon, where 'they seemed lifted into a finer air' (I: vi, 109), or their parallel meeting in 'the magic place' (I: xii, 174) of the Brys' conservatory. Intensified by the contrast with material constructs, these give glimpses of a reality behind the façades and a setting where 'the real Lily' (I: xii, 172) might unfold. For many readers, as with Selden himself, such images of a world outside society, and the strongest intimations of freedom, are summed up by Lily's seal: '*Beyond!* beneath a flying ship' (I: xiv, 191).

But individual interpretations will differ. For some '*Beyond!*' might suggest a sphere of authenticity, of romantic or spiritual possibility. For others, located in these settings, such hints are an illusion, effects produced (like the *tableaux vivants*) by the 'vision-making influences' (I: xii, 170) of luxury. Readers disappointed in Selden might suspect that the 'word which made all clear' (the novel's final sentence) is his own, self-gratifying fantasy; and they might, instead, regard Lily's visit to Nettie and her baby as the most powerful epiphany in the novel. With its strong, climactic position in the narrative, this episode seems to reverse everything that the text has hitherto marked as negative – the terrain of the dingy, the mundane and domestic, the story of the bad woman, the division between the decorative and the dull. Here, and in the moment's reprise as Lily dies, she seems to find at last a sustaining vision of what a better life might be. But whether the episode suggests wider possibilities of renewal, outside the 'house of mirth', or is present only as temporary, delusive, consolation, the novel leaves ambiguous.

Questions of privilege

As most reviewers noted, *The House of Mirth* was the work of an insider. Its author, Edith Wharton, was born into the social group to which Lily Bart aspired: a well-to-do, white, social elite, of Anglo-Dutch stock. She married within this group; and, though eventually divorced, maintained, lifelong, her social position, her wealth and all the advantages these brought. Unlike the 'irresponsible pleasure-seekers'[11] in *The House of Mirth*, Wharton believed in using her privilege to some purpose. Pursuing her craft, as novelist and cultural analyst, she

---

11 Wharton, *A Backward Glance*, p. 207.

discovered her own, more expansive, sphere – her 'new citizenship' in 'The Land of Letters', as she expressed it,[12] and in so doing, she moved far from the accepted course of the society into which she was born.

However, her background has, from the start, prompted many critics to inquire about assumptions she might have carried into her fiction – into constructions of character, for example, or narrative emphasis. The viewpoint of *The House of Mirth* largely remains with characters for whom luxury and beauty are the norm and dwells at length on the glittering surfaces of the rich; and one might ask, for instance, how far the text takes for granted the superiority of this enclosed world and the structures that support it (inherited money, servants, leisure). While Mrs Peniston is obviously a figure of satire, some might suggest that the text, more generally, shares Mrs Peniston's snobbery in its representation of outsiders, or of less acceptable 'types' (from the ridiculous intellectual, Lady Cressida to the monstrous philistine, Norma Hatch). From that, a number of questions might follow. To what extent, for example, does the focalisation draw readers in, to share Lily's revulsion from the world of the 'dingy', or her recoil from those who threaten her? And, in any case, just how are we invited to respond to her demise – the extinction of her beauty? (Is this a tragedy, an elegy, an impersonal, sociological case study, a melodrama – or none, or all, of these?) Wharton's class was under pressure at the turn of the century, from new forces – newly wealthy 'robber barons', those without 'breeding', immigrants, the poor (see Text and contexts, **pp. 26–41**). Is *The House of Mirth* an anti-democratic lament for the rise of such groups; or is it a wider critique of a turbulent, divided society? Critics have long ceased to seek simple answers to such questions. Whatever the focus of attention (class, for example, or gender), it is rare to find any seeming evidence of Wharton's conservatism or elitism left uncountered by arguments about her own questioning, even her radicalism. There are many approaches which prioritise other kinds of inquiry, but fresh waves of interest – as now, at the novel's centenary, in Wharton's racial politics – continue to give urgency to debate (see Critical history, **p. 79**).

Lily's story is not Edith Wharton's, and biography should be used with caution. *The House of Mirth*, nevertheless, reaches back into Wharton's own earlier New York world. Making Lily some ten years her junior, Wharton places Lily in a fictional representation of her own society, negotiating the same cultural forces, up to the early 1900s – the date of the novel's writing. As she herself emphasised: 'the circle I described in it was that in which I had lived since my eleventh year, and which, in all essentials, had remained unchanged in the interval between my childhood and the writing of the book'.[13] Lily grows up on the edges of that circle; she has the prospect of security, but, disinherited, is expelled beyond its boundaries.

A closer knowledge of that society, and of how Wharton herself emerged from it, brings out significant features of the text and of the alternative path she wrote for Lily. Though the novel has a sharply contemporary pitch, read with Wharton's life (and her autobiographical reflections on her life) in mind, a

---

12 Wharton, *A Backward Glance*, pp. 22, 119.
13 Edith Wharton, Introduction, *The House of Mirth*, World's Classics edition, London: Oxford University Press, 1936, p. v.

different set of elements comes into the foreground: lingering voices and images from a refined class, now under threat; ideals and possibilities glimpsed, but never realised; mid-nineteenth-century manners, morals and assumptions, still operative even in the whirl of modernity. The next section, therefore, focuses, in particular, on Wharton's life before *The House of Mirth* – on her family background and her interests and experiences as a girl, young woman and wife in leisure-class America.

The author: Edith Wharton (1862–1937)

'Why, the beginning was in my cradle, I suppose—'

(II: iv, 264)

Edith Jones: family, tradition and early life

Born Edith Newbold Jones in 1862, Edith Wharton's beginnings lay in a conservative, close-knit world. Her parents Lucretia (Rhinelander) and George Frederic Jones came from prosperous New York families. These were not the new multimillionaires of the extravagant Gilded Age – the Rockefellers, Goulds, or Wharton's fictional Welly Brys, whose impact Wharton would register so sharply in her novels (see Text and contexts, **pp. 33–41**). Rather, they were quietly affluent, Manhattan stock, traceable back some 300 years to colonial ancestors (of Anglo-Dutch lineage, they were among those regarded as New York aristocracy). Amply funded by income from New York land holdings, George Frederic did not have to work, and the couple enjoyed a leisured life.

The Jones's habits and attitudes followed the pattern of their class: 'everything in our family life was ordered according to convention', Wharton commented.[14] This was the 'world of copy-book axioms' (I: i, 43),[15] which Mrs Peniston's stiff regime in *The House of Mirth* perpetuates into the twentieth century. Her stifling world view is reinforced in Wharton's own reminiscences, particularly in glimpses of her chilly, scornful mother, disapproving of anything or anyone she thought not 'nice'. Wharton later suspected her father of having had imaginative potential, 'shrivelled' by his wife's 'matter-of-factness',[16] a situation echoed by her characterisation of Hudson Bart and his wife when she presented Lily's early life. But, like Lily's philistine circle, this set had no intellectual or cultural interests. They enjoyed a social round with friends and relations – giving dinners, visiting the theatre and entertaining at their winter town house and seaside summer home. Lucretia's ruling passion, which her daughter shared, appears to have been elegant attire; and Wharton long remembered the excitement of unpacking her mother's annual order of Paris gowns: 'The enchantment of seeing one resplendent dress after another shaken out of its tissue-paper.'[17]

---

14 Edith Wharton, 'Life and I' (an autobiographical fragment), in *Novellas and Other Writings*, selected Cynthia Griffin Wolff, New York: The Library of America, 1990, p. 1092.
15 Wharton uses the same phrase of her own family in *A Backward Glance*, p. 25.
16 Wharton, *A Backward Glance*, p. 39.
17 Wharton, *A Backward Glance*, p. 20.

In later life, Wharton acknowledged the values in this society. The New York of her childhood had been swept away – in part, by the currents of change the novel identifies. As she exclaimed in 1936: 'It seems like going back to the Pharaohs to try to re-enter the New York world in which *The House of Mirth* originated.'[18] In *A Backward Glance*, she contrasted the new moral fluidity with the firm standards that governed her parents' group. Her less-guarded autobiographical fragment, *Life and I*, depicts more of its strains. There, her account of a happy, uneventful, childhood is secondary to her fears, her frustrations and her dawning awareness of worlds beyond its limits. In *The House of Mirth*, the shelter and tradition of this older order, as well as its constrictions, remain visible throughout the text.

Her parents' last-born child, and only daughter, Edith Jones was expected to grow up in her mother's mould – well mannered, well dressed, and well spoken; she would make a social debut, marry a man from the same milieu, establish her own household and manage her servants. 'Lily' or 'Puss', as she was known, shared such expectations, and, unlike her fictional namesake, she would accomplish all of these. But, as she realised early, her 'external life', as she called it, would never completely satisfy her. She was aware of being 'different', of possessing energies she did not know how to use; regarding herself as the least good-looking in her family, she became painfully self-conscious.[19] But in narrating her own story, Wharton gives a view of inner resources – redemptive values and energies, sensed only as shadowy potentialities in *The House of Mirth*. This inner world was illumined for her, first, in words. Even before she could read, she had a fierce compulsion to 'make up' stories, and this world, she said, became her refuge.

Her home life, and her governesses' teaching, in contrast, were 'an intellectual desert'.[20] In after years, she lamented her lack of a rigorous education, deploring the influence of theories that young people should avoid taxing study, for fear of brain fatigue. (Girls were further disadvantaged, by widespread worries that learning was unfeminine, off-putting to men, and, at worst, damaging to their reproductive health.) In *The House of Mirth*, raised to be ornamental, Lily, tragically, leaves her other qualities and abilities undeveloped. Wharton, in contrast, found her own way to what she needed. Two sets of encounters were crucial: her introduction to Europe and her explorations in her father's library. Understanding what such encounters meant to Wharton highlights the ironies and gaps in *The House of Mirth*. Lily is within reach of these meanings but fails to apprehend them: though Europe and reading expand her ambitions, it is largely to her detriment. For Wharton, both were a revelation.

The family's move to Europe (a temporary economy measure after the Civil War) was for Edith Jones, aged four, a permanent transformation. These six years gave her fluency in languages and, for the rest of her life, put her in touch with 'that background of beauty and old-established order!'[21] The shock of returning to America reverberates throughout her writing:

18 Wharton, Introduction to *The House of Mirth*, p. v.
19 Wharton, 'Life and I', p. 1089.
20 Wharton, 'Life and I', p. 1089.
21 Wharton, *A Backward Glance*, p. 44.

I shall never forget the bitter disappointment produced by the first impressions of my native country. I was only ten years old, but I had been fed on beauty since my babyhood, & my first thought was: '*How ugly it is!*' I have never since thought otherwise, or felt otherwise than as an exile in America.[22]

Her revulsion from the United States deepened into a profound sense of cultural alienation – not merely from visual ugliness but also from a nation committed, as she saw it, to commercial growth, money-making, mass culture; and she chose, eventually, an expatriate life in Europe. In her writing, not least in *The House of Mirth*, her vision of the barrenness of American culture would prove richly productive. As a child, however, books proved her deliverance; and she found her way back to the European tradition through the shelves of her father's 'gentleman's library'. Free to explore, she absorbed an array of subjects: philosophy, art criticism, histories, diaries, poetry. Her mother insisted on giving prior approval to any fiction and prohibited most contemporary novels – an edict, Wharton claimed, that saved her from 'ephemeral rubbish';[23] but she immersed herself in the classics – in English, French and German.

Reading led to writing. She experimented with genres – even blank-verse tragedy and sermons; and in her novella *Fast and Loose*, written secretly when she was fourteen, juxtaposed a sensational love romance with witty mock reviews.[24] Her family were suspicious of artists in general, but her mother, somewhat surprisingly, took some interest in her efforts; and, when Edith was sixteen, arranged for a private printing of her *Verses*. That year, too, the *Atlantic Monthly* (North America's most distinguished periodical) accepted one of her poems.

However, when her solitary bookishness seemed to threaten her social chances, her parents took action, bringing her 'out' in 1879, at seventeen, a year earlier than was usual (see Text and contexts, **p. 42**). Her social debut was less dazzling than the one she reports of Lily Bart, but she recalls shedding her shyness and becoming caught up in the whirl of the ensuing season. Yet, even so, 'all the delights of society'[25] failed to eclipse her sense that there could be richer pleasures.

As in Lily's story, her father's ill-health broke off her second season. Though the family sought a warmer climate in Europe, George Frederic declined, dying when Edith was just twenty. Unlike the fictional Barts, however, his family were not left impecunious, nor did his widow die of disgust – Lucretia would live until 1901, keeping her social position; Edith herself inherited more than $20,000 in a trust fund. (Throughout her life, further legacies came her way, some with the kind of fortunate timing she avoided in Lily's history.) Recalling her father's death, Wharton expresses sadness but not the dreariness with which she infuses Lily's similar experience. Instead, she highlights her elation in rediscovering Europe – in being 'drunk with seeing & learning'.[26]

---

22 Wharton, 'Life and I', pp. 1080–1.
23 Wharton, *A Backward Glance*, p. 65.
24 This has now been published: Edith Wharton, *'Fast and Loose' and The Buccaneers*, ed. Viola Hopkins Winner, Charlottesville, Va. and London: University Press of Virginia, 1993.
25 Wharton, 'Life and I', p. 1094.
26 Wharton, 'Life and I', p. 1095.

During this time, she began to acquire a romantic history – though one less variegated than Lily's. A brief engagement, to Harry Stevens in 1882, ended amid rumours that (like Lily's disapproving Mrs Dillworth) Harry's formidable mother had scotched the match. Observers speculated that, as the widow of a self-made millionaire, she had found the Jones clan stand-offish. Newspaper gossip, echoing Lucretia Jones's earlier anxieties, took a different view:

> The only reason assigned for the breaking of the engagement hitherto existing between Harry Stevens and Miss Edith Jones is an alleged pre-ponderance of intellectuality on the part of the intended bride. Miss Jones is an ambitious authoress, and it is said that, in the eyes of Mr. Stevens, ambition is a grievous fault.[27]

As conduct books emphasised, a broken engagement was, inevitably, a painful issue; and for the man to instigate the break, the reason had to be exceptionally strong. As one writer explained: 'By thus releasing himself he not unfrequently leaves the lady in an embarrassing position before the public, not to mention the possible injury that may be inflicted upon the deepest feelings of her heart.'[28] However, as biographers have suggested, for Wharton, as for Lily, perhaps more painful still was an engagement that never happened. A young lawyer, Walter Van Rensselaer Berry, later became for her, she said, that 'one friend' who seems 'an interpretation, of one's self, the very meaning of one's soul'.[29] But though they became close, a declaration never materialised; and her mother encouraged the attentions of Edward ('Teddy') Wharton, an old acquaintance from a respectable Boston family. Engaged in March 1885, they married in April, in 'a very quiet' New York wedding. Described in the society column, beneath another nuptial party, held in a house 'elegantly decorated with orchids, tropical ferns and roses', and 500 guests,[30] this seems a contrast with the weddings that provoke Lily Bart's envy. But as a debutante, Edith Jones, had succeeded.

Mrs Edward Wharton: marriage, travel and home

An advice book for women in 1900 pointed to the common lament that 'a girl's vision of marriage extends no further into the future than the wedding-day, and that this limited view is responsible for many matrimonial mistakes.'[31] In *Life and I*, Wharton recalled her own deep ignorance as a bride of twenty-three – and her mother's refusal to enlighten her (see Kathy Fedorko, Critical readings, **p. 120**). In *The House of Mirth*, she represents Lily's similarly limited (though, at nearly thirty, possibly less ignorant) vision. She can picture herself as 'the mystically veiled figure' (I: viii, 123) at the centre of attention but who, faced with potential husbands, deliberately refuses to let her imagination 'range beyond the day of plighting' (II: vi, 287).

27 Newport *Daily News*, cited: R. W. B. Lewis, *Edith Wharton*, p. 45.
28 Maude C. Cooke, *Social Etiquette*, Boston, Mass.: c. 1896, p. 136.
29 Wharton, *A Backward Glance*, p. 115.
30 'Weddings Yesterday', *New York Times*, 30 April 1885, p. 4.
31 Helen Churchill Candee, *How Women May Earn a Living*, New York: Macmillan, 1900, p. 258.

As Wharton's text engages readers in surmise about Lily's sexuality and relationships (see Katherine Joslin, Critical readings, **pp. 96–105**), biographers have speculated, in turn, about Wharton's own marital relations and how far she drew on these in her writings. Whatever her private experiences, they were inseparable from the wider problems of her culture. Where the 'niceness' of young women, and the capture of a socially suitable husband, were at a premium, other aspects of marriage could be swept aside, to inflict lasting damage. She and Teddy had enthusiasms in common (the outdoors, small dogs), and biographers emphasise his devotion. It seems probable, however, that marriage, even in its early days, lacked intensity. Edith Wharton's bouts of illness and depression throughout her thirties, her affair in her forties, her problems with Teddy's increasing mental and emotional instability, the relief of her divorce in her early fifties – all seem, cumulatively, symptoms of an increasingly unsatisfactory partnership.

Written twenty years into the Whartons' marriage, *The House of Mirth* opens the institution up to scrutiny. Though matrimony is Lily's goal, the text shows little to recommend it. Apart from the glow of Nettie Struther's kitchen, most glimpses of life beyond the wedding day reveal indifference, boredom or brutality – sometimes, as with Gus Trenor, all three. Married, Jack Stepney becomes a stolid prude, George Dorset a dangerously smouldering volcano. Selden, as a lawyer, ruminates on the fall-out of divorce. (With Teddy deteriorating mentally as Wharton worked on the novel, such scenes seem resonant.) And a caustic narratorial aside offers a particularly disturbing vision: angling for Percy Gryce, Lily must submit to boredom and more boredom, 'all on the bare chance that he might ultimately decide to do her the honour of boring her for life' (I: iii, 60).

The Whartons' marriage lasted about a quarter of a century. As a leisure-class wife, however, Edith Wharton managed to establish many of the friendships and interests she would value as an independent woman and writer. Teddy was supported on an allowance, and the Whartons' time was at their own disposal. The couple settled into a pattern – months of travel in Europe, summer and winter at their homes in America – which, together or separately, they followed for many years. Wharton's writing draws richly on these experiences.

Travel abroad was an enthusiasm Wharton shared with Old New Yorkers; though, as she explains, their pleasures had centred on scenery and shopping, not 'cultivated sight-seeing'.[32] For Edith Wharton, travel meant more. In early marriage, it kept her in touch with her dream of authorship. Chartering a steam yacht in 1888, the Whartons explored the Aegean, visiting islands where no steamer had previously landed; and Edith chronicled the cruise in a vivid journal, now rediscovered and published (in 1992) as *The Cruise of the Vanadis*.[33] She captured beautiful scenes and atmosphere, but she also observed closely, drawing out literary associations and histories. Exploring Italy, France and (later) Morocco, travel writing became a key genre for her, another form of cultural investigation; and place remained a central motif throughout her fiction.[34] But, as *The House of*

32 Wharton, *A Backward Glance*, p. 63.
33 Edith Wharton, *The Cruise of the Vanadis*, with photographs by Jonas Dovydenas, text by Edith Wharton Restoration, Lenox, Mass.; London: Bloomsbury, 2004.
34 See Janet Beer Goodwyn, *Edith Wharton: Traveller in the Land of Letters*, Basingstoke: Macmillan, 1990.

Mirth exemplifies, it is a rare character in her texts who approaches another country with anything like her own knowledge and intellectual curiosity. Typically, here, only Selden and Lily display any sensitivity, each taken briefly by the radiance of a Mediterranean scene. In spite of the Barts' 'dread of foreignness' (I: iii, 71), Lily, like Wharton, feels the 'romantic adventure' of a cruise, a 'thrill of the nerves' as she hears Greek idylls read aloud (II: ii, 234). But in the text such memories and moments vanish, undercut by the next turn of the drama. For Wharton, they remained, as an enriching treasure.

When at home, gardening and work on her houses rivalled writing in Wharton's creative passions. Interested in every aspect, she studied her subjects and sought advice from a professional architect, Ogden Codman. Becoming a connoisseur of elegant eighteenth-century Italian and French furniture increased her loathing of the dark monumental fittings of mid-century interiors like Mrs Peniston's. She detested, equally, modern, open American rooms, with brash electric lighting (a sign of vulgarity throughout *The House of Mirth*). She had rooms remodelled to create intimate spaces and to open up views and natural light, and she experimented similarly with gardens. *The Decoration of Houses* (1897) grew out of the collaboration with Codman. A success on publication, today the book's examples of 'simple' proportions (rooms in Florence's Pitti Palace, among them) seem hardly useful models for the ordinary reader. But the text itself remains invaluable as a gloss to the sites that figure significantly throughout her fiction and as an index to her general precepts on a harmonious and civilised culture.

In *The House of Mirth*, in Lily's spiralling downward course, she has no centre, no 'one spot of earth' (II: xiii, 359) from which to draw her strength. In Wharton's autobiography, an ever-present theme is her search for a place where she could live and work, true to her own conceptions of 'grave endearing traditions' (II: xiii, 359). Authorship opened new horizons. Her first book of stories, *The Greater Inclination* (1899), she said, 'broke the chains which had held me so long in a kind of torpor. For nearly twelve years I had tried to adjust myself to the life I had led since my marriage; but now I was overmastered by the longing [. . .] to break away from the world of fashion and be with my own spiritual kin.'[35]

The world which Wharton wished to escape was that in which Lily strives to keep a foothold. The life of this circle – its entertainments, ship arrivals, visitors, departures for its luxurious country 'cottages' – was charted, as it is in *The House of Mirth*, in the press's society columns. The Whartons appear regularly in the lists of the invited, for example, at a Vanderbilt ball in August 1895, 'a function of magnificent and expensive details' (see Text and contexts, **pp. 38–9**) or at 'an elaborately appointed' farewell dinner for Mrs Astor in February 1900; and Mrs Wharton is among the 'fashionable women' taking a box at an American Rose Society charity event at the Waldorf-Astoria in March 1901 (the boxes 'will be arranged as rose bowers, with little tables for the serving of tea to their guests [. . .] and the ballroom of the Astoria will be made to resemble an Italian garden, with beds of roses').[36]

35 Wharton, *A Backward Glance*, pp. 122–3.
36 *New York Times*, 29 August 1885, p. 3; 11 February 1900, p. 9; 19 March 1901, p. 9.

Whereas 'Lily was in her element on such occasions' (I: xii, 167), Wharton found them vacuous and draining, and she tired of the 'flat frivolity' of the Newport social scene.[37] Her purchase, in 1901, of a 113-acre estate, with a lake, in the hills of West Massachusetts, at last gave her fresh scope. Lenox was itself a fashionable resort: Baedeker's Guide, in 1893, dubbed it 'the Newport of the Berkshires', commenting that 'it makes an even greater impression of wealth and luxury than the real Newport'.[38] But here Wharton could shape her space, in the model of the civilised life. Styling her house ('The Mount') on an English stately home, Belton House in Lincolnshire, she set it off with splendid Italianate gardens. Here, each summer, she could write, enjoy excursions in her chauffeur-driven motor (then an unusual sight) and, above all, discover the stimulus of literary fellowship. In *The House of Mirth*, in Lily's early fantasy, Wharton presents a faint reflection of her own more serious aspirations: to attain a position where she might 'make her influence felt in the vague diffusion of refinement and good taste' (I: iii, 70). Lily's vision of a gracious life remains unfocused, and, with possibility extinct, her solitude is one of the bleakest elements of the final phase of the narrative. Edith Wharton, in contrast, celebrated the richness her friends brought to her life and work. Walter Berry became the companion to whom she could read her compositions in progress, and her most scrupulous critic. Henry James, above all, inspired with talk, with humour and with kindness. She now had the environment where she could develop her craft: it was here she completed her first novel, *The Valley of Decision* (1902), a historical romance of Italy; and it was here that, taking up James's admonition to 'DO NEW YORK!' (see Introduction, **p. xiii**), she settled to work on *The House of Mirth*.

Edith Wharton's career: *The House of Mirth*, and after

The first instalment of *The House of Mirth* appeared in *Scribner's Magazine* in January 1905, the month of Edith Wharton's forty-third birthday; and she came to regard the book as a turning point in her career. By this time, she had become a highly regarded author. She had seen poems and stories printed in prestigious magazines since the late 1870s, and, over the previous eight years, she had brought out nine books – including *The Valley of Decision*, three short-story collections,[39] two novellas,[40] a translation of a German tragic drama and compilations of her travel articles on the Italian landscape and its buildings. (One of these, *Italian Villas and Their Gardens*, 1904, became a standard work.[41]) She enjoyed good reviews and, with her growing publications, further commissions followed. Yet, so she claimed, she still lacked confidence, and although the subject of *The House of Mirth* had been in her mind as early as 1900 (see Text and contexts, **p. 4**), she failed to make much progress. As she recalled, the writing halted 'between my critical dissatisfaction with the work, and the distractions of

37 Wharton, *A Backward Glance*, p. 143.
38 James Muirhead, ed., *The United States: [. . .] A Handbook for Travellers, 1893*, Leipzig: Karl Baedeker, 1893, p. 139.
39 *The Greater Inclination*, 1899, *Crucial Instances*, 1901, and *The Descent of Man and Other Stories*, 1904.
40 'The Touchstone', 1900, and 'Sanctuary', 1903.
41 This was followed by *Italian Backgrounds*, 1905.

a busy and hospitable life'.[42] She was jolted into action when *Scribner's Magazine*, let down by another contributor, suddenly requested her story at four months' notice. With the challenge of seeing her first chapters serialised in print, while she was still working out her story, she was compelled to set aside self-criticism and stick to a routine; and she succeeded in delivering her novel within the deadlines This experience, she said, transformed her 'from a drifting amateur into a professional' and gave her 'the kingdom of mastery' over her tools.[43]

The House of Mirth caused a sensation. Announced as 'The Greatest Novel of the Year' by Scribner's, it dominated best-seller lists well into 1906. Although some denied that the rich were as vacuous, unpleasant and unscrupulous as the novel suggested, all acknowledged Wharton's credentials. As one disputant insisted, in a long-running debate in the *New York Times*: 'Mrs Wharton from peculiar circumstances of birth and surroundings is better qualified than any other writer of American fiction to describe this condition of society [. . .], and that she has the ability to do so no one will question.'[44] Demands for a stage adaptation followed, and, although the production flopped, Wharton's collaboration with the (then famous) playwright, Clyde Fitch, generated fresh publicity (see Performance/adaptation, **pp. 148–51**). A French translation, by a young writer, Charles Du Bos, brought it to a still wider international audience.[45]

Wharton's success confirmed her place as the pre-eminent novelist of modern American culture; and she went on, in further fictions, to analyse the entire spectrum of society. From the domain of the leisure classes in *The House of Mirth*, she turned to its rising aspirants in *The Custom of the Country* (1913) and, in *Ethan Frome* (1911) and *Summer* (1917), meditated on the lives of the New England country people beyond society's notice. Though she had concluded *The House of Mirth* as Lily entered her thirties, she herself found, in her forties, new experience, new vitality. She embarked on an brief affair with the journalist, Morton Fullerton; and, charting its painful intensities in her secret 'Love Diary', she exclaimed that it brought her 'the wine of life', 'the only moments of real life I have ever known'.[46] After the affair, her divorce from Teddy in 1913 released her from a relationship which had become ever more destructive. Teddy had sold the Mount, and Wharton came to a decision to make France her permanent home. She remained there throughout the First World War, turning her energies to war work – efforts acknowledged by the award of Chevalier of the Legion of Honour in 1916. In *A Son at the Front* (1923), she recreated in fiction the impact of the war on rich Americans, but also returned to her earlier world in *The Age of Innocence* (1920) (winning the Pulitzer Prize for this novel in 1921). In 1923, she returned briefly to the United States to be awarded Yale University's Doctor of Letters (the first the university had bestowed on a woman – some forty years before it would admit women to its degrees). She used her observations in *The Mother's Recompense* (1925), *Twilight Sleep* (1927), and other novels, where she turned to the new American post-war scene. These, her ghost stories (collected in 1937, the year she

---

42 Wharton, *A Backward Glance*, p. 207.
43 Wharton, *A Backward Glance*, p. 209.
44 Letter, signed 'Lenox', *New York Times*, 16 December 1905.
45 The novel was serialised in the *Revue de Paris*, 1906, followed by book publication.
46 Edited by Kenneth M. Price and Phyllis McBride, 'The Life Apart (*L'âme close*) [French: the enclosed soul]', was published in *American Literature* 66, December 1994, pp. 663–88.

died) and her unfinished novel, *The Buccaneers*, published posthumously, returned to some of the unspoken subjects of her earlier fictions and paved the way for later, non-realist readings.

Approaching her seventies, Wharton declared herself outmoded – 'the literary equivalent of tufted furniture and gas chandeliers', as she described herself in a letter to F. Scott Fitzgerald;[47] a younger generation, novelists such as Fitzgerald himself or the then-popular Sinclair Lewis were in tune with the new age. But all her writings have re-emerged for readers as acute, formally innovative, observations of a complex social phase. Her visions of a culture dominated by crazes, cults, advertising and spending, fragmented families and serial divorce, are nightmares of Late Capitalism, which seem, in retrospect, the culmination of all she had dreaded – the antithesis of 'the old-established order' she had discovered as a child in Europe. *The House of Mirth* was the text in which she, early on, identified such forces.

Literary contexts

In the densely layered canvas of *The House of Mirth*, it is not always possible (or helpful) to separate literary and cultural elements, and these, in the period, are often closely intertangled. ('Literature' itself was then a broad term, encompassing, not just imaginative writing, but the work of thinkers in fields from sociology or political comment, to science and philosophy.) In this and the following section, therefore, aspects of both literature and culture will feature under each main heading. Where appropriate, extracts from newspapers, guidebooks, social commentary and gossip columns will give a flavour of some of the text's contemporaries. Even such brief snatches of other writings can greatly assist in our understanding of the nuances of Wharton's satire, her perfect pitch in discriminating the different notes of topical debate: these are the voices of the culture with which *The House of Mirth* is in dialogue.

Literary antecedents and contemporaries; allusion, quotation and art

Much critical debate has centred on the novel's generic affinities: whether its closest relations are European or American; whether it belongs in a realist or a naturalist tradition; whether Wharton's own attempts to distance herself from women's writing or sentimental fiction have obscured key elements of her text. Aspects of all these, and others, figure in her writing (see Critical history). Wharton's title of 'Henry James's Heiress', bestowed by the British critic Q. D. Leavis in 1938, has also coloured readings of her texts (see Critical history, **pp. 68–9**); and James's heroines in *Daisy Miller* (1879) or *The Portrait of a Lady* (1881), a study of a young American, an 'intelligent but presumptuous girl',[48]

---

47 Edith Wharton, letter F. Scott Fitzgerald, 8 June 1925, quoted in R. W. B. Lewis and Nancy Lewis, eds, *The Letters of Edith Wharton*, New York: Scribner's, 1988, p. 481.
48 Henry James, Preface, *The Portrait of a Lady*, Vol. I, London: Macmillan, 1928, p. xiv.

offer interesting precursors to Wharton's Lily. But James's own relationship to European realism connects Wharton with broader literary currents (see Janet Beer and Elizabeth Nolan, Critical readings, **pp. 106–15**). Kathy Fedorko suggests a different set of affiliations, in popular and literary Gothic (see Critical readings, **pp. 116–26**). Besides these, many of the text's plot devices (orphanhood, ill-timed encounters, illicit letters, debts, disinheritance, blackmail) have their roots in nineteenth-century popular or sensation fiction (novels such as those, in the United States, of the prolific, best-selling, Mrs E. D. E. N. Southworth).

Alongside the satiric realism, the dynamics of emotion (displays of feeling, restraint), as Hildegarde Hoeller argues, take the text, too, into the realms of American sentimental writing (most famously exemplified by Susan Warner and Maria Cummins).[49] Though the text also satirises sentimental fiction, as in Lily's daydreams of exotic European marriages ('an English nobleman' or 'an Italian prince' (I: ii, 70), its tones colour Lily's relations with Selden and inform her final renunciations. In its engagement with the new, however, the novel might be read alongside the analysts of the city, or the 'Woman Question' (see Texts and contexts, **pp. 41–56**). Many of the text's concerns reverberate in other American novels of the first quarter of the century, among them: David Graham Phillips's *Susan Lenox: Her Fall and Rise* (1917), Sinclair Lewis's *Main Street* (1920), F. Scott Fitzgerald's *The Beautiful and Damned* (1922) and Willa Cather's *A Lost Lady* (1923). All these share some of the text's main ingredients: a focus on money, commodity and the objectification of beauty; hints of evolutionary decline; the waste of female creative energies in a debased and vacuous culture. Such themes remain highly topical, and Lily's story retains its force, as a model and a site for reworking, in the fiction of novelists today (see Pamela Knights, Critical readings, **pp. 127–41**).

In presenting a 'frivolous society' of 'irresponsible pleasure-seekers',[50] the text draws richly on Wharton's reading. Packing *The House of Mirth*, like all her writing, with allusion, she gives the narratorial commentary a range far beyond that of any of the characters. Although it seems unlikely that any single reader will pick up all her subtle notes, Wharton's irony usually gives sufficient hint. Any annotated edition (though none can be comprehensive) will serve to suggest the novel's panoramic scope of reference and to identify specific sources which individuals may be interested in pursuing.

Wharton's references contribute to her drive to investigate – her attempt to grasp essential characteristics of a personality or a social group. This was one of the major projects of the realist novel, with its emphasis on capturing everyday details, to present a larger whole (see Critical history, **pp. 74–5**). However, in presenting readers with an array of particulars, a realist text also sought ways of guiding their judgement, of highlighting the most significant features. Allusion serves helpfully in this process, in presenting readers with what the modern critic, Catherine Belsey, calls in her definition of Classic Realism, a '*hierarchy of*

---

49 Hugely popular heroines included Ellen Montgomery in Susan Warner (Elizabeth Wetherell), *The Wide, Wide World* (1851), and Gerty Flint in Maria Cummins, *The Lamplighter* (1854). Hildegard Hoeller studies Wharton's complex relationship to such fictions in *Edith Wharton's Dialogue with Realism and Sentimental Fiction*, Gainesville, Fla.: University Press of Florida, 2000.

50 Wharton, *A Backward Glance*, p. 207.

discourses'.[51] Allowed an overview of individual characters' levels of cultural understanding, readers are placed in a privileged position, to see their place in the narrative's scheme of values. Within such a hierarchy, Selden's appreciation of La Bruyère, a seventeenth-century French moralist, seems to suggest a greater range of apprehension than, for example, Percy Gryce's penchant for (unread and unreadable) Americana. However, Wharton's irony will often take a further twist – that even the most sensitive (or intellectually pretentious) characters comprehend very little. Through all these references, Wharton keeps in view a vision of the Arts as a source of deeper values which are absent in this society: the 'mighty sum of human striving' (II: xiii, 359) without which Lily is lost.

Allusions, then, provide a touchstone. As in her details of furnishings or architectural finish, an aesthetic choice will often precisely place a character's class, taste and morality. Cheap reproductions of both American and European art, as often in Wharton's works, code their admirers' limitations. The paintings from Thomas Cole's 'Voyage of Life', for example, the chosen décor for the walls of the dreary Bart relations (I: iii, 65), were a popular allegorical sequence. Sold on a mass market, they act as an index to a banal, middle-class sensibility, concerned only that art be genteel; Mrs Peniston's selections (the replica of the Dying Gladiator among them) are similarly dull and respectable. Such references heighten for the reader, in contrast, the subtleties of Wharton's narrative itself. Challenging, complex and disturbing, *The House of Mirth* is not the kind of book most of its characters would understand or approve.

Wharton's allusions also bring into the text hints of thematic and structural parallels, from the title onwards. As the *New York Times* review first suggested, and critics since have reaffirmed, the biblical reference to Ecclesiastes, for example, in Wharton's final choice of title, indicts the whole upper-class society: 'Vanity of vanities; all is vanity' (Eccles. 1:2).[52] Wharton's earlier title, 'A Moment's Ornament', keeps the attention on Lily. Janet Beer Goodwyn locates its source in William Wordsworth's lyric, 'She Was a Phantom of Delight': 'A lovely Apparition, sent / To be a moment's ornament'; and explores its special significance for nineteenth-century readers, as an image of the 'perfect Woman'.[53] Taken cumulatively, such references cast new cross-lights on the action, as Wharton layers associations, opening up narratives within the narrative. Even a passing touch can intensify an episode locally, while hinting at broader sets of affinities throughout the text. 'Bellomont', an ironic echo of 'Belmont', the beautiful estate of Shakespeare's *The Merchant of Venice*, sets the scene for a wider arena of conflict – the stage where Lily plays out her choices, rivalries, debts and desperate bargains. Even the despised Cole paintings, as Killoran notes, reflect the narrative's passage from life to death, figured in the frequent images of voyaging, floating, seas and ships (given form in 'dreamlike scenery in which people set out on allegorical sea journeys of childhood, youth, manhood, and old age as angels guide their way'[54]).

51 Catherine Belsey, *Critical Practice*, London: Methuen, 1980, p. 70.
52 Helen Killoran, for example, makes this point in her study *Edith Wharton: Art and Allusion*, Tuscaloosa, Ala. and London: University of Alabama Press, 1996, p. 16.
53 Beer Goodwyn, *Edith Wharton: Traveller in the Land of Letters*, p. 57.
54 Killoran, *Edith Wharton: Art and Allusion*, p. 23.

The text is full of pictures of women; legends of other stories colour the view of Lily. Readers have glimpsed her likeness, for instance, in the imprisoned figures of fairy tale and literary ballads – the Sleeping Beauty, or Tennyson's 'The Lady of Shalott' (1832; revised, 1842). Such images hover both in story and in scene, drawing into the text hints of their reworkings in art and illustration. Selden's final view of Lily, for example, reflects many Victorian pictures of a dead, or dying, beauty. The Lady of Shalott was a favourite subject, and Pre-Raphaelite treatments of Tennyson's poem offer a number of famous examples. (Dante Gabriel Rossetti's illustration, in Moxon's edition, of 1857, is particularly worth attention.) Turning to later nineteenth-century models, Cynthia Griffin Wolff emphasises the prominence of Art Nouveau as a pervasive cultural style and reads Lily's purity in terms of its repeated floral motif: the lily (see Critical history pp. 70–2).

In popular culture, the Gibson Girl (see Edith Thornton, Critical readings, pp. 84–95), provides another hugely influential style note.[55] Awareness of American portraiture makes a further contribution, especially the work of the society favourite, John Singer Sargent (1856–1925), an artist Wharton is believed to have satirised in various fictions. (The self-satisfied Popple in *The Custom of the Country* and Paul Morpeth in *The House of Mirth*, have struck many critics as resemblances.) Sargent's beautifully draped, jewelled and ornamental women, seem emblems of Lily's idealised picture of her future: 'in a drawing-room, diffusing elegance as a flower sheds perfume' (I: ix, 89). Her actual fate is rendered in the more sombre tones – the 'dark pencilling', 'morbid blue-', or 'dull chocolate-' (II: x, 329) – of a realist painter such as Thomas Eakins (1844–1916). A series of 'gallerylike still portraits', to use Killoran's summary,[56] captures her social decline, from the first view at the station until the final scene. All these styles represent ways of framing Lily – for Selden, for Rosedale, for other spectators, and for the reader, positioned alongside.

Lily's own self-conscious poses form part of such a sequence. In the most elaborate of these, at the climax of the Brys' entertainment, Wharton again creates effects through reference to a popularised pictorial art. *Tableaux vivants*, 'living pictures', were all the rage as an amusement throughout the period, for all ages and classes, in private homes and in charity functions, ranging from low-cost versions in schoolrooms to the extravaganzas of the very rich. Their subject matter was diverse, from biblical scenes to comic vignettes – but 'Old Masters' feature frequently. The more expensive tableaux, staged by well-known leisure-class women, were featured in the society columns. Even a brief example gives a flavour:

> Mrs. George J. Gould threw open Georgian Court to the public this afternoon and evening for a Colonial bazaar and entertainment in aid of the Women's Auxiliary of All Saints' Memorial Church, of which she is an attendant. [. . .] At least a thousand persons took advantage of the opportunity to view the interior of the court and incidentally aid the

---

55 An extensive survey of cultural models of femininity of the period may be found in Martha Banta, *Imaging American Women: Idea and Ideals in Cultural History*, New York: Columbia University Press, 1987.
56 Killoran, *Edith Wharton: Art and Allusion*, p. 25.

association. [. . .] A series of tableaux vivants, arranged by Mrs. Gould, was an enjoyable feature of the entertainment. Miss Marjorie Gwyne Gould posed as 'The Christian Martyr' after Gabriel Max's famous painting, 'The Last Token.' Miss Vivian Gould, Master George Jay Gould, and Miss Hope Hamilton posed in a picture of a Watteau fan. Tea was served to the patrons by women who were attired in Japanese costumes.[57]

Wharton's description closely echoes the notes of such items. At the Wellington Brys', for instance: 'The scenes were taken from old pictures, and the participators had been cleverly fitted with characters suited to their types' (I: xii, 170). At 'An Hour with Gibson's Models' ('A Unique Entertainment Given at the Pratt Institute'), similarly: 'Twelve tableaux were shown, the principals being posed by Miss Fletcher, in reproductions of famous illustrations by C. D. [Charles Dana] Gibson. The young men and women taking part in the tableaux had been carefully selected as reproducing the types chosen by the artist.'[58]

The specific subject of Lily's triumph has been the focus of considerable critical attention: the portrait 'Mrs [Richard Bennett] Lloyd' by the eighteenth-century British artist Joshua Reynolds (1723–92). Mrs Lloyd's own pose in the painting, draped like a dryad, in revealing classical robes, pictured in the act of writing a name on a tree, generates multiple interpretative possibilities – layerings of text, artifice, acting and performance – in ways that continue to produce fresh readings. Lily imitates a portrait, which itself seeks to replicate an earlier Renaissance ideal of a still-earlier classical scene. Cynthia Griffin Wolff, for example, notes the allusion to Shakespeare in a contemporary review of Reynold's exhibit: 'Mrs. Lloyd [. . .] a beautiful figure in a loose, fancy vest, inscribing her husband's name on the bark of a tree. The idea is taken from *As You Like It*.'[59] Margot Norris points to an earlier model: Angelica from the Italian poet, Ariosto's *Orlando Furioso* (c. 1532).[60] Whatever the specific source, all such images raise questions about Lily as an object for male fantasy – an artwork, a collector's item, the centre of speculation. They also prompt inquiry about character. In the narratives of such intertexts, what further roles do characters play? Is Lily complicit with her destiny or caught in a plot outside her making? Cast as a prince, or as Lancelot, how is Selden to be read? All such connotations complicate the narrative, forestalling simple response.

The mythic strains of the text offer a further set of analogies; many of these are introduced through a character's consciousness and take readers back into an older classical tradition: Greek drama, Roman legend. Lily's casual acquaintance with Aeschylus' *Eumenides* brings the horrific vision of the Furies into the broader narrative, closing for vengeance on her cowering self. The images of a trapped creature – or prisoner, or victim – are present in her admirers' viewpoints,

57 *New York Times*, 22 February 1903, p. 7.
58 *Brooklyn Eagle*, 26 February 1897, p. 4.
59 Cited from a review in a London newspaper, the *Morning Post*, in 1776: Cynthia Griffin Wolff, 'Notes' to Edith Wharton, *The House of Mirth*, Harmondsworth: Penguin, 1986, p. 335.
60 Margot Norris, 'Death by Speculation: Deconstructing *The House of Mirth*', in Edith Wharton, *The House of Mirth*, ed. Shari Benstock, Boston, Mass.: Bedford Books of St Martin's Press, 1994, p. 439.

too. Selden views her as a 'captured dryad', with an air of 'sylvan freedom' (I: i, 47). Later, he casts her as the chained Andromeda and places himself in the role of Perseus, her rescuer (I: xiv, 196). (Andromeda, a beautiful woman, had been appointed as a sacrificial victim to placate a savage sea-monster.) Rosedale does not share Selden's close knowledge of the classics, but draws on a half-remembered story. Like Selden, he flatters himself, as a hero, in his compliments to Lily: 'There was a girl in some history book who wanted gold shields, or something, [. . .]; and she was crushed under 'em: they killed her. [. . .] What I want is a woman who'll hold her head higher the more diamonds I put on it' (I: xv, 214).

What Rosedale recalls here is another doomed woman: the mythical Tarpeia, who betrayed Rome to the invading Sabines, for the promise of gold bracelets but, rewarded instead by trickery, was crushed under their shields. Elaine Showalter (see Critical history, **pp. 72–3**) suggests that such comparisons often reflect back on the ego of the man who makes them. At the turn of the century, to view a woman as a dryad (a fragile, elusive creature) was a fashionable male fantasy. So, Selden's poeticising is a cliché; Lily's 'sylvan' self is as artificial as any other stylish drawing-room feature. Elizabeth Ammons takes a similar view, suggesting that another legend lurks here: that of Pygmalion (Selden), who falls in love with a beautiful statue and wishes it brought to life (a scene echoed at the *tableaux*). For Ammons, like Showalter, what masquerades as love is a desire to possess, to dominate.[61] Showalter points, too, to Wharton's awareness of nineteenth-century revisions of classical tales, which she reworks in turn, often with a subtle critique of gender constructions. Tarpeia, for example, was the subject of various poems, which questioned her reputation as the epitome of the materialistic traitor and rewrote her as the victim of her culture. Showalter instances: 'Louise Guiney's well-known poem of the 1890s that dramatised the paradox of a woman's being condemned by her society for the mercenary and narcissistic values it has encouraged.'[62]

As a psychological study, *The House of Mirth* repeatedly reverts to questions of heritage and expectation – what has shaped Lily, what she might achieve. Lily fails either to fulfil the part she has been fashioned for or to renew herself through any other kind of agency. What kind of society is hers and what kind of place can an individual woman expect in it? The mesh of allusion keeps such questions constantly alive.

The social analysts and the state of the city

Wharton's inquiries also draw on other, broader contexts – overlapping discourses of degeneration and discussions of the state of the city and its gulfs of money and class. With a new century in prospect, many writers saw the urgency of social analysis – taking stock, in order to speculate about the future of America.

Social theory colours *The House of Mirth*, and many interrelated strands are informed by Wharton's keen interest in the new social sciences, philosophy and

61 Elizabeth Ammons, *Edith Wharton's Argument with America*, Athens, Ga.: University of Georgia Press, 1980, p. 36.
62 Elaine Showalter, 'The Death of the Lady (Novelist): Wharton's *House of Mirth*', *Representations* 9, winter 1985, p. 140.

models of evolution. Her cultural critique, as various critics have pointed out,[63] adapts from ethnography and social-anthropology methods of analysing the group as well as the individual. She turns on her own circle the sort of scrutiny nineteenth-century thinkers such as E. B. Tylor or Edward Westermarck devoted to so-called 'primitive' tribes.[64] Wharton would elaborate her method most explicitly in her 1920 novel, *The Age of Innocence*, but her anthropological eye is evident in *The House of Mirth*, in her study of the social nuances, habits and habitat of a select Manhattan class. In the kind of details noted earlier – for example, the seeming trivia of Mrs Peniston's domestic arrangements (see Text and contexts, pp. 7–8) – she depicts the household altars, belief systems, customs, rituals, sacred objects, taboos and survival tactics of a threatened group. When Lily offends those who hold power in the tribe (its elders such as Mrs Peniston, gossips like Grace Stepney, or its rich, the Judy Trenors and Bertha Dorsets), she unleashes the forces which will expel and destroy her.

In presenting this elite circle and hinting at what makes it vulnerable, Wharton shades her analysis with contemporary fears about social 'degeneration'. Drawing on Darwinian theories of evolution, anxieties about national and cultural decline were pervasive throughout the period. (Max Nordau's *Degeneration* [1895] in translation from the German, was the most famous expression of such concerns.) The 'signs' of degeneration were manifold, encompassing a range of cultural and social 'weaknesses' from 'decadent' sexualities (homosexuality, 'mannish' women) and 'morbid' novels, through disease and feeble-mindedness, to 'polluted' blood. Accounts such as George M. Beard's widely read *American Nervousness* (1881) described the assault on sensitive natures of a pressured, modern lifestyle; the refined elite, he suggested, were the most susceptible, as the 'lower orders' were less finely tuned. Such pressures rack many of the characters; and George Dorset's delicate digestion, for instance, or Lily's insomnia can be read directly in terms of many of Beard's case studies.[65] (Edith Wharton herself was treated for 'nervous' illness during the 1890s.)

At their most extreme, such anxieties underpinned the advocation of eugenics, the science of breeding healthy national stock through mating the 'finest' evolutionary specimens and attempting to eliminate degenerative and decadent forms. Theories that the older, white stock (the descendants of early Dutch and Anglo-Saxon colonists, such as Wharton's own family) was in decline fuelled racist polemics; and many discussions of the socially disadvantaged, poor, or inadequate, are marked by eugenicist discourses. In the United States, deeply embedded in the dominant culture, they entered even such radical reformist writings as those of the feminist writer, Charlotte Perkins Gilman (see Text and contexts, pp. 45–7). White, aristocratic politicians, such as President Theodore Roosevelt (a friend and distant relative of Wharton's by marriage) openly warned

---

63 See, for example, the essays by Pamela Knights and by Nancy Bentley in *The Cambridge Companion to Edith Wharton*, ed. Millicent Bell, New York: Cambridge University Press, 1995, pp. 20–46, 47–67; and Nancy Bentley, *The Ethnography of Manners: Hawthorne, James and Wharton*, Cambridge: Cambridge University Press, 1995.

64 For example, Edward B. Tylor's *Primitive Culture* (1871) and *Anthropology* (1894) (both in Wharton's library), John F. McLennan, *Primitive Marriage* (1865) and Edward Westermarck, *History of Human Marriage* (1894).

65 See Knights, Introduction, *The House of Mirth*, pp. vii–vii; xxvi–vii.

of 'Race Suicide': the weakening of white America by an 'underclass' (including immigrants, African Americans, the unemployed) and by the rise of new, unregulated fortunes. The tenements, poverty, the sickness of the city and the desperate state of many of its populace, were, collectively, the symptom, in such views, of deeper sickness threatening the nation. Fears of Jews, particularly those (like Simon Rosedale) economically successful, added currents of anti-Semitism to such arguments. The well-educated, white leisure classes were urged to breed, to replenish the race. Wharton gives a satirical edge to eugenicist thinking in Percy Gryce's concerns about Lily's headache: 'he wondered rather nervously if she were delicate, having far-reaching fears about the future of his progeny' (I: vi, 102). In Nettie Crane (later Struther), she offers a more sympathetic inflection: Lily had known her 'as one of the discouraged victims of over-work and anaemic parentage: one of the superfluous fragments of life destined to be swept prematurely into that social refuse-heap of which Lily had so lately expressed her dread' (II: xiii, 352–3).

But for some readers, such fears hold a more central place in *The House of Mirth*. Such elements as Lily's inability to find a suitably refined mate, her attraction to Lawrence Selden for his air of 'superiority' and his appeal to 'the fastidious element in her taste' (I: vi, 101); and her seemingly instinctive revulsion from the Jewish Rosedale have roused debate about Wharton's attitudes (see Critical history, p. 79). The figures who set the plot in motion, appearing ominously outside Selden's door, are marked as socially 'other', diseased or ethnically different: the cleaning woman, Mrs Haffen, with her pock-marked face and unpleasantly bald scalp, and Mr Rosedale, with his overfamiliar tone. But what strikes some readers as Wharton's conservative anxiety may be for others only Lily's individual revulsion – countered by Wharton's more fully rounded portraits in the broader narrative. For these readers, the evidence of Rosedale's kindness, or Nettie Struther's humanity, for example, offer positive images which challenge anti-Semitic or class stereotyping and rebut eugenicist scare stories.

With the advent of a new century, these debates about national decline were inseparable from discussion of progress. Visions of the city, New York in particular, were central to many investigations; and in urging Wharton to 'DO NEW YORK!' (see Introduction, p. xiii), Henry James was directing her to a vibrantly topical subject. The modern metropolis, with its crowds, noise and hurry, its buildings (seemingly in a state of constant demolition or construction), its incomers (from immigrants to millionaires), its distinctive social worlds, struggles and pressures, seemed to defy representation. In his own short novel, *Washington Square* (1880), James himself had examined 'old' Manhattan, under threat from what he viewed as the depredations of new commercial forces;[66] and, following his injunction to Wharton, he too would attempt to capture the impact of modernity, in his impressionistic documentary travelogue, *The American Scene* (1907). From the very start of *The House of Mirth*, Wharton took up the challenge directly. Placing her heroine in the afternoon throng at Grand Central Station, she presented her readers in 1905 with the rush of the contemporary:

---

66 For discussion of parallels with *The House of Mirth*, see Christopher Gair, 'The Crumbling Structure of "Appearances": Representation and Authenticity in *the House of Mirth* and *The Custom of the Country*', *Modern Fiction Studies* 43 (2), 1997, pp. 349–73.

for commentators of the day, the vast transport terminals, like Grand Central, epitomised the energies of the modern world. Here, poised, radiant, set apart from the dull crowds (the estimated 50,000 persons a day who passed through this great station),[67] Lily begins her journey still in touch with her familiar habitat, her small, select circle of older Manhattan; but during the course of the novel, Wharton precipitates her into the faster-paced, changing, twentieth-century city.

From the pleasant façade of Selden's bachelor 'flat-house' to the 'blistered brown stone front' of Lily's down-at-heel boarding house (I: i, 40; II: x, 333) Wharton's evocation of New York's finely graded social spaces builds on, but also significantly extends, other writers' treatments.[68] The late nineteenth century had seen a swelling stream of inquiry into the city's ills, by sociologists, economists, philanthropists and researchers. Such writers explored the strata which, within *The House of Mirth*, constitute the realm of the 'dingy' from which Lily recoils. In *A Hazard of New Fortunes* (1890), for example, the highly regarded realist author William Dean Howells (see Critical history, **p. 74**), had focused on a middle-class milieu of work (magazine journalism). In the city as Howells presents it, even the cosy enclave of literary endeavour is affected by wider disturbances – currents of political conflict, between capitalism and socialism, enacted in violent labour struggles. Many writers went further into the city's lower depths, finding a compelling subject in the desperate conditions of its tenement areas, particularly on the Lower East Side, and in the character of its 'under classes'. In *The House of Mirth*, a narrative aside remarks: 'Affluence, unless stimulated by a keen imagination, forms but the vaguest notion of the practical strain of poverty' (I: vii, 112). Socially concerned studies of day sought to rouse awareness; and documentary investigations into poverty – such as the photo-journalist, Jacob Riis's pioneering *How the Other Half Lives* (1890) – made a strong impact. Inquiries extended to other American cities, and, in the case of Jack London, to exploration, in 1902, in the slums of London, related in the resonantly titled *The People of the Abyss* of 1903. Fiction contributed to public concern. In *Maggie: A Girl of the Streets* (privately issued under a pseudonym in 1893, before publication in 1896), the naturalist novelist (see Critical history, **pp. 77–8**) Stephen Crane shocked many readers with his story of life in the tenements, as he took his heroine from work in the sweatshops to prostitution and violent death. Notes of alarm would continue to sound, as, for example, in Ernest Poole's *The Voice of the Street* (1906), and James Oppenheim's *Dr. Rast* (1908).

In *The House of Mirth*, poverty threatens Lily throughout her story. Wharton stops short of taking her heroine into the tenements, and Lily's death coincides with the final erasure of her funds. Had she lived, her alternatives remain unspecific, but the sordid fate of penniless women, as unveiled in *Maggie*, hovers in the text. It seems hinted at, for instance, in the story of Nettie Struther's sexual betrayal and near-fatal decline, and in the repeated motif of the 'abyss', which looms closer as Lily descends. Lily's appeal to Gerty, which goes unanswered, is haunted by such stories: 'There are bad girls in your slums. Tell me—do they ever

67 George H. Daniels, *New York Central*, Four-track Series, New York: New York and Hudson River Railroad Company, 1896, p. 250.
68 For a fuller view, see Douglas Tallack, 'New York New York', The 3Cities Project, available on-line at <http://www.nottingham.ac.uk/3cities/tallack2.htm> (accessed 15 April 2005).

pick themselves up? Ever forget and feel as they did before?' (I: xiv, 202). Another contentious city novel of the new century resonates in Lily's dilemma: Theodore Dreiser's *Sister Carrie* (1900). This, too, moved into the abyss, with the descent of the central male character into dinginess, poverty and extinction. At the same time, however, to the disgust of many readers, it traced the course of its eponymous heroine on a trajectory upwards. Casually seduced by ever more glittering men, and ever-larger cities, Carrie ends the novel, single, rich and successful, her name in lights, a star in Manhattan musical theatre. Readers were shocked by the lack of moralising and by Carrie's complete absence of remorse or introspection. A highly ambiguous success story, like *The House of Mirth*, *Sister Carrie* is concerned with the forces of commodity and consumerism, female beauty and male voyeurism,[69] and the construction of 'personality' in the modern age, but it reaches only the borders of Wharton's specific social realm. Wharton makes plain that, in rejecting Trenor's or Rosedale's sexual bargains, Lily refuses to sell herself for a life inside the 'little illuminated circle' (I: xiv, 187). But, for Lily, life outside that circle is a dark, almost unthinkable prospect. Her fears seem confirmed, in the narrative, by her struggles in Mme Regina's workroom and the glimpses of the 'fagged profiles' of fellows in this 'underworld of toilers' (II: x, 321, 325). Beneath this, the text hints at lower and darker worlds still, the lives of those, unlike the working-girls, who live beneath the level of want. But other elements in the text allow room for more positive visions.

Bleak as some city narratives were, they did not necessarily reinforce the worst fears of the conservative elite; and many writers went to great lengths to emphasise that though poverty was a social evil, the poor themselves were not innately depraved. (It was hardship not corruption, which, for example, led women to 'fall'.) Pioneering studies such as Robert Hunter's *Poverty* (1904) attempted objective views of the causes of social conditions, with suggestions about amelioration: Hunter, a settlement worker (see Text and contexts, **pp. 31–3**), famously defined the 'poverty line' as $460 a year. In trying to understand the value of any sum of money of the period – those in *The House of Mirth* included – it is tempting, but simplistic, to seek a direct equivalent in twenty-first-century terms; and there is debate about the meaningfulness of any such exercise.[70] An example would be the $300 Lily donates to Gerty's charity work – 'a liberal fraction' of the price of the dressing case she covets (I: x, 148). Depending on the parameters used for the calculation, this translates into a range of 'equivalents', a century on, from, approximately, $6,600 (c. £3,500) to $129,400 (£69,150).[71] Far more helpful, therefore, in trying to assess what constituted poverty or riches in Lily Bart's day is to look at the relative powers of spending between different groups. Wharton herself gives the clue to degrees of value, in Gerty Farish's exclamation, that the smallest of Mrs George Dorset's pearls 'would pay the rent of our Girls' Club for a year' (I: xii, 169).

69 For a close discussion of this aspect, see Lori Merish, 'Engendering Naturalism: Narrative Form and Commodity Spectacle in U.S. Naturalist Fiction', *Novel*, 29 (3), 1996, pp. 319–45.

70 For a full discussion, see John J. McCusker, *How Much Is That in Real Money? A Historical Price Index for Use as a Deflator of Money Values in the Economy of the United States*, 2nd edn, Worcester, Mass.: American Antiquarian Society, 2001.

71 Samuel H. Williamson, 'What is the Relative Value?' Economic History Services, June 2005, available on-line at <http://www.eh.net/hmit/compare> (accessed 1 June 2006).

Contemporary studies of the New York poor sharpen the picture. One such, a survey by Louise More, a sociologist, published two years after the novel, documented the budgets of 200 low-income families. More's evidence contributes to a positive view of the poor, giving a strong image of dignity, even in penury – the kind of vision Wharton offers readers in the view of Nettie Struther's shining kitchen, 'extraordinarily small and almost miraculously clean' (II: xiii, 353). For readers of *The House of Mirth*, More's carefully itemised lists of annual earnings and spending make clearer, moreover, the scale of Lily's purchasing habits and expectations. We can picture more strongly, for instance, the magnitude of Gus Trenor's $1,000 cheques, or the extent of Mrs Peniston's (far from meagre) $10,000 legacy by contemplating them alongside the reckonings in one of More's case studies. In the following example, this woman, left alone after her husband, a bookseller, had fallen on hard times, taken to drink and been removed to the penitentiary, supported herself and three children on a total of $260 a year. Her thirteen-year-old daughter made summer earnings ($14) in an artificial flower factory (a less exclusive version of Lily's work at Mme Regina's millinery establishment); otherwise the family were dependent upon the mother's earnings from sewing ($70) and a few dispensations from charity. Itemised the expenditures for the year were:

Food	$130.00
Rent	$92.75
Clothing	$18.00
Fuel	$13.00
Medicine	$1.00
Moving expenses	$3.00
Sundries	$2.25
Total:	$260.00

The family spent nothing on recreation, insurance, furniture, books or papers or car fares; they saved nothing, but they kept out of debt. Noting that this existence 'was not without physical deterioration for each member of the family'; Louise More adds: 'They were sent to Sea Breeze for two weeks in the summer, and the boy was sent with a Fresh Air party to Valhalla. The girl comes to clubs at the Settlement, which is the only recreation she has.'[72]

Many social commentators were interested in crusades for civic improvement and in the kind of charitable attempt More describes here to save families from sinking entirely. In *The House of Mirth*, Wharton picked up these topical themes in Gerty's endeavours with the Girls' Club and Carry Fisher's brief zeal for municipal reform. In Gerty's efforts, in particular, Wharton represents a broad movement of philanthropy, whose most famous worker was Jane Addams, known worldwide for her influential 'Settlement' work, at Hull House in Chicago. Nettie's rehabilitation, in a fresh-air cure in the mountains, sponsored through Lily's casual beneficence, is paralleled in many real-life documents of the time;

---

72 Louise Bolard More, *Wage-Earner's Budgets: A Study of Standards and Cost of Living in New York City*, New York: Henry Holt, 1907, pp. 153–5.

and, while some readers might view her rescue merely as a sentimental cliché,[73] knowing the contexts complicates easy judgement. For example, the following account by a French observer, describes the impact of a charity worker, Grace Dodge, and her activities in New York:

> She established her Association of Working-Girls' Societies in 1884, in a bare room on Tenth Avenue. At first she gathered around her, without requiring any fee, about a dozen girls who spent their days behind the counter in a shop, or in working for factories. At the end of a month there were sixty of them, and they agreed to pay twenty-five cents a week apiece. The same society now has a large house for which it pays one hundred and twenty-five dollars a month, sub-letting part of it for eighty-five dollars, which reduces the Society's rent to forty dollars, amply covered by the fees for membership. [. . .] [T]here are classes in cooking, embroidery, and sewing. There are also weekly practical talks, [. . .] The subjects are very characteristic of American ways; for instance, 'Men Friends;' 'How to find a husband;' 'How to make money and how to save it.'[74]

Gerty's artless comment about the rent that one of Mrs Dorset's pearls could buy gains a sharper edge in such a context; and Lily's transient interest in good works is further glossed here by the emphasis on the important role that richer women might play:

> For three dollars a week a girl may enjoy all the benefits of Holiday House [an annex on Long Island] and all the delights of the country. The clubs pay the travelling expenses; they all have fresh-air funds, and also arrange for this with the Working-Girls' Vacation Society, made up of rich girls, who, while they traverse the world for their own pleasure, do not forget that other young girls, tied down to their work, have neither opportunity nor means for travelling [. . .]. The frantic luxury of New York is atoned for by an equal outlay of intelligent philanthropy.[75]

Even brief extracts such as these serve to throw into sharp relief Lily's extravagances – lilies-of-the-valley at $2 the dozen, or the $300 lost in one night's bridge at Bellomont; and they provide fuller understanding of the nature of lives *The House of Mirth* has space only to hint at. Although some early critics suggested that Wharton's own privileged background limited her outlook (see Critical history, **pp. 66–8**), the text keeps in view the more precarious living of those outside the hot house. Nettie's presentation may be too strongly marked, for some readers' taste, as a figure of redemption and moral awakening, at the

73 For example, the director Terence Davis, who omitted Nettie in his screen adaptation, remarked in a talk that he had, in this respect, improved on Wharton. Address at 'Edith Wharton in London' Conference, 14–17 July 2003.
74 Mme Blanc (Th. Bentzon), *The Condition of Women in the United States: A Traveller's Notes*, trans. Abby Langdon, Boston, Mass. 1895; rpt. New York: Arno, 1972, pp. 241–2.
75 Blanc, *The Condition of Women in the United States*, pp. 243–4.

climax of Lily's narrative. But other figures, cumulatively, add depth to the novel's social perspectives. Here Wharton acknowledges the desperate at every level, from the genteel Miss Silverton to the coarse Mrs Haffen, driven to blackmail when her husband loses his work. These may be the spectres of Lily's nightmares, but, in a narrative sensitive to the shifts and turns of unemployment (a sharply topical theme), they also offer notes of realism in Wharton's broader cultural analysis.

Money, status and display

For the heroine of *The House of Mirth*, 'the only way not to think about money is to have a great deal of it' (I: vi, 105); but a sustained analysis of money, and monied groups, lies at the centre of *The House of Mirth* and, thus, warrants its own section here. If in comparison with novelists such as Crane or Dreiser Wharton only sketches the world of poverty, her major contribution was to map, in fiction, the landscape of the extremely affluent. She captures its contours in a state of transition, as the traditional leisure class of Wharton's own kind was invaded by newcomers to Manhattan, those with extravagant wealth, of more recent origin. Wharton's interest was not unique, but no other novelist had her insider's knowledge, or her rigour, attention to nuance or cultural grasp. In *A Hazard of New Fortunes*, Howells had portrayed the tensions within a millionaire family, giving a view into these ranks, but he stopped short of a full treatment. Other contemporaries interested in this terrain have long been largely forgotten – among them, for example, David Graham Phillips, whose essays, *The Reign of Gilt* (1905), would be reviewed alongside *The House of Mirth*; and Clyde Fitch, the novel's stage adaptor (see Performance/adaptation, **pp. 148–51**). In short-lived 'society' fictions, riches served as a backdrop rather than as a subject for investigation. Other, more searching, writings concentrated on the economic rather than social dimensions of riches. Journalistic 'muckrakers', as Theodore Roosevelt termed them, and Naturalist novelists, actively addressed the dangers of the most powerful forces and set out to expose corruption. Ida Tarbell's *The History of the Standard Oil Company* (1904), for example, presented an unsparing report on the abuses of the Rockefeller monopoly; and Frank Norris's novel *The Pit: A Story of Chicago* (1903) traced the damaging reverberations of the business world (commodity speculation on the wheat exchange) within the emotional life of individuals. Novels by the socialist, Upton Sinclair, conducted similarly vigorous attacks. Critics have also seen parallels in European novels of the city, such as George Gissing's *The Whirlpool* (1897).[76] Though largely turning their lens on cities elsewhere, such accounts give insights into the kinds of fortune we might imagine behind *The House of Mirth*'s rising characters.

Wharton captures the tensions during a period of immense economic change in the United States, which was to sweep away the Old New York of which Wharton's family had been a part (see Text and contexts, **p. 13**). This class had its roots in the earliest Anglo-Dutch settlers, who regarded themselves (and were

---

76 C. S. Collinson, '*The Whirlpool* and *The House of Mirth*' *Gissing Newsletter*, 16, 1980, discussed in Killoran, *Art and Allusion*, p. 19.

regarded) as the aristocracy of New York and whose income came from long-settled wealth, tied up in land and property. In *The House of Mirth* and throughout her fiction (as in her later novels, *The Custom of the Country* and *The Age of Innocence*), she presents the collisions and accommodations as newcomers rose into the leisure-class ranks. In Old New York, solid comfort, without obvious excess, had been the mark of good taste;[77] and the flagrant spending on new consumer goods, exercised by the incomers, became the object of endless fascinated commentary. Social reporters vied with each other to analyse the phenomenon of the new American fortunes (such as those of the Vanderbilts or Goulds), made in the cut-throat worlds of business, industry, mining and transport, in the post-Civil War United States ('The Gilded Age'), and to describe ever-greater ostentation in spending. Spectacularly lavish mansions, along Fifth Avenue, on Long Island, or at resorts like Newport, were transforming genteel leisure-class enclaves and stunning all observers. Often mentioned in relation to their houses, the Gryces, Welly Brys, Simon Rosedale, the Gormers, all represent millionaires at different stages of social ascent. Alarming as these were to the established upper echelons (women such as Mrs Peniston), in painting them onto her fictional canvas, Wharton made the most of her opportunities. In *The Custom of the Country*, for example, she would adopt a varying focus, taking readers into the view of both invader and invaded, at crucial points of encounter. In that novel, she tracked the career of Undine Spragg – a more deadly version of Louisa Bry or Mrs Hatch – in her trajectory across two continents. In *The House of Mirth*, she places the reader as an observer, enabling us, as Lawrence Selden does, to be part of an audience, as the new rich attempt to gain entrance and acceptance in the inner circles: '[Selden] enjoyed spectacular effects [. . .] all he asked was that the very rich should live up to their calling as stage-managers, and not spend their money in a dull way' (I: xii, 168).

In *The House of Mirth*, as in the New York of the period, if fortunes were judiciously deployed, the boundaries between old and new money could prove permeable; rich and generous newcomers, especially if prepared to acquire acceptable manners, were assimilated; and intermarriage between groups consolidated their names. Lily traverses the different sets, from the established wealth of the Trenors in their dignified Hudson Valley estate to the extreme outpost of Mrs Hatch in the brash Emporium Hotel. Further to understand the nature and social impact of this 'new money' and to appreciate more about *The House of Mirth*'s own emphases and its timing and significance as a cultural document, it is helpful to look at some non-fictional responses from the period. Some of these are in themselves noteworthy and remain landmarks of United States critical writing; others represent more ephemeral, but no less relevant, records of the time. (These are now preserved only in historical archives but are typical of the kind of newspaper pieces or discussions that would have been everyday fare to Wharton's own first readers.) *The House of Mirth* shapes its character-types, its descriptions of their lifestyle and its observation of the shock waves they create from such raw materials. Even brief extracts such as those which follow make clear how astutely

---

77 For an analysis of these economic changes, as registered within American Literature, see Richard Godden, *Fictions of Capital: The American Novel from James to Mailer*, Cambridge: Cambridge University Press, 1990.

Wharton's satire tuned itself in to the hot topics of the hour, catching the notes of current commentary, from Society Column to cultural theory.

One major question captured by the novel was concern about the force of such wealth, as economists, across the political spectrum, wondered how, long term, it might shape society. Unlike European aristocracy, Americans had no traditions of expenditure, no inherited responsibilities as a guide. *The House of Mirth* presents readers with memorable images of this unprecedented flow of money, as it invades and changes the old New York of Wharton's family; and Wharton's text taps into her upper-class contemporaries' anxieties – as expressed here, for example, by the conservative social philosopher, E. L. Godkin:

> It is only of late years that we have had among us a class capable of equalling or outdoing the European aristocracy in wealth. American fortunes are now said to be greater than any of those of Europe, and nearly, if not quite, as numerous. But the rich American is face to face with a problem by which the European was not, and is not, troubled. He has to decide for himself, what is decided for the European by tradition, by custom, by descent, if not by responsibilities, how to spend his money. [. . .] great wealth has not yet entered into our manners. No rules have yet been drawn to guide wealthy Americans in their manner of life.[78]

Although 'tradition' and responsibility, as Wharton presents it, can itself be suffocating, the text implies the dangers of life without duties, rules or boundaries. Mrs Hatch's vulgar hotel world emerges as a 'limbo', void of meaning or purpose, where 'wan beings' drift in a state of 'stifling inertia' (II: ix, 313–14). For Selden, Lily imperils herself by remaining here; and although Lily herself accords Mrs Hatch herself more sympathy, the narrative description depicts this existence outside 'inherited obligations' as a 'vast gilded void', without 'traditional functions' (II: ix, 314–15). As Wharton later wrote, she discovered her key to her subject here: that, in telling the story of 'a society of irresponsible pleasure-seekers', she realised that significance lay in 'what its frivolity destroys'; it gained 'tragic implication [. . .]' in its power of debasing people and ideals'.[79] Lily Bart, her heroine, is a victim of this world without ideals.

Wharton's satire also picked up notes from less conservative critiques, those who regarded all riches as corrupting. She did not share radical political visions of the redistribution of wealth, but her presentation of the rich suggested depths of decadence that shocked (and were refuted by) many readers. As one correspondent exclaimed in the *New York Times*:

> Are the gentlemen who dwell in Fifth Avenue palaces, own splendid country seats, and wear purple and fine linen every day, truly represented by the Trenors, the Dorsets and Rosedales of Mrs. Wharton's story? Are the wives of these men as heartless and immoral as Mrs. Wharton's

---

78 E. L. Godkin, *Problems of Modern Democracy: Political and Economic Essays*, New York: Scribner, 1896, pp. 311–22.
79 Wharton, *A Backward Glance*, p. 207.

fashionable women? Does education, refinement, religion and morality dwindle and shrivel in the opportunity and medium in which they are supposed to have their root? [. . .] If so, why do we send missionaries to Japan (or Timbuctoo, for that matter) when the most conspicuous circle in the greatest city of America, according to Mrs. Wharton's showing, knows but one evangel, the evangel of self-indulgence?[80]

Wharton's images have parallels in appraisals by some of the most extreme social philosophers, those who advocated drastic measures to cure social divisions. In the following passages, for example, we see a set of observations on the millionaire lifestyle which add weight to what some saw merely as Wharton's exaggerations and distortions. Henry George, the writer here, was one of the most outspoken commentators of the Progressive Era, who opposed accumulation of fortune and campaigned for civic improvement funded from a 'Single Tax' on landownership – the source of many leisure-class incomes. His repeated references to Rome, in 'How Our Princes Live', published, like *The House of Mirth*, in 1905, unequivocally associates New York with other decadent empires:[81]

Do not those whom we may call Princes of Privilege live with much of the circumstance of princely wealth? It may be answered that their sumptuous style of living outdoes that of many princes born to the purple, making startlingly apparent to the stranger the wide breach existing between them and great multitudes in the Republic who are beset by want or the fear of it.

Like Wharton, Henry George demonstrates the changes in the fabric of New York society by describing the grandiosity of its architectural developments. Here, like Van Alstyne summing up its 'social aspects' for Selden (I: xiv, 197), he turns his eye on the ever-greater dimensions of the constructions on Fifth Avenue:

A little north of the Whitney house on Fifth Avenue a still larger palace is being completed. It is the residence of Mr. William A. Clark, the Montana and Arizona copper king [. . .]. The ambition of Senator Clark respecting his house may be measured by the corner-stone, which weighs sixteen tons. This stone had to be brought from the quarry in a specially built railroad car. A single mantelpiece is expected to cost $100,000. Impatient at delay in getting bronze fittings and ornaments, a famous foundry was purchased and enlarged specially to meet the needs of this splendid house, which also is to contain a theater capable of seating five hundred persons.

We might describe palace after palace of our Princes of Privilege that for a couple of miles stud Fifth Avenue as thickly as the sumptuous residences of the nobles graced the undulations of the Palatine Hill in Rome before the imperial régime made it the sole abode of the Emperors.

---

80 Letter from M. L. Livingston, *New York Times*, 4 November 1905.
81 Henry George, *The Menace of Privilege: A Study to the Dangers to the Republic from the Existence of a Favored Class*, New York: Macmillan, 1905, pp. 63–71.

Reading *The House of Mirth* in such contexts highlights the sharp edge of even passing moments. Wharton reveals the dynamics of social competition and assimilation, as older families are drawn into the show of flaunted privilege:

> I hear Mrs. Trenor wants to build out a new ball-room, and that divergence from Gus on that point keeps her at Bellomont. The dimensions of the Brys' ball-room must rankle: you may be sure she knows 'em as well as if she'd been there last night with a yard-measure.
>
> (I: xiv, 198)

Display could take many forms but was key to status. *The House of Mirth* alerts readers to the 'hundred shades of manner and aspect' through which discriminations could be made: 'from the pattern of the men's waistcoats to the inflexion of the women's voices' (II: v, 272).

In her analysis of the relative ranks, and the power play, of monied groups, Wharton dramatises in fiction insights of a kind then being presented by social scientists. Of these, Thorstein Veblen's *The Theory of the Leisure Class* (1899), an innovative work of sociology, has remained the most famous; and many of his terms, which remain current today, offer a helpful framework for discussing Wharton's vision of social manoeuvres. Veblen suggests that 'Conspicuous Consumption', 'Conspicuous Waste', or 'Conspicuous Leisure', are the modes through which the elite, the rich and the leisure classes mark themselves off from the lower orders. All these modes involve degrees of display, which require the possession of superabundant resources (money and time) over and above the level needed for mere survival or comfort. Such shows of expenditure vary, in scale and in tastefulness, but all are intended to demonstrate the owner's financial standing and to establish superior social status. For a woman like Judy Trenor, 'her social talents, backed by Mr. Trenor's bank-account' almost always 'assured her ultimate triumph in such competitions' (I: iv, 76). However, the efforts of the newly rich (like Wharton's Brys and Gormers) offered the most spectacular examples of 'Conspicuous Consumption'. Veblen's terms are evident, here, in an instance proffered by Henry George:

> With others the sign of power is to be revealed only through the luxury of the table. [. . .] The striving for novelty entails much expense. A hostess may offer her guests peaches and apples artificially sun-marked with her monogram; muskmelons raised in slings; grapes ripened in bags; [. . .] Though it be the dead of winter, she may have growing strawberry plants, or dwarfed cherry trees, amid flowers and ferns, as the centrepiece of her table, each guest picking the ripe fruit at pleasure.[82]

The Welly Brys' lavish *tableaux vivants* and marble pleasure halls represent a similar, though slightly more artistic show: 'baits [. . .] to attract the desired prey' (I: xii, 167), the fashionable guests who will help to establish their social position. Wharton tracks the Brys in their advance, registering their appearance at

---

82 George, *The Menace of Privilege*, p. 71.

Monte Carlo in Veblen's terminology: seen again through Selden's eyes, they are part of a 'consciously conspicuous group [. . .] with the air of chief performers gathered together by the exigencies of the final effect' in a show 'staged regardless of expense' (II: i, 222).

According to Veblen, as the newly rich consolidated their fortunes, they turned to the quieter forms of 'Conspicuous Leisure' – that is, labour spent in expensive occupations which consumed considerable amounts of time, while, patently, producing nothing. Wharton captures one such second-generation millionaire in the figure of Percy Gryce. Whereas Gryce's father made his money 'out of a patent device for excluding fresh air from hotels' (I: ii, 57), Percy defines himself as a collector. In his custodianship of his Americana (books, documents and memorabilia with American historical connotations), he enjoys an expensive and exclusive pastime and 'could assert a superiority that there were few to dispute' (I: ii, 54). Although the collection represents a lifetime's boredom to Lily, she is all too aware of the message it sends out: that those who enjoyed such leisure had made their fortunes and no longer needed to toil (as Lily's downtrodden father had), in the exhausting world of business.

However, it was the more flamboyant manifestations of money that caused greater ripples, as the press and the new cinematic media detailed the displays of the rich, for outsiders of lower rank to marvel at, or envy. In *The House of Mirth*, Wharton shares Veblen's interest in distinguishing the 'canons of taste' at different social levels. Her narrative skilfully merges intellectual commentary with pastiche of popular journalism – the notes of *Town-Talk* and the other papers that relay the activities of Lily's set. Wharton blends into her descriptions echoes of the society columns, which went to extraordinary lengths to regale readers with every last detail and fed the appetite for gossip, evident, in the text, at every social level. The seemingly superior Mrs Peniston, relying on first-hand witnesses, finds Lily 'deplorably careless in noting the particulars of the entertainment' at the Van Osburgh wedding and takes pride in her own former meticulousness: 'I used to keep the *menu* of every dinner I went to [. . .] and I never threw away my cotillion favours till after your uncle's death' (I: ix, 144). Mme Regina's milliners, or the admiring Nettie, consume the columns eagerly: 'I used to watch for your name in the papers, and we'd talk over what you were doing, and read the descriptions of the dress you wore' (II: xiii, 354).

As it can be difficult for readers today to envisage the scale of such spectacles, the following extract, from a considerably more exhaustive account of a 'Great Ball in Newport', offers a sample. (Mr and Mrs Edward R. Wharton were among the 500 or so invited.) The ball was given by Mrs William K. Vanderbilt in honour of her daughter Consuelo, soon to become engaged to the Duke of Marlborough, who was also present. (To everyone's disappointment, the engagement was not announced that evening.[83]) When Mrs Bart 'followed in imagination the career of other beauties' (I: iii, 69), it was this kind of alliance, we can safely assume, that she pictured for her daughter, with Lily as the centrepiece of the spectacle. Such transatlantic matches between rich American beauties and landed European

---

83 Consuelo herself recalled the Whartons as an obviously incompatible couple: Consuelo Vanderbilt Balsan, *The Glitter and the Gold* (1953), Maidstone: George Mann, 1973, p. 216.

aristocracy were a phenomenon of the day, fascinating to the public and to social critics. (Wharton's final, unfinished novel, *The Buccaneers*, also centred on this theme.) Mrs Vanderbilt, in her 'marble palace', here demonstrates the ultimate in competitive display, staging a ball 'probably outdoing any private social function ever given in this country.' The details of the 'favors' (party gifts for the guests) and the themed decorations anticipate, and even outstrip, the extravaganzas recounted in celebrity magazines today. The reference to the workers (including those of other races) whose labour created them echo in repeated images in *The House of Mirth*: as in Selden's reflections that Lily 'must have cost a good deal to make, that a great many dull and ugly people must, in some mysterious way, have been sacrificed to produce her' (I: i, 39):

> Chiefs of decorators, caterers, and illuminators, had been engaged since early Summer in their arrangements. In Paris a well-known house had a large force making favors for some time, and away off in China natives had been engaged manufacturing a special lot of Chinese lanterns, all of pure white, for the exterior display [. . .] There was general dancing until midnight, and then the first supper was served, which was immediately followed by the cotillion, which was danced in the gilt drawing room off the hall. It is of Louis XIV style, embellished with African marble. [. . .] The favors cost $5,000 [. . .]. They were numerous, beautiful, and in great variety, all white and gold. There were hand-painted sachet bags, complete bagpipes as played by French peasants, fans, hat boxes, large oars with silver blades, hand glasses, and books.[84]

The movement of this passage, between a sense of the brilliance of the scene and a sharp awareness of its construction, also enters Wharton's depiction of Selden's or Lily's consciousness. At the Wellington Brys', where 'one had to touch the marble columns to learn they were not of cardboard' (I: xii, 168), they appreciate the entrancing illusions but never lose sight of their cost or their purpose as a piece of staging for social advancement. Of the Vanderbilts' spectacle, we are told:

> Some truly entrancing effects were [. . .] created with flowers and other objects. [. . .] At the south side of the hall is a large bronze drinking fountain, surrounded with an immense beveled plate-glass mirror. With the purpose to make that spot cool and inviting, the basin was filled with water plants in full flower. The tall lotus of the Nile stood up above the score or more of pink and white nymphal blossoms, and the delicate lilac flowers of a mass of hyacinths, and the tiny fairy lamps, and all around seemed to swarm a flock of humming-birds. At one side of the mirror was a group of pale pink hollyhocks standing fifteen feet high. Seemingly hovering around the open flowers were butterflies and bees [. . .] imported for the occasion. They were very lifelike. [. . .] Each of the supper tables held a wreath of pink hollyhock flowers, tied with pink ribbons. The veranda for reclining purposes was decorated with green

84 *New York Times*, 29 August 1895, p. 3.

bay trees in pyramid forms, while down on the terrace and lawn were groups of huge latina palms, all lighted up with colored butterfly fairy lamps.

The Vanderbilt decor suggests, here, the kind of pastoral artifice Wharton deploys to complex effect in her image of the Brys' conservatory, where her central characters allow themselves a rare moment, as if out of time: 'Hanging lights made emerald caverns in the depths of foliage, and whitened the spray of a fountain falling among lilies. The magic place was deserted [. . .] Selden and Lily stood still, accepting the unreality of the scene as a part of their own dream-like sensations' (I: xii, 174).

Whereas Wharton is careful to place Selden and Lily, her central characters, both at once within and outside the scene, as participants and critical audience, she keeps her social 'types' at a distance. The discussion of 'types', a word, then often placed in quotation marks, was key to the period, emerging from the nineteenth-century interest in classification and taxonomic systems – in every sphere from insects to racial groups or intellectual tendencies. The *tableaux vivants* place this discourse at the centre of the narrative, with the clever matching of painting and person in 'characters suited to their types': Carry Fisher as a 'typical Goya' or Mrs Van Alstyne as 'the frailer Dutch type', for instance (I: xii, 170). But Wharton's inquiry goes further. In seeking to understand the changing culture, she exhibits a range of types, capturing their behaviour in action and, at the same time, articulates the world view of the upper-class circles, for whom identifying the 'right type' (or keeping out the 'wrong' one) was an act of social survival. From Lily's viewpoint at the start of the novel, Mr Rosedale, 'a plump rosy man of the blond Jewish type' (I: ii, 48), is clearly unacceptable, but during her narrative, Wharton brings her in contacts which extend her (and the reader's) horizons.

Again, in its analysis of types, almost any thread of *The House of Mirth* can be traced through into the hot topics of the day. As an illustration of Wharton's grasp, take, for example, the representation of the parvenu, significant throughout Lily's narrative. Here, through Lily's and Carry Fisher's contacts with aspirants at different levels of the social ladder, Wharton gives sharp vignettes of a type keenly discussed by commentators: the wife of the newly enriched man, still in the process of striving to become 'a lady'. Louisa Bry and Mattie Gormer embody such figures and, as a fresh divorcée, Mrs Norma Hatch represents a still newer variety. As Simon Rosedale realised, it was through the influence of a wife that many a newcomer made the last successful move into society. For those men who arrived, already married, the transformation of a spouse into a lady was an urgent matter. Vast numbers of etiquette books were aimed at this market, and, as informal social secretaries, Carry and Lily perform a similar function. On the outskirts of her own class, Lily is in fact playing a direct role in transforming it – an ambiguous act of betrayal for which Selden berates her in the Norma Hatch episode. However, Wharton's treatment of the parvenu remains in tune with more complex analyses, such as this editorial from *Vogue* (then an avant-garde publication):

At every turn she is made to realize that she is a social 'out,' and that her want of ancestors is very damaging. Her personal idiosyncrasies, her infelicities of language, her gaucheries of behavior, her lack of repose, betray continually that she is one of the newly arrived at wealth [. . .] Her guests, usually selected with a view to pushing herself on, are invariably her contemptuous critics who attend her balls for the supper, or accept theatre or opera invitations as free show opportunities. It is a game on both sides. The guests lend themselves for use as social ladders, taking their pay in sumptuous fare and costly amusement.[85]

Like *Vogue*, *The House of Mirth* makes clear that for these social groups – old and new – 'It is a game on both sides'. Like *Vogue*, too, the text resists simply sneering at the incomers' crudities but conveys both humour and sympathy; this editor's advice is echoed, for example, in Carry Fisher's exasperation at Mrs Bry: 'If she'd be natural herself—fat and vulgar and bouncing—it would be all right [. . .] but she keeps up the humbug even with me' (II: i, 226):

> Even those who have little sympathy with the ambition of the newly enriched one for social recognition, can not but pity her when she undergoes the ordeal of contact with the 'ins.' Assured of their position, they contrive in the subtlest manner possible to make the poor 'out' realize her costume, physical and linguistic deficiencies. [. . .] If the parvenu could be persuaded to be simple and unaffected and to give up pretending to be other than she is, her social pathway would be shorn of many disagreeable experiences and mortifying explanations. Her voice, her footstep, her carriage, her vulgar self-consciousness, her address, all emphatically testify that she is not a lady, and neither diamond tiaras nor lavish expenditure can obscure this humiliating truth. In breeding and culture, and in the indefinable charm which results from refined associations the parvenu will always be at a disadvantage, a fact she would show wisdom in acknowledging, at least to herself. [. . .] Parvenu, give up pretending you've always been a butterfly![86]

The issue of what is an act and what is natural goes to the heart of the narrative. Lily comes to question the superiority of 'the sacred precincts', suggesting to Selden that 'as far as I can see there is very little real difference in being inside or out' (II: ix, 320), but also to see clearly, even as they destroy her, how the 'ins' exert their power.

The 'Woman Question' and Lily Bart

The issue of the parvenu represents a single strand of Wharton's far broader investigation. Any novel of the period, centred, as is *The House of Mirth*, on a woman's destiny was caught up, intentionally or not, in what was termed the 'Woman Question'. This multifaceted discussion encompassed many of the issues outlined so far. In the United States, early feminist debate had acquired a

85 Editor's column, *Vogue*, 11 April 1895.
86 Editor's column, *Vogue*, 11 April 1895.

significant public presence with the pioneering Seneca Falls Convention (19 July 1848). Organised by two reformers, Lucretia Mott and Elizabeth Cady Stanton, this proclaimed the equality of women – a radical proposition, which divided even those who supported the extension of women's rights. But the emerging movement gathered force. Addressing topics from civic duty to female invalidism, child-rearing to suffrage, dress reform to girls' education, the 'Woman Question' opened up for scrutiny long-held assumptions about women's natures, roles, living space and opportunities. *The House of Mirth* canvasses the whole cycle of female options, from girlhood through to old age. With Lily at the centre, the leisure-class (or would-be leisure-class) woman commands most attention. This section will highlight some of the most significant types and give a sense of the contexts for Wharton's treatment.

Lily's story unfolds against a paradigm of what was expected of the proper young lady. In a leisure-class lady's history, the conventional sequence of events was a social debut, followed, within a few seasons at most, by courtship, an engagement and a wedding. A debut, as Edith Wharton's own experience witnessed, gave a strong message about priorities. Although the detail of practices varied, the model of femininity it prescribed is made clear in etiquette manuals:

> The mamma determines the time, when by a proper celebration, her daughter shall be accepted by the world as a fully matured woman, who may receive the homage of gentlemen if she desires their attention. She marks this transition of her daughter from girl-life to young ladyhood by inviting only fitting friends to her house, where she may present this daughter to them as a member of their circle. This ceremony should convey the information to the world that the young lady has been graduated in all the accomplishments and knowledge necessary to make her acceptable to society. In fact, it should mean that she has been instructed in all that deft wisdom which will be required by a *belle* of her circle and a queen of a household, for which she is, as all women are, a candidate.
>
> Especially is it assumed that she has been thoroughly taught that when she enters society she must obey its social laws to the letter, and assume all its duties and its sometimes wearisome bondage. [. . .] A *début* is a barrier between an immaturity of character and culture and an admission of the completion of both. Previous to this event a young girl is not supposed to be sufficiently interesting to her elders among her own sex, and certainly not worldly-wise enough to associate with gentlemen.[87]

But obeying 'social laws to the letter' holds little potential for narrative. The 'wearisome bondage' of a rule-bound society featured in a strong line of women's writings. It was a major theme, for instance, in Margaret Fuller's polemical *Woman in the Nineteenth Century* (1845) as it was in Louisa May Alcott's more cautious *Little Women* (1868) or *Rose in Bloom* (1876). Alcott's Jo March

---

87 (No author), *Social Etiquette of New York* (1878), New York: Appleton, 1887, pp. 41–2.

rejecting the stiff manners of 'calling', Nan (in *Jo's Boys*, 1886) choosing spinsterhood, a medical career and the vote, or Rose rebelling against the constraints of corsets, grew out of a current of protest, even within seemingly safe 'domestic' fiction. Sentimental best-sellers such as 'Susan Warner' [Elizabeth Wetherell]'s best-selling *The Wide, Wide, World* (1851) and *Queechie* (1852) offered a female *Bildungsroman*, a life story demonstrating women's strengths and potential. As Susan K. Harris points out, even here, as in the many mid-century fictions that moved towards a formulaic resolution, through marriage, motherhood and home, it was the characters' questions, disobedience, creativity and energy that meant most to readers; not the conventional 'happy' (or 'womanly') endings.[88]

By the 1890s, however, the image of the so-called 'New Woman' was beginning to enlarge perceptions about women's possible choices and to allow more open arguments that female existence was not necessarily bound into husband, home and children. Though often pilloried in the press, or the object of vicious caricature (as de-sexed, ugly, love-starved, or degenerate), her supporters framed the New Woman as a strong evolutionary model. 'New Woman' writing (for example, the short stories of Charlotte Perkins Gilman) had begun to propose blueprints for action and positive models of emancipation. The most adventurous, radical texts – from Gilman's 'The Yellow Wall-Paper' (1892) to Kate Chopin's *The Awakening* (1899) – explicitly challenged the pieties of wifehood and motherhood, presenting the sanctuary of home as claustrophobic and stifling. Gilman's anonymous narrator disintegrates under the strains of a protective husband and a new baby; Chopin's Edna Pontellier abandons her social duties, her marriage and her children for sexual arousal, new forms of freedom. (Each narrative, like *The House of Mirth*, closes on the ambiguous ending of its central female character.)

Edith Wharton was not a women's rights activist, nor even politically in sympathy with the women's movement. If there are New Women in *The House of Mirth*, they are seen at a distance – possibly those busy with their music and proofs in the little restaurant where Lily takes her lonely cup of tea (II: xi, 342). While the text presents independent women – Kate Corby or Carry Fisher, for instance – it tinges them with satire; and in Carry's case hints that, in spite of all her energetic 'causes', she is happiest at home and hearth, together with her small daughter. Gerty Farish seems to live with a freedom Lily cannot manage: she can cross social boundaries, without forfeiting respect, and lives in her own small flat, in a modest self-sufficiency. But in her unspoken, unrequited love for Selden, her resolute cheerfulness and even her philanthropy, she seems closer to the self-abnegating spinster of a Victorian subplot rather than a new twentieth-century figure. Lily's delight in Nettie's baby and her final comfort in its visionary presence have struck some as signifying a 'solution' to Lily's emptiness – one which reinforces the conventional woman's stories that New Woman writing challenged. Yet many readers have found in *The House of Mirth* one of the most searching explorations of women's lives. At every social level, as Ammons and other feminist critics point out (see Critical history, **p. 72**), the text gives glimpses of women in unsatisfying, damaging or debilitating roles. Like Gilman

---

88 Susan K. Harris, *19th-century American Women's Novels: Interpretive Strategies*, Cambridge: Cambridge University Press, 1990.

and Chopin, Wharton is interested in the woman who strays from the path but, here, through digression and carelessness rather than in any dramatic, transgressive gesture.

Echoing Wharton's own earlier history, in *The House of Mirth*, external events – Mr Bart's sudden collapse and death – disrupt the heroine's course as a debutante. In Lily's musings in the dark at Bellomont and in scraps of memory and gossip throughout the text, Wharton presents a decade dissipated in indiscretions, fancies, 'chances' thrown away (I: i, 44; II: i, 227). Yet in her distressed outpourings to Gerty, Lily identifies with the fallen women of the slums. Her self-condemnation is unequivocal: 'I am bad—a bad girl—all my thoughts are bad—I have always had bad people about me' (I: xiv, 202). To modern readers, Lily's sins might seem negligible. Though, like Chopin's Edna, she smokes and gambles and, possibly, even (in the period term) 'brightens' her hair (I: i, 39), she seems imprudent rather than wilfully rebellious. However, though the incident with which the novel opens – tea at a bachelor's flat – seems trivial, it is the start of a fatal sequence. (For Wharton's own commentary, see Critical history, p. 59.) Warnings against infringing such social regulations remained a constant in etiquette books even in the new twentieth century and give the measure of Lily's misdemeanour:

> A sine qua non to all bachelor entertaining is a chaperon. The married woman can not be dispensed with on such occasions. The host may be gray-headed and old enough to be a grandfather many times over, but, as an unmarried man, he *must* have a chaperon for his women-guests. If he object to this, he must reconcile himself to entertaining only those of his own sex.
>
> The age of this essential appendage to the social party makes no difference, so long as the prefix 'Mrs.' is attached to her name. She may be a bride of only a few weeks' standing,—but the fact that she is married is the essential.[89]

As Wharton herself had experienced, even minor jolts in a romantic history could cause ripples in society. Unmarried 'girls' were figured in everyday discourse, as in fiction, as blank pages, 'buds', fruit and flowers with the bloom still on them, vulnerable to any blemish. In *The House of Mirth*, Mrs Peniston expresses the rigour of an older generation: 'It was horrible of a young girl to let herself be talked about; however unfounded the charges against her, she must be to blame for their having been made' (I: xi, 163). Among the novel's younger set, expediency replaces moral absolutes; but this blame structure still holds force. No matter how delicately handled, bringing a girl's name before the public could wound both her modesty and her reputation. Warnings like the following (written in 1905, as *The House of Mirth* was serialised) spell out the dangers:

> We are accustomed to seeing the sign 'Hands off!' hung upon dainty fabrics,—pure, spotless materials that would be injured and stained by the

---

89 Marion Harland and Virginia Van de Water, *Everyday Etiquette: A Practical Manual of Social Usages*, Indianapolis, Ind.: Bobbs-Merrill, 1905, pp. 105–6.

touching of a gloved or bare hand. People who admire the pure beauty of the article thus marked do not resent the sign. They see the wisdom of it and are willing to obey the mandate. For a fabric once soiled never looks the same again. All the chemicals in the country can not give it the peculiar pristine freshness that was once its chief beauty. [. . .] We would not be—we are not—prudes, but the bloom of the peach is beautiful, and once rubbed off it can not be replaced. The snow-white fabric is too fair to be carelessly handled.[90]

From the very first page of the novel, Lily's freshness and surface – her 'purity of tint' (I; I, 38) in every aspect – come under question. Her observers are fascinated by her blushes, her glow, her air of youth; and she herself is frightened by the telltale signs that her surface is flawed or fading. Constant small abrasions, rather than any single incident, damage Lily's bloom. But the effect is the same: marked through carelessness, bad luck or malice, 'the truth', as she tells Gerty, 'is that once she's talked about she's done for' (II: iv, 265). In a further twist, Wharton suggests that simple nineteenth-century morality is inadequate in twentieth-century stories. Lily is technically innocent but regards herself as worse than the 'lowest' of women because she has refused the route of sexual favours.

If how women are judged is one central theme of the novel, how they might occupy themselves is another. In Lily's ambitions and its depictions of other, wealthier, women, *The House of Mirth* touches on many other aspects of leisure-class women's lives which fascinated observers, inside and outside the women's movement. The details of the obligations of the social round, and of leisure pursuits, may be found in many contemporary journals; the extracts interleaved below exemplify some more general issues.

Husband-hunting was conventionally a young lady's most important occupation. Among the New Women who began to question this priority, one of the most vocal was Charlotte Perkins Gilman (then Stetson). In her ground-breaking book *Women and Economics* (1898), she presented the strains the hunt imposed on women. Marriage itself was, she argued, a competitive market, where women competed for survival – acquisition by the men most able to support them:

> From the day laborer to the millionaire, the wife's worn dress or flashing jewels, her low roof or her lordly one, her weary feet or her rich equipage—these speak of the economic ability of her husband. The comfort, the luxury, the necessities of life itself which the woman receives are obtained by the husband and given her by him.[91]

Readers differ over Wharton's personal views about fellow women and argue whether *The House of Mirth* presents women's friendship as well as their rivalry

---

90 Harland and Van de Water, *Everyday Etiquette*, pp. 245–8.
91 Charlotte Perkins Stetson (later Gilman), *Women and Economics: A Study of the Economic Relation between Men and Women as a Factor in Social Evolution* (1898), reprinted, ed. Michael Kimmell and Amy Aronson, Berkeley, Calif.: University of California Press, 1998, pp. 9–10. A search engine will lead readers to online numerous editions, including the excellent Kimmell and Aronson one here: <http://ark.cdlib.org/ark:/13030/ft896nb5rd/>.

(see Critical history, **p. 75**), but the narrative leaves us in no doubt of the ruthlessness of a Bertha Dorset or Judy Trenor in competition over a man. Newspaper readers like Nettie, or Mrs Bart, might be dazzled by the careers of fashionable beauties, but, as Gilman suggests here, glamour also disguised struggle, degradation and dependency. Allowed only a passive, 'innocent' part, a young woman was deeply disadvantaged (especially when, unlike the dull Evie Van Osburgh, she had no mother to manoeuvre on her behalf):

> Marriage is the woman's proper sphere, her divinely ordered place, her natural end. It is what she is born for, what she is trained for, what she is exhibited for. It is, moreover, her means of honorable livelihood and advancement. *But*—she must not even look as if she wanted it! She must not turn her hand over to get it. She must sit passive as the seasons go by, and her 'chances' lessen with each year. Think of the strain on a highly sensitive nervous organism to have so much hang on one thing, to see the possibility of attaining it grow less and less yearly, and to be forbidden to take any step toward securing it! This she must bear with dignity and grace to the end.[92]

Wharton presents a similar view through Lily's clear-eyed awareness of her situation. Like Gilman, she spells out her difficulties for Selden and contextualises her seemingly narrow ambitions: 'a girl must [marry], a man may if he chooses' (I: i, 46).

If to be single was a strain, to become a wife brought further pressures, and the specialised position of the successful woman in the life of a rich man was the subject of much attention. The society hostess had a central role in spending and displaying her husband's wealth. Mrs Trenor complains about the burden – 'as if [having a baby] were anything to having a house-party!' (I: iv, 74) – but revels in her power. Lily's ideal future is to deploy her social knowledge and aesthetic refinement, through helping a rich man spend his money graciously; and it is for this, in part, that Rosedale appreciates her. Knowing that 'it's only the showy things that are cheap', he realises that the next step in his social advancement, from Wall Street to Fifth Avenue, is to acquire an expensive and decorative wife: 'I wanted money, and I've got more than I know how to invest; and now the money doesn't seem to be of any account unless I can spend it on the right woman' (I: xv, 213).

As well as presiding over a man's drawing room, the woman herself embodied its most valuable item, its chief exhibit. She was the trophy and the chief ornament through which the wealthy man could best signify his prowess. This role was plainly described by Veblen in *The Theory of the Leisure Class*, as well as by Gilman in *Women and Economics* the previous year. As Lily reminds Selden, a man was valued for himself, a woman for her decorative qualities. To be viewed as 'useful', as Gerty is, would be to cancel her chances of being placed in a man's collection: 'Who wants a dingy woman?' (I: i, 46). A lady, as her elaborate and constraining clothing signified, had to appear as if she never had to lift a finger to work:

---

92 Gilman, *Women and Economics*, pp. 87–8.

It has come about that obviously productive labour is in a peculiar degree derogatory to respectable women, and therefore special pains should be taken in the construction of women's dress, to impress upon the beholder the fact (often indeed a fiction) that the wearer does not and can not habitually engage in useful work. Propriety requires respectable women to abstain more consistently from useful effort and to make more of a show of leisure than the men of the same social classes. It grates painfully on our nerves to contemplate the necessity of any well-bred woman's earning a livelihood by useful work. It is not 'women's sphere'. Her sphere is within the household, which she should 'beautify', and of which she should be the 'chief ornament'. The male head of the household is not currently spoken of as its ornament.[93]

In a novel so interested in show and performance of all kinds (see, for example, Critical readings, **pp. 96–105**), costume is a central motif, both as symbol and as social indicator. In *The House of Mirth*, as in Gilman's and Veblen's analyses, beauty and dress represent women's economic capital and weaponry and demand considerable attention. As Lily tells Selden, 'We are expected to be pretty and well-dressed till we drop—' (I: i, 46).[94] Wharton keeps in view Lily's struggles to maintain both her looks and her stylishness, in many different fashionable settings: 'clothes have grown so frightfully expensive; and one needs so many different kinds, with country visits, and golf and skating, and Aiken and Tuxedo—' (I: xv, 208). As ever, she grounds the detail precisely. Lily is not of the class who would ever buy ready-made costumes from a department store. Like Wharton's mother, the truly upper-class New York lady ordered her dresses directly from Paris or, at second-best, from a French-trained dressmaker. American magazines, such as *Vogue* and the *Delineator*, offered readers close descriptions of Paris fashions, as well as patterns and plates (see Figures 1–5, **pp. 48–51**) to help the less affluent keep up to the moment. In such elaborate garments, as with designer clothes today, the details spoke volumes:

> The first figure which we illustrate is an exquisite evening dress by Paquin. It is made of white chiffon, which falls in broad folds. The lower edge of the skirt is embroidered with spangles of silver and mother of pearl, and a similar trimming appears on the front of the corsage. This is hemmed on both sides by two narrow silver galons, attached to the *décolleté* line by two bunches of roses, which are also repeated on the bracelets.[95]

Lily tells Gus Trenor that she has 'had to give up Doucet' (I: vii, 118) (Jacques Doucet, a renowned Parisian couturier). The Van Osbrugh set, however, can afford the real thing and can tell the difference; as Mrs Peniston affirms, 'we knew

---

93 Thorstein Veblen, *The Theory of the Leisure Class: An Economic Study of Institutions* (1899), London: Unwin, 1970, p. 126.
94 For more on costume in *The House of Mirth*, see Clair Hughes, *Dressed in Fiction*, Oxford and New York: Berg, 2006, pp. 134–56.
95 *The Delineator*, August 1905, p. 176. (Illustrated, see Figure 1.)

'Keeping up Appearances' fashion items from the *Delineator*, summer season, 1905

THE LOWER EDGE OF THE SKIRT IS EMBROIDERED WITH
SPANGLES OF SILVER AND MOTHER OF PEARL, AND A SIM-
ILAR TRIMMING APPEARS ON THE FRONT OF THE CORSAGE.

Figure 1 Evening dress by Paquin (August 1905, p. 176).

Figure 2 The summer millinery (August 1905, p. 180).

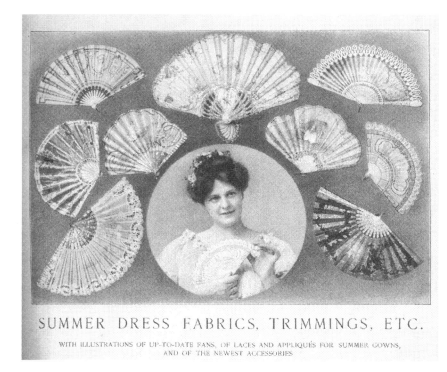

SUMMER DRESS FABRICS, TRIMMINGS, ETC.

WITH ILLUSTRATIONS OF UP-TO-DATE FANS, OF LACES AND APPLIQUÉS FOR SUMMER GOWNS,
AND OF THE NEWEST ACCESSORIES

Figure 3 Accessories: up-to-date fans (June 1905, p. 953).

Figure 4 'Beauty in every Jar':
advertisement for Milkwood Cream
(September 1905, p. 459).

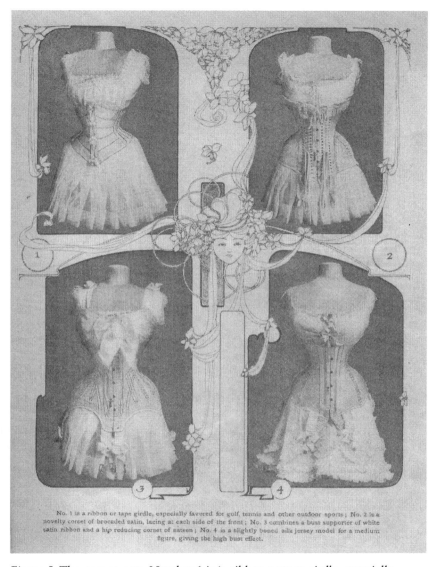

No. 1 is a ribbon or tape girdle, especially favored for golf, tennis and other outdoor sports; No. 2 is a novelty corset of brocaded satin, lacing at each side of the front; No. 3 combines a bust supporter of white satin ribbon and a hip reducing corset of sateen; No. 4 is a slightly boned silk jersey model for a medium figure, giving the high bust effect.

Figure 5 The new corsets. Number 1 is 'a ribbon or tape girdle, especially favored for golf, tennis and other outdoor sports' (September 1905, p. 337).

at once, from the fold in the back, that it must have come from Paquin' (I: ix, 144).

For readers today, it can be hard to picture why Lily fell into debt. These extracts from a newspaper interview with a 'Smart Woman' indicates how far her allowance would have had to stretch. On being asked what it cost her to dress, the Smart Woman produces (and prices) all her gowns:

> And soon the 'creations' were spread all about, rainbow heaps on chair and couch. Their description will give an idea of the necessary sinews of war of any woman who presumes to be smartly gowned. [. . .] The black velvet gown cost $300, the yoke and sleeves of the Russian lace alone being worth £175. The Chantilly gown and its blue replica are $300 or $350 apiece. The other gowns described cost on an average $200 apiece. This may be taken as the bottom figure for a dinner or evening gown in which any woman who pretends to be 'smart' can appear. [. . .] As this particular Smart Woman seldom goes to balls, she has only three ball gowns.[96]

As explained earlier (see Text and contexts, **p. 30**), it is a largely meaningless exercise to attempt to translate the currency of early nineteenth-century life into today's monetary equivalents, but viewing even a selection of this woman's expensive wardrobe gives us a sense of the lifestyle taken for granted in Lily's circles and illuminates the scale of Lily's sartorial obligations: 'the girl pays [. . .] by going to the best dress-makers, and having just the right dress for every occasion, and always keeping herself fresh and exquisite and amusing' (II: viii, 305). To make even clearer the extent of her expenses in relation to the spending power of the day, we might keep in mind the mere $260 which supported the entire family in Louise More's survey of annual outgoings (see Text and contexts, **p. 31**):

> Some of the other things which go to make up the Smart Woman's wardrobe are the following:
>
> | | |
> |---|---:|
> | Carriage coat of black broadcloth, lined with cream satin | $250 |
> | Tailor-made cloth jacket. | 85 |
> | Gray coaching coat | 35 |
> | Riding habit | 200 |
> | Opera cloak, cream satin brocade, trimmed with ermine | 300 |
> | Opera cloak, café-au-lait lady's cloth, trimmed with mink | 165 |
> | Trottoir, or sidewalk skirt for shopping | 50 |
> | Rainy-day skirt, three and one-half inches from ground | 50 |
> | Golf skirt, two inches from ground | 50 |
> | Breakfast dress, figured foulard | 50 |
> | White flannel yachting suit | 150 |
> | Two China silk kimonas, $40 dollars each | 80 |
> | Two silk matinées, $15 each | 30 |
> | Teagown | 150 |

---

96 'What it Costs to Be in the Fashion', *New York Times*, 12 January 1902, p. 6.

One dozen shirt and fancy waists, from the ordinary plain cheap
shirtwaist at $16, to the imported waist of Cluny lace at $150   500
Six hats, ranging from $30 to $75 each   300
Russian blouse of best quality of Russian sable, matching the
carriage robe.. 2,000

Total (omitting the coral collar and jewelled purse), $12,275. But to go with
these clothes certain conventional jewels are necessary. [Total, including
other items omitted here: $31,525.][97]

This woman's 'rainbow heaps on chair and couch' unwittingly foreshadow Lily's
final review of her dresses at the climax of *The House of Mirth*. There, in one of
the most memorable scenes of the novel, Wharton transforms Lily's own systematic examination of her possessions into a reading of a decorative, and seemingly
wasted, life:

> An association lurked in every fold: each fall of lace and gleam of
> embroidery was like a letter in the record of her past. She was startled to
> find how the atmosphere of her old life enveloped her. But, after all, it
> was the life she had been made for [. . .] She was like some rare flower
> grown for exhibition, a flower from which every bud had been nipped
> except the crowning blossom of her beauty.
>
> (II: xiii, 357)

In such central images of overspecialisation and waste, *The House of Mirth*,
again, makes a crucial intervention into current debates: the issue of the purposeful life. The topic had been given a high profile in a famous speech by Theodore
Roosevelt in 1899 (known as the 'Strenuous Life' speech). There he had exhorted
Americans that: 'A mere life of ease is not in the end a very satisfactory life, and,
above all, it is a life which ultimately unfits those who follow it for serious work in
the world.'[98] Roosevelt's main audience was the male citizen, but with the expansion of wealth into new social groups, many were also worried about the problem
of bringing up girls, like Lily, fit for nothing but a life of leisure. The anxieties
behind the novel are here forcefully articulated in a *Vogue* editorial; their expression gains weight when we recall that the Editor here is addressing the magazine's
own fashionable readers, women like Lily herself. Similar discussions appeared in
the pages of *Scribner's Magazine*, where *The House of Mirth* was serialised and
would have been familiar to the novel's readers:

> As the leisure-class girl is increasing in numbers as the country grows in
> wealth, the question as to what she shall do with her life becomes ever
> more vitally the concern of the community. At present not only is she a
> drone, but by her mode of life and her influence she puts the emphasis of
> approval upon what is really unworthy. Idleness, one of the most
> vicious, the most fundamental and ineradicable faults of the human

97 'What it Costs to Be in the Fashion', *New York Times*, 12 January 1902, p. 6.
98 Theodore Roosevelt, 'The Strenuous Life: A Speech Delivered to Chicago's Hamilton Club on
     10 April 1899', available at <http://www.bartleby.com/58/1.html>.

race, is presented as the most covetable of possibilities; indeed, an order of caste is founded upon it, and every social force is invoked to emphasize the alleged superiority of the idle over those whose industry, fidelity and energy create and maintain the necessaries, the comforts, the luxuries for which the world of to-day is noted, and whose untiring labor makes possible the existence of classes in the community whose lives are devoted to the conservation of culture. Self-absorption and laziness are qualities encouraged in the leisure-class girl and woman— impossible foundation for nobility of life.

The effect of the purposeless life on the one who leads it is belittling and unsatisfying to the last degree. In youth, even after the twentieth mile-stone has been passed, there come many days when a realization of the emptiness of life brings keenest discouragement. And as the years advance, these times of depression come around more frequently, until the now elderly woman becomes, like thousands of her class, a mere human vegetable, endured for her social position and the favors which she can dispense, but regarded as an infliction and shunned whenever it is safe to do so.[99]

In Lily's story, Wharton brings out the double sets of concerns we see here: for her heroine herself and for the society which creates her. As Lily tells Selden:

I am a very useless person [. . .] I was just a screw or a cog in a great machine I called life, and when I dropped out of it I found I was of no use anywhere else. What can one do when one finds that one only fits into one hole? One must get back to it or be thrown onto the rubbish heap—

(II: xii, 348)

One answer to such emptiness (and to wider civic ills), as *Vogue*'s editor went on to suggest, was the work of the women's clubs, where the rich girl might assist the less fortunate. Although Lily rejects Gerty's choice of such a route as impossibly dingy, it is her brief contact with Nettie, through Gerty's club, which ignites a temporary glow of self-worth and, more deeply, her first insight into the 'mysterious links of kinship' (II: xiii, 359). Her vision of a future outside the leisure class is concentrated, as it is in the editorial above, in the sad figures of the ageing Miss Silvertons, trying to sell their amateur handicrafts through the genteel 'Women's Exchanges' (II: viii, 303). Readers today who might wonder whether these were, in truth, the only options would find a different vision in advice books to women, often themselves written by women. Here, for example, an author addresses a woman, like Lily, who needs work and who is 'about to determine the extent of her money value to the world'. She suggests a wide range of occupations, among them typewriting, insurance, advertising, real estate, law, medicine, hack-writing, architecture and interior decoration, hairdressing, skin care and editing. The key to success, however, is a positive attitude:

---

99 Editor's column, *Vogue*, 20 September 1900.

First of all, she must realize that it is not enough that from her proud estate she is willing to enter business. That attitude is in itself a handicap. The truth, a hard one, too, is that the world is already full of workers, and there really is no place for untried hands. Then you must *make* a place, and to do this the woman that works must be of the right sort or her work is desultory and ineffectual. Failure is not always the fault of the occupation chosen, nor of the woman's talents, but comes because she lacks those traits of character that force success. [. . .] It is of the greatest importance that you should be able to distinguish your abilities from what may be called your tastes or inclinations. The latter are far pleasanter to follow, but may not always be profitable [. . .] Become acquainted with a woman worker and you usually find she has been unfortunate; she is sure to have trials and grievances to fill her mind, and must resolutely stamp on them in order to keep her spirit soaring. One of the most persistent trials may be her self-consciousness in her altered surroundings, and a sense of the injustice of being forced into the world.[100]

Lily's failures in the commercial workplace, on the bench at Mme Regina's millinery business, are anticipated in such discussions. With her 'charming listless hands', her 'untutored fingers', Wharton presents her as the epitome of the desultory, ineffectual, untrained worker described here: Lily, too, mistakes her tastes and inclinations for the signs of professional ability, but in Mme Regina's 'temple of art no raw beginners were wanted' (II: x, 322–6).

Taking stock of her own life in her memoir, *A Backward Glance* (1934), Wharton presents her work on *The House of Mirth* as a narrative of fulfilment – of her own evolution into a professional author and of the joy she found through her writing. In *The House of Mirth*, she was exploring the opposite kind of story. Lily finds no sphere to exercise her powers. First seen in a gap of time between trains and appointments, she spends much of her narrative waiting – for invitations, visits, offers. Sick of her old self, she longs for a new part, but she can neither renew herself nor turn into the various kinds of self that different men propose for her. Distractions, wrong turns and missed opportunities mark every stage of her journey; she never finds a worthwhile focus for her vague aesthetic leanings, let alone any joy in creative work. Once out of the world of leisure, she remains stranded 'in a great waste of disoccupation' (II: xi, 342). In *The Fruit of the Tree* (1907), her next novel, Wharton created a modern heroine, Justine Brent, a competent professional nurse. But in *The House of Mirth* she left readers with a vision of Lily as a dying species, an evolutionary failure.

The critic, Lionel Trilling, in a much-quoted definition, described the novel of manners as picking up 'culture's hum and buzz of implication'.[101] Reading *The House of Mirth* within its contemporary contexts – even the small sample represented here – opens up the text to the hum and buzz of a vast range of overlapping dialogues. All these and many other voices meet in Lily's story – or, as Wharton

---

100 Candee, *How Women May Earn a Living*, pp. 3–10.
101 Lionel Trilling, 'Manners, Morals and the Novel', in *The Liberal Imagination: Essays on Literature and Society*, London: Secker and Warburg, 1951, p. 206.

described it, 'the "conversation piece" of which she forms the central figure'.[102] Although Lily falls silent, her readers continue to discuss her. Encountered after its centenary, through the lens of its own period or as a work for the new millennium, *The House of Mirth* remains remarkable for its insights, for its energy and for its witness to creative powers, which, unlike its heroine, its author recognised, and learned how to use.

---

102 Wharton, Introduction to *The House of Mirth*, p. vii.

2

Critical history

Early critical responses

The House of Mirth, published in 1905, attracted a good deal of critical attention in both America and Britain from the moment of its publication. Wharton's previous work (see Text and contexts, **p. 19**) testifies to an author building a reputation as a creative artist and cultural commentator. So, when *The House of Mirth* was published, critics reacted to its difference from her previous work by foregrounding Wharton's confident treatment of the social milieu of leisure-class New York while also acknowledging the transatlanticism of its subject matter. Many of the early responses to the book were concerned with what they constructed as the amorality of Wharton's narrative, particularly with regard to the conduct of her heroine and the careless destructiveness of those around her. In her introduction to the 1936 World's Classics edition of the novel, Wharton makes comic reference to the moral outrage expressed by some of her readers:

> What picture did the writer offer to their horrified eyes? That of a young girl of their world who rouged, smoked, ran into debt, borrowed money, gambled, and – crowning horror! – went home with a bachelor friend to take tea in his flat! And I was not only asking the outer world to believe that such creatures were tolerated in New York society, but actually presenting this unhappy specimen as my heroine! [. . .] it seems incredible that the early success of *The House of Mirth* should in some measure have been one of scandal! But so it was, to my own amusement, and to the immense satisfaction of my publishers. Ah, golden days for the novelist were those in which a lovely girl could besmirch her reputation by taking tea between trains at a bachelor's flat![1]

Notwithstanding her levity, Wharton's point here is a serious one with regard to the superficiality of critical reaction to the portrayal of the real compromises and restrictions faced by women at the turn of the century.

---

1   Wharton, Introduction to *The House of Mirth*, pp. ix–x.

Commentators inevitably read details of Wharton's background and personal life into the narrative of *The House of Mirth*, a critical tendency that would haunt her throughout her writing career, and which she was powerless to halt. Reviewers were, however, united in agreement about the superior quality of the writing and structure of the text, and Wharton herself, in her autobiography, describes the writing of *The House of Mirth* as coincident with the realisation of her full powers as an artist. As she says: 'It was good to be turned from a drifting amateur into a professional [. . .] I was really like Saul the son of Kish, who went out to find an ass, and came back with a kingdom: the kingdom of mastery over my tools.'[2]

Contemporary reviews

A survey of early critical responses to *The House of Mirth* gives a sense of the varied reaction to the novel on both sides of the Atlantic. With the exception of Olivia Howard Dunbar who, writing in the *Critic*, claimed that the novel fails to achieve the standards set by earlier collections of short stories, reviewers acknowledged Wharton's confident and skilful handling of her material in *The House of Mirth*. There was, however, divergence of opinion on other matters, not least the morality of Lily's story. In offering a scathing critique of the text, to take an example here, one commentator employs the tone of moral outrage which Wharton herself ridicules. Dismissing the work as an example of 'fashionable' social fiction which 'will not last', the *Independent* critic places Wharton into relation with her compatriot – the novelist and short-story writer Robert Grant (1852–1940) – and laments the trend among American artists for producing work of a 'sensational kind' which takes as its subject 'the most corrupt class of people in the world':

> This [. . .] class of writers find their ethics by what may be called the dredging process. Formerly we got all our morals and golden texts from the lives of saints and the Holy Scriptures, whether we were writing or actually living them. But now it is the fashion to get them out of the cesspools of vice. The author who can portray the most sins in the best style is the most popular literary preacher now.
>   And, according to this standard, Mrs. Wharton should stand very high. She has selected a situation in that circle of society where conditions make for the destruction rather than the development of honor and virtue. The heroine, a capable, well poised woman, is inmeshed in it. And this is the tragedy – that a creature so morally sane should be subjected to a process sure to prove disintegrating. Her acting, her subterfuges, her pitiful treacheries are simply the threads of a common web which entangles with her every person in her set. She is surrounded by men and women whose esthetic sensibilities are so highly developed that they have become emasculated. Their pleasures are self-indulgences

---

2   Wharton, *A Backward Glance*, p. 209.

founded upon some social form of almost every vice. Meanwhile beauty is her own spirit's art of expression, just as religion might be a nun's. The need of money, the petty intrigues and delicately veiled temptations which follow, sully conscience and damage self-respect.[3]

Taking an opposing view, the reviewer for the *Outlook* dismisses readings of *The House of Mirth* as a frivolous 'society' novel, instead noting its deep moral significance. Here the text is identified as an exceptional and memorable work of art which ranks alongside the finest examples of American literature. Describing Wharton's rendering of Lily's story as a piece of 'expert workmanship', the commentator claims: 'It would be difficult to find a carelessly written sentence, an obscure phrase, a halting paragraph, in the text of the book.' This appraisal also recognises the universality of the novel's theme across time and across continents and, in making connections between *The House of Mirth* and the writings of artists including Gustave Flaubert and George Eliot, it recognises Wharton's indebtedness to European literary traditions:

> To say that this novel is far and away the best novel of society written by an American is to give it pre-eminence in a very small class; for the society novel, in the strict sense of the term, has never laid hold of the imagination of the writers of a country engrossed in settling the more pressing problems of life [. . .] Mrs. Wharton knows at first hand the world she describes, and her story is free from those exaggerations, misplaced values, and happy-go-lucky descriptions of society life which make the great majority of so-called society novels cheap imitations. *The House of Mirth* gains immensely by reason of its moderation, firm handling of the facts, discriminating emphasis, and freedom from didacticism. Mrs. Wharton has escaped the danger of setting up moral sign-posts on the road, and has given her novel a concentrated and tragic moral significance.
>
> For *The House of Mirth* is deeply moralized because it is deeply humanized; it is impossible to touch life at first hand without saturating fiction with the moral element; for morality, as Mr. Morley[4] says, is not *in* the nature of things; it *is* the nature of things. *Père Goriot, Madame Bovary, Anna Karénina, Vanity Fair, Adam Bede, The Scarlet Letter*[5], must be counted great human documents, not because they set out to be text-books of character, but because they touched the very sources of life. From its title to its closing paragraph, *The House of Mirth* is a judgment as searching, penetrating, relentless as life itself; and yet it

3   'Mrs. Wharton's Latest Novel,' *Independent*, 59, 20 July 1905, pp. 150–1.
4   John Morley, Viscount Morley of Blackburn (1838–1923), British MP, political writer, biographer, journalist, philosopher, historian, editor and essayist.
5   *Père Goriot* (1834–5), by French realist novelist Honoré De Balzac (1799–1850); *Madame Bovary* (1857), most famous work of Gustave Flaubert (1821–80), French novelist of the realist school; *Anna Karénina* (1875–77), by Leo Tolstoy (1828–1910), Russian writer of realistic fiction; *Vanity Fair* (1847), by English novelist, William Makepeace Thackeray (1811–63); *Adam Bede* (1859), by George Eliot (1819–80); *The Scarlet Letter* (1850), by American writer Nathaniel Hawthorne (1804–64).

never for a moment ceases to be a story of absorbing interest. No tract
for the times could have been more scathing and opportune; but no
novel of the hour is farther removed from the didactic mood and manner. The kind of society which it describes with merciless veracity has
existed in every generation, and is to be found in every city. The story is
laid in New York, but it has been told again and again of Rome, Paris,
London, and it might be told of Boston, Chicago, New Orleans, San
Francisco.[6]

In some quarters, contradictory readings of the novel provoked direct critical
disagreement and debate. As Olivia Howard Dunbar had been less than compli-
mentary about Wharton's craftsmanship in the December 1905 issue of the
Critic, so in its January 1906 number, Alice May Boutell sprang to the author's
defence, branding her a 'genius'. Noting her 'keen sense of disappointment' at the
earlier review's cursory treatment of *The House of Mirth*, Boutell takes issue with
Dunbar's assertion that 'It is certainly not [...] a "great" novel',[7] insisting
that: 'There can be no question as to the supreme excellence of the book as a work
of art.'[8]

Despite the occasional dispute over the quality of the novel's craft and the
more fiercely contested question of its morality or otherwise, there were some
points of agreement across the range of critical responses. The influence of the
work of European artists on the novel's composition, for example, is a common theme addressed in contemporary reactions, including another favourable
response penned by the reviewer for the *Literary Digest*. This commentator
identifies *The House of Mirth* as 'Mrs. Wharton's most masterly achievement',
noting that the brilliance and power of the text lies in its 'pitiless psychological dissection of a beautiful young woman'.[9] Here, comparisons are drawn
between Lily Bart and the heroines of Thackeray and Eliot,[10] but the portrait drawn by Wharton is judged to have 'surpassed' those of her European
predecessors.

Wharton drew on the literary traditions of Europe and her own work attracted
significant critical attention across the Atlantic – in France and in Britain.
On its publication, *The House of Mirth* was reviewed in the French *Revue
des Deux Mondes* and *Mercure de France* and in a number of English journals
including the *Times Literary Supplement*, the *Spectator* and the *Bookman*. The
English reviews were generally positive in tone. The *Times Literacy Supplement*
piece, for example, praises Wharton's transition from a writer known primarily for her shorter fictions to a competent practitioner of the novel form.
It also recognises that the text is infused with ironic intent. Describing *The
House of Mirth* as 'an exceptional book', the English reviewer notes Wharton's

---

6 'A Notable Novel,' *Outlook*, 81, 21 October 1905, pp. 404–6.
7 Olivia Howard Dunbar, 'A Group of Novels', *Critic*, 47, December 1905, pp. 509–10.
8 Alice May Boutell, 'A Burst of Enthusiasm', *Critic*, 48, January 1906, pp. 87–8.
9 'The Abode of the Fool's Heart', *Literary Digest*, 31, December 1905, p. 886.
10 Becky Sharp, the heroine of Thackeray's *Vanity Fair* (1847) and Gwendolen Harleth of George
Eliot's *Daniel Deronda* (1876).

lack of sentimentality and credits her with a rich literary imagination from which 'something entirely new has been conceived and embodied':

> Mrs. Wharton has shown again and again in her short stories that she possesses not only an extraordinary mastery over technique, but also the real spirit of comedy, watchful, sympathetic, and ironic too. She takes a more prolonged flight in this book, and with it marks the highest point she has yet reached. She brings all her humour and sureness of touch, and adds a sustained fire and beauty beyond anything she has written hitherto.[11]

Wharton's biographer R. W. B. Lewis gives further insight into the early critical reception of the text, discussing the responses of several of Wharton's intimates. He describes the rather 'huffy' response of Charles Eliot Norton, distinguished Harvard professor and long-time friend of Wharton, who took exception to the 'immorality' of the heroine, and the warm words of Howard Sturgis, a member of Wharton's 'inner circle', who, while he is fulsome in his praise, makes allusions to the superiority of Henry James:

> How good! How good! It is to *my* mind the best thing you have done, so sustained, so closely woven, so inevitable, so living! I am lost in admiration [. . .] Except perhaps for our beloved Henry, I think you are head and shoulders above any other writer of fiction of the present day in English.[12]

Lewis's survey of the general tenor of press reviews concurs with the overview given above. He concludes that 'For all its huge commercial success, *The House of Mirth* did not earn uniform approval.'[13] He also points out that despite early protestations about the 'immoral' nature of the narrative and a concentration on the unsuitability of Wharton's subject matter, the superior quality of the writing was widely acknowledged, and debates instigated at the time of publication continue to resonate in much later readings of the text:

> The unfavourable commentary had the air of being made knowingly in a lost cause. What permeates the reviews of *The House of Mirth* is the sense, as of a settled fact, that Edith Wharton was one of the two or three most serious and accomplished writers of fiction on the American scene and that the new novel was undeniably her most important work to date. The hostile sought to pick flaws in what was taken for granted to be a novel of distinction. Amid the favourable, the issue was whether *The House of Mirth* could be adjudged a masterpiece or whether it fell just short of that final accolade. It may be added that enlightened critical opinion remains today at that same stage of uncertainty.[14]

11 'Fiction: The House of Mirth', *Times Literary Supplement*, 1 December 1905, p. 421.
12 R. W. B. Lewis, *Edith Wharton*, p. 152.
13 R. W. B. Lewis, *Edith Wharton*, p. 154.
14 R. W. B. Lewis, *Edith Wharton*, p. 154.

Wharton's correspondence about *The House of Mirth*

Edith Wharton was a prolific letter-writer who, in her correspondence, exchanged views on life, literature and art with some of the most eminent intellectuals, writers and scholars of her day. Her letters from the period of the novel's publication provide further insight into the way in which it was received by those whose critical opinions she valued most – those with whom she shared a professional as well as a personal relationship. These letters give a sense of Wharton's pleasure at the novel's popular success; writing to William Crary Brownell, of Scribner's, she expressed delight at sales figures of 100,000 and noted that she had arranged a meeting with the well-known theatrical agent Elisabeth Marbury to discuss the many offers she had received to dramatise the story. Particularly worthy of note in her correspondence with Brownell is her satisfaction at his praise of the novel's composition:

> I am so surprised & pleased, & altogether taken aback, that I can't decently compose my countenance about it. I was pleased with bits, myself; but as I go over the proofs the whole thing strikes me as so loosely built, with so many dangling threads, & cul-de-sacs, & long dusty stretches, that I had reached the point of wondering how I had ever dared to try my hand at a long thing – So your seeing a certain amount of architecture in it rejoices me above everything.[15]

In her autobiography, Wharton recalls the lack of confidence which had plagued her as she sought to make the transition from travel writer and author of short stories to novelist:

> After 'The Valley of Decision,' and my book on Italian Villas, the idea of attempting a novel of contemporary life in New York began to fascinate me. Still, I hesitated. 'The Valley of Decision' was not, in my sense of the term, a novel at all, but only a romantic chronicle, unrolling its episodes like the frescoed legends on the palace-walls which formed its background; my idea of a novel was something very different, something far more compact and centripetal, and I doubted whether I should ever have enough constructive power to achieve anything beyond isolated character studies, or the stringing together of picturesque episodes.[16]

As has been noted elsewhere in this volume, Wharton was an intimate friend of Henry James with whom she kept up a regular and long-term correspondence; the two often exchanged views on their respective writings. Following the publication of Wharton's 1902 novel, *The Valley of Decision*, Henry James had, in fact, advised her to engage with 'the American Subject' (see Introduction, **p. xiii**). His

---

15 Quoted in   R. W. B. Lewis and Nancy Lewis, eds, *The Letters of Edith Wharton*, 1988, pp. 94–5.
16 Wharton, *A Backward Glance*, p. 205.

response to *The House of Mirth*, reproduced below, is full of praise with just a hint of criticism that gestures towards the gentle professional jealousy that characterised their relationship:

> Half an hour ago, or less, I laid down the November *Scribner* [. . .] Let me tell you at once that I very much admire that fiction, & especially the last three numbers of it; finding it carried off with a high, strong hand & admirable touch, finding it altogether a superior thing. There are things to be said, but they are—some of them—of the essence of your New York donnée[17]—& moreover you will have said them, to a certainty, yourself. The book remains one that does you great honour—though it is better written than composed; it is indeed throughout *extremely* well written, and in places quite 'consummately.' [. . .] There are fifty things I should like to say—but, after so long an interval there are so many in general, & I think that my best way to touch on some of the former would be by coming back to the U.S. to deliver a lecture on 'The question of the *roman de moeurs*[18] in America—its deadly difficulty.' But when I do that I shall work in a tribute to the great success & the large portrayal, of your Lily B[art]. She is very big & true—& very difficult to have *kept* true—& big; & all your climax is very finely handled.[19]

To give a flavour of Wharton's exchanges with other correspondents about the novel, also reprinted here are extracts from letters to historian and writer William Roscoe Thayer and Dr Morgan Dix. To Thayer, whose assessment of *The House of Mirth* had evidently, in common with many reviews, drawn attention to Wharton's own background, she offers a robust defence of her work:

> I am particularly & quite inordinately pleased with what you say of my having—to your mind—been able to maintain my readers' interest in a group of persons so intrinsically uninteresting, except as a social manifestation. I knew that my great difficulty lay there, & if you think I have surmounted it, I shall go about with a high head.—But—before we leave the subject—I must protest, & emphatically, against the suggestion that I have 'stripped' New York society. New York society is still amply clad, & the little corner of its garment that I lifted was meant to show only that little atrophied organ—the group of idle & dull people—that exists in any big & wealthy social body. If it seems more conspicuous in New York than in an old civilization, it is because the whole social organization with us is so much smaller & less elaborate—& if, as I believe, it is more harmful in its influence, it is because fewer responsibilities attach to money with us than in other societies.—

---

17 A set of artistic principles on which a literary work is based.
18 Social novel.
19 Henry James to Edith Wharton, 8 November 1905, from *Henry James and Edith Wharton: Letters 1900–1915*, p. 53.

> Forgive this long discourse—but you see I had to come to the defense
> of my own town, which, I assure you, has many mansions outside of the
> little House of Mirth.
>   [. . .]
> I wish you felt a little more kindly toward poor Lily![20]

The correspondence between Wharton and Morgan Dix, rector of Trinity Church
in New York, again addresses one of the most contentious issues surrounding the
novel's publication: its morality. In a letter dated 1 December 1905, Dix had
written: 'This book places you at the head of the living novelists of our country or
of the English-writing authors of our day. It is a terrible but just arraignment of
the social misconduct which begins in folly and ends in moral and spiritual
death.'[21] In her response to the rector, Wharton stresses the moral dimension of
the novel:

> Few things could have pleased me more than the special form which
> your commendation has taken; for, lightly as I think of my own equip-
> ment, I could not do anything if I did not think seriously of my trade; &
> the more I have considered it, the more has it seemed to me valuable &
> interesting only in so far as it is 'a criticism of life.'—It almost seems to
> me that bad & good fiction (using the words in their ethical sense) might
> be defined as the kind which treats of life trivially & superficially, & that
> which probes deep enough to get at the relation with the eternal laws;
> & the novelist who has this feeling is so often discouraged by the
> comments of readers & critics who think a book 'unpleasant' because it
> deals with unpleasant conditions, that it is a high solace & encourage-
> ment to come upon the recognition of one's motive. *No* novel worth
> anything can be anything but a novel 'with a purpose,' & if anyone who
> cared for the moral issue did not see in my work that *I* care for it, I
> should have no one to blame but myself—or at least my inadequate
> means of rendering my effects.[22]

The first critics

Early critics of Edith Wharton, as has already been noted, often focused on her
class background when writing about her fiction. In 1914 and 1922 respectively,
John Curtis Underwood and Katharine Fullerton Gerould offered different, but
equally class-conscious appraisals of Wharton's work. In *Edith Wharton: A Critical Study*, Gerould compares Wharton's society fictions, including *The House of
Mirth*, with *Ethan Frome* (1911), her novella of New England working-class life.
She argues that the author's most successful literary engagements are those
informed by her own social milieu:

---

20 Edith Wharton to William Roscoe Thayer, 11 November 1905 from Lewis, ed., *The Letters of
    Edith Wharton*, pp. 96–7.
21 Quoted in R. W. B. Lewis and Nancy Lewis, eds, *The Letters of Edith Wharton*, pp. 99–100.
22 Quoted in R. W. B. Lewis and Nancy Lewis, eds, *The Letters of Edith Wharton*, pp. 98–9.

the people who have leisure to experience their own emotions, and the education to show them how the emotions fit into the traditions of the race, are more interesting in themselves than the people whose emotions are bound to be on a more nearly animal plane [. . . Edith Wharton] did not abandon her civilized and sophisticated folk, for any length of time, to deal with rustics. Let us hope that she never will abandon them.[23]

In *Literature and Insurgency*, which includes a discussion of *The House of Mirth*, Underwood takes an opposing view, suggesting that Wharton's artistic achievement is limited by her inability to transcend the bounds of her privileged upbringing:

If Lily and her creator had had more red blood, and less blue blood or mere anæmic sawdust in their veins, the heroine might have realized life at last as she sank deeper and deeper towards the bedrock of existence as men and women have made it in America to-day. The author might have varied her treatment gradually through each successive circle of Lily's Inferno. In the final tragedy she might come to grips with life herself – in a style, and in a setting that somehow should have represented more of the misery, more of the struggle and its transient rewards, its doubtful prophecies and promises, for millions on Manhattan Island, than the narrow stage setting here provided for the final appearance of the ineffectual central figure.

And just so far as Lily Bart is ineffectual, incompetent, unfit to rouse any genuine interest or sympathy from any man or woman not of her own type, just so far we are constrained to feel that Mrs. Wharton is ineffectual and incompetent herself; that she has been trying to gain and retain our attention under false pretenses; that, on the whole, whatever the author's intention, the book tends to over-emphasize false and artificial values; that the author's time and energy to a great extent has been wasted as well as our own.

[. . .]

In sporadic instances, by spurts and by dashes, Mrs. Wharton, like the class of which she is so strikingly an example, suggests something better than brilliancy, begins to realize it, rises and subsides, and fails to repeat.

In this failure to make good repeatedly, to get down to some solid working basis, to devote her undoubted talents to some lasting and disciplined service to herself and to the rest of the world, she remains highly typical of the type and the more selfishly enlightened section of Twentieth Century American plutocracy that she so ably interprets and represents.[24]

Another very good example of this kind of attitude to Wharton's work can be found in an – unintentionally comic – review of her novel, *The Age of Innocence*,

23 Katherine Fullerton Gerould, *Edith Wharton: A Critical Study*, New York: D. Appleton and Company, 1922, pp. 6–7.
24 John Curtis Underwood, *Literature and Insurgency*, New York: Mitchell Kennedy, 1914, pp. 360–1, 390.

1920, by Vernon L. Parrington which opens: 'The note of distinction is as natural to Edith Wharton as it is rare in our present day literature. She belongs to the "quality," and the grand manner is hers by right of birth. She is as finished as a Sheraton sideboard.'[25] A bizarre combination of critical condescension and deference to class characterizes much of the criticism written after her death in 1937, although there are moments of analytical acuity in essays by Edmund Wilson and Q. D. Leavis, both published in 1938.

In 'Henry James's Heiress: The Importance of Edith Wharton', Q. D. Leavis, bestows upon the author a label that she had railed against throughout her career. While an intimate friend of James and an admirer of his earlier work, Wharton's lack of appreciation for his later writings and her frustration at being considered his imitator is made apparent in her correspondence. Writing to William Crary Brownell, describing a pleasant day spent in the company of Henry James she notes: '[He] talks, thank heavens, more lucidly than he writes.'[26] In another letter to the same recipient she complains: 'I have never before been discouraged by criticism [. . .] but the continued cry that I am an echo of Mr. James (whose books of the last ten years I can't read, much as I delight in the man), [. . .] makes me feel rather hopeless.'[27]

Nevertheless, a year after Wharton's death, Leavis insists on the influence of James in her work. She does, however, credit Wharton with building on the Jamesian legacy and with becoming a significant figure in the development of American letters. Wharton's coming of age as an artist in her own right, Leavis claims, coincides with the publication of *The House of Mirth*:

> She was taking up Henry James's work where he left it off with *The Bostonians* and *The Portrait of a Lady*. And in this novel [*The House of Mirth*] she turned [. . .] from an amateur into a professional novelist. The American novel grew up with Henry James and achieved a tradition with Mrs. Wharton. He, she points out in a passage of great interest, was never at home in twentieth century America – 'he belonged irrevocably to the old America out of which I also came' and whose traces, as she said, remained in Europe where he went to seek them. 'Henry James was essentially a novelist of manners, and the manners he was qualified by nature and situation to observe were those of the little vanishing group of people among whom he had grown up, or their more picturesque prototypes in older societies – he often bewailed to me his total inability to use the "material," financial and industrial, of modern American life.' [. . .] Unlike James, she rightly felt herself qualified to deal with the society that succeeded 'the old America' and she stayed to write its natural history, to write it in a form as shapely and with a surface as finished as if she had had a number of predecessors in her chosen task.[28]

25 Vernon L. Parrington J., 'Our Literary Aristocrat', *Pacific Review*, 2, June 1921, pp. 157–60.
26 Quoted in R. W. B. Lewis and Nancy Lewis, eds, *The Letters of Edith Wharton*, p. 88.
27 Quoted in R. W. B. Lewis and Nancy Lewis, eds, *The Letters of Edith Wharton*, p. 91.
28 Q. D. Leavis, 'Henry James's Heiress: The Importance of Edith Wharton', *Scrutiny*, 8.3, December 1938 (pp. 261–76), pp. 263–4.

Leavis acknowledges the competence with which Wharton portrays the disintegration of Lily Bart, likening her narrative techniques to those of her European precursors in the realist novel and, in doing so, recognises influences other than James: 'Mrs. Wharton never ceases to be first of all a novelist. Her social criticism is effected in the terms that produced Middlemarch society and the Dodsons in *The Mill on the Floss*, and often challenges comparison with analogous elements in Jane Austen.'[29]

In 'Justice to Edith Wharton', while noting that 'the language and some of the machinery of *The House of Mirth* seem old-fashioned and rather melodramatic', Edmund Wilson concedes that 'the book had some originality and power'.[30] In common with Q. D. Leavis, Wilson identifies the novel as a significant turning point in Wharton's literary career. For him too, this was the moment at which she emerged from the shadow of Henry James, as whose 'lesser disciple' she was often described, to become 'an historian of the American society of her time'.[31] 1905, he suggests, marked the beginning of a fifteen-year period during which she produced her best writing, work 'of considerable interest both for its realism and its intensity'.[32] Noting Wharton's brilliance as 'a passionate social prophet',[33] Wilson, in fact, reverses the debate about James/Wharton influences to claim that *The Ivory Tower*, James's unfinished novel and his only satire of 'plutocratic America', is derivative of Edith Wharton.[34]

Despite Leavis's and Wilson's recognition of Wharton's development of a distinct voice, however, the assumption that Wharton was but a pale and inadequate imitation of Henry James tends to be the prevailing theme in the criticism written between her death and the publication of R. W. B. Lewis's biography *Edith Wharton* in 1975, although in 1953 and 1965, Blake Nevius and Millicent Bell,[35] respectively, wrote fuller, more generous assessments of her work than that judgement would seem to allow. Considerable damage had been done to Wharton's reputation by the publication of Percy Lubbock's *Portrait of Edith Wharton* in 1947. His account of her fiction as trifling and derivative set the tone for a kind of brushing aside of her achievement. Wharton did receive attention from eminent American critics like Lionel Trilling, although the attention was of a denigratory kind, as in his essay, published in 1956, 'The Morality of Inertia', an ultimately dismissive commentary on her 1911 novel, *Ethan Frome*. Richard Poirier in his important book *A World Elsewhere: The Place of Style in American Literature* (1966) did, however, give considerable space to *The House of Mirth*, and Irving Howe, in his volume *Edith Wharton: A Collection of Critical Essays* (1962) wrote a full, if grudging, account of the novel's importance. An extract from Howe's essay is reproduced on the following page.

29 Leavis, 'Henry James's Heiress', p. 264.
30 Edmund Wilson, 'Justice to Edith Wharton', in Irving Howe, ed., *Edith Wharton: A Collection of Critical Essays*, Englewood Cliffs, NJ: Prentice-Hall, 1962, p 21.
31 Wilson, 'Justice to Edith Wharton', p. 19.
32 Wilson, 'Justice to Edith Wharton', p. 19.
33 Wilson, 'Justice to Edith Wharton' p. 20.
34 Wilson, 'Justice to Edith Wharton', p. 20.
35 Blake Nevius, *Edith Wharton: A Study of Her Fiction*, Berkeley, Calif.: University of California Press, 1953; Millicent Bell, *Edith Wharton and Henry James: The Story of Their Friendship*, London: Peter Owen, 1965.

Mrs. Wharton, if not a great writer, is a genuinely distinguished one [. . .] The early stories hardly prepare one for the work to come. For with *The House of Mirth* (1905), a full-scale portrait of a lovely young woman trapped between her crass ambitions and her disabling refinements of sensibility, Mrs. Wharton composed one of the few American novels that approaches the finality of the tragic. The book is close in philosophic temper to European naturalism, though constructed with an eye toward 'well-made' effects that are quite different from the passion for accumulating evidence that we associate with the naturalistic novel. At its best Mrs. Wharton's style is terse, caustic, and epigrammatic – a prose of aggressive commentary and severe control. At points of emotional stress, however, she succumbs to a fault that is to mar all her novels except *The Age of Innocence*: she employs an overcharged rhetoric to impose upon her story the complexities of meaning it cannot support and intensities of feeling it does not need. If not her most finished work, *The House of Mirth* is Mrs. Wharton's most powerful one, the novel in which she dramatizes, with a fullness and freedom she would never again command, her sense of the pervasiveness of waste in human affairs and the tyranny that circumstance can exert over human will and desire.[36]

R. W. B. Lewis, Cynthia Griffin Wolff: the pioneers

In 1968, the Wharton papers – manuscripts, diaries, letters and a host of other private documents – were opened to the research community for the first time since their arrival at Yale University after Wharton's death. The first major study of Wharton's life and works to be published after the archive was opened was R. W. B. Lewis's *Edith Wharton*, in 1975, followed by Cynthia Griffin Wolff's *A Feast of Words: The Triumph of Edith Wharton*, in 1977. While very different, Lewis's critical biography and Wolff's psycho-critical study have both played a critical role in shaping the work which was to follow, laying the ground for new and varied interpretations of Wharton's work. Both biographers pay attention to *The House of Mirth*, recognising it as one of Wharton's greatest literary achievements. Lewis discusses the considerable commercial success of the novel and the substantial income that it brought to its author; he notes that within two months of publication, 140,000 copies were in print, figures that far exceeded the expectations of the publishers, prompting William Crary Brownell to remark that they were witnessing 'the most rapid sale of any book ever published by Scribner'.[37] Lewis indicates that the novel's popularity assured Edith Wharton earnings of more than $20,000 in 1905.

In her study of Edith Wharton, Cynthia Griffin Wolff offers a perceptive and innovative reading of *The House of Mirth* which, as has been noted (see Text and contexts, p. 24), assesses the significance of art, in particular Art Nouveau, in the

36 Irving Howe, 'The Achievement of Edith Wharton', in Howe, ed., *Edith Wharton: A Collection of Critical Essays*, 1962, pp. 1–18.
37 R. W. B. Lewis, *Edith Wharton*, p. 151.

novel. Noting that '*The House of Mirth* is built upon a series of explicit allusions to the art of the day',[38] Wolff presents a comprehensive account of contemporary artistic forms and styles in order to aid the modern reader in an appreciation of Wharton's indebtedness to visual art. According to Wolff, late nineteenth-century art was 'designed to capture the spirit of America (the ideal republic), and this "ideal" was most often embodied in the figure of "Perfect Womanhood" '.[39] She describes the ways in which symbolic images of 'chaste' and 'virtuous' women and girls – 'sexless females, draped in white' – dominated the large-scale murals that adorned public buildings and identifies a similar idealisation in the apparently more realistic likenesses of women in the portraiture of the period.[40] Wharton's writing, Wolff argues, demonstrates deep scepticism towards the notion of 'realistic' representation of the woman:

> Edith Wharton, who knew a great deal about art, was not impressed by the virtuosity of surfaces [. . .] Wharton recognized the difference between superficial rendering and a genuine understanding of psychological complexities, and she gives a sceptical view of the society portraitist in *The Custom of the Country*: 'All [new society] asked of a portrait was that the costume should be sufficiently "life-like," and that the face not too much so; and a long experience in idealizing flesh and realizing dress-fabrics had enabled Mr. Popple to meet both demands. "Hang it," Peter Van Degen pronounced, standing before the easel in an attitude of inspired interpretation, "the great thing in a man's portrait is to catch the likeness – we all know that; but with a woman's it's different – a woman's picture has got to be pleasing. Who wants it about if it isn't?" '[41]

Wolff's piece suggests that the popular Art Nouveau movement of the day, which again focused almost exclusively on the figure of the woman, develops such idealisation of the woman in one important respect – by introducing a sexual element: 'Now, the woman's capacity to be decorative is her chief attraction [. . .] there is a latent sexuality in the Art Nouveau woman. Her layers of clinging drapery and the fullness of her hair often offer a promise, if not more, of concealed passion.'[42] It is an engagement with these various contemporary artistic representations and the identification of the woman as the 'object' of art that Wolff believes informed Wharton's craft and which she claims pervade the *House of Mirth*. Such women:

> come to view themselves not as persons but as objects – to be admired, to be sustained in their beauty. The men around them [. . .] have significance principally as connoisseurs or collectors. It is this exquisite, empty

38 Cynthia Griffin Wolff, *A Feast of Words: The Triumph of Edith Wharton*, New York: Oxford University Press, 1977, p. 112.
39 Wolff, *A Feast of Words*, p. 112.
40 Wolff, *A Feast of Words*, p. 112.
41 Wolff, *A Feast of Words*, p. 113.
42 Wolff, *A Feast of Words*, pp. 114–15.

image of self that has contaminated Lily's life; it is, ultimately, this confusion between the ideal and the real that leads to her tragedy.[43]

The radicalisation of Wharton criticism

Lewis's and Wolff's influential reconsiderations of Edith Wharton's life and work have since been supplemented by Shari Benstock's *No Gifts from Chance: A Biography of Edith Wharton* (1994), which brought fresh insights to the story of Wharton's life, and, as this Guide is in preparation, an important new biography by the eminent British critic and biographer, Hermione Lee, is due to be published on Wharton's birthday in 2007. This biography will pay particular attention to the author's life in Europe after 1907.

It was the ground-breaking work of Lewis and Wolff that signalled the moment at which there began to be differentiation in critical readings of Wharton's fiction and non-fiction. Wharton's substantial and varied body of work includes short stories, novellas, novels, autobiographical writing, literary and cultural criticism, art history, travel-writing and an interior-design manual, all of which have proved a rich source of interest for critics. In terms of her fiction, however, it is *The House of Mirth* that has received more critical appraisal than any of her other novels; it lends itself to a multiplicity of readings and interpretations, including those centred on manners and customs, feminism, race, genre, morality and social and economic considerations. The novel features as a subject of discussion in all the major critical work published in the 1980s and 1990s. Elizabeth Ammons's *Edith Wharton's Argument with America*, 1980, takes as its subject the situation of women in turn-of-the-century American society, and Carol Wershoven's *The Female Intruder in the Novels of Edith Wharton*, 1982, considers the ways in which women can enter and influence social structures. Wai-chee Dimock, who published the first Marxist reading of the novel,[44] and Amy Kaplan[45] made important contributions to Wharton studies in the 1980s as did Elaine Showalter[46] and Judith Fryer.[47] Two of the most influential of these studies – those by Elaine Showalter and Amy Kaplan – will be discussed in more detail here.

In 'The Death of the Lady (Novelist): Wharton's *House of Mirth*', Showalter, one of the founders of feminist literary criticism in America, offers a feminist reading of Lily's story. She identifies the text as 'the novel of the woman of thirty', a 'genre' that, she points out, might also include Kate Chopin's *The Awakening* (1899), whose heroine Edna Pontellier, in common with Lily and other turn-of-the-century female protagonists, dies around the time she enters her fourth decade. Showalter's article explores 'the problem of female maturation in narrative terms' and poses

43 Wolff, *A Feast of Words*, p. 115.
44 Wai-chee Dimock, 'Debasing Exchange: Edith Wharton's *The House of Mirth*', *PMLA*, October 1982, pp. 738–92.
45 Amy Kaplan, *The Social Construction of American Realism*, Chicago, Ill.: University of Chicago Press, 1988.
46 Showalter, 'The Death of the Lady (Novelist)', pp. 133–49.
47 Fryer, *Felicitous Space*, 1986.

the questions: 'What can happen to the heroine as she grows up? What plots, transformations, and endings are imaginable for her?'[48] Lily in transition and in crisis, is read here in relation to wider cultural and literary contexts, as representative of a moment of social change and reconfigured gender identities; the text itself is seen as 'pivotal in the historical tradition from one house of American women's fiction to another, from the homosocial women's culture and literature of the nineteenth century to the heterosexual fiction of modernism'.[49] Drawing on the work of Elizabeth Ammons, Showalter discusses *The House of Mirth* in terms of its examination of the possibilities available to women and to women writers at the turn into the twentieth century. 'The fiction of this transitional phase in women's history and women's writing,' she claims, 'is characterized by unhappy endings, as novelists struggled with the problem of going beyond the allowable limits and breaking through the available histories and stories for women.'[50] She also makes connections between the situation of Lily, who maintains the manner and morality of the 'lady' and in every crisis 'rises magnificently to the occasion' to Wharton herself – the 'lady' novelist:

> Wharton refuses to sentimentalize Lily's position but rather, through associating it with her own limitations as the Perfect Lady Novelist, makes us aware of the cramped possibilities of the lady whose creative roles are defined and controlled by men. Lily's plight has a parallel in Wharton's career as the elegant scribe of upper-class New York society, the novelist of manners and décor. Cynthia Griffin Wolff calls *The House of Mirth* Wharton's 'first Kunstlerroman,'[51] and in important ways, I would agree, Wharton's *House of Mirth* is also a fictional house of birth for the woman artist. Wolff points out that *The House of Mirth* is both a critique of the artistic representation of women – the transformation of women into beautiful objects of male aesthetic appreciation – and a satiric analysis of the artistic traditions that 'had evoked no conventions designed to render a woman as the maker of beauty, no language of feminine growth and mastery'. In her powerful analysis of Lily Bart's disintegration, Wharton 'could turn her fury upon a world which had enjoined women to spend their artistic inclinations entirely upon a display of self. Not the woman as productive artist, but the woman as self-creating artistic object – that is the significance of the brilliant and complex characterization of Lily Bart.' In deciding that Lily cannot survive, that the lady must die to make way for the modern woman who will work, love, and give birth, Wharton was also signalling her own rebirth as the artist who would describe the sensual worlds of *The Reef, Summer*, and *The Age of Innocence* and who would create the language of feminine growth and mastery in her own work.[52]

48 Showalter, 'The Death of the Lady (Novelist)', p. 133.
49 Showalter, 'The Death of the Lady (Novelist)', p. 134.
50 Showalter, 'The Death of the Lady (Novelist)', p. 135.
51 The story of an artist's maturation.
52 Showalter, 'The Death of the Lady (Novelist)', pp. 135–6.

Much critical analysis of *The House of Mirth* has centred on the issue of genre. Amy Kaplan's *The Social Construction of American Realism* (1988) enters into these long running debates, offering a discussion of the novel as a realist text (see also Beer and Nolan's essay in Critical readings, **pp. 106–15**). Emerging around the time of the Civil War in the 1860s and flourishing until the end of the century, American literary realism is a contested term,[53] but can be broadly defined as the attempt to create a faithful representation of reality, in an effort to understand society. Typical characteristics include: a wealth of true-to-life detail, including meticulous description of character and setting; omniscient, third-person narration which purports to present an objective account; an absence of intrusive, authorial commentary; and a concentration on the ordinary. William Dean Howells, to whom Kaplan refers, was a well-known practitioner of American literary realism, whose novels included: *A Modern Instance* (1881) and *The Rise of Silas Lapham* (1885). Howellsian realism is concerned with grasping the significance of everyday experience and the ordinary; as the extract below demonstrates, Kaplan's reading extends this definition, contrasting the 'realism' of *The House of Mirth* with the more traditional understandings of the term often associated with Howells. Kaplan's analysis takes as its starting point the opening section of the novel in which the beautiful and vibrant Lily Bart stands out against the drabness of the crowd at Grand Central Station:

> The opening scene describes Lily Bart in precisely those idealistic terms which Howells dismissed as unrealistic: artificial, polished, painted, and covered with a 'fine glaze,' she appears behind a veil, like a mysterious heroine of a romantic novel. Howell's aesthetic of the common, in contrast, advocates representing the members of the crowd, who exhibit for Selden 'the dinginess, the crudity of this average section of womanhood'. The lady indeed represents all that is uncommon and superfluous, useless and rarefied, as far away from the businessmen of her own class as from the working world of the lower-class women. Epitomizing the unreal qualities of modern life, the lady of leisure seems a most inappropriate subject matter according to the producer ethos underlying Howells's theory of realism, to which Wharton herself subscribed. Yet Wharton's opening scene can be read as a critique of Howellsian realism by posing the figure of Lily at center stage and then decentering her by revealing her social production. Just as Selden first views Lily against the crowd of average women rushing through the station, the reader approaches the coming scene of upper-class luxury and intimacy against a crowded society in flux.[54]

Kaplan goes on to consider Wharton's depiction of 'crowds' other than that at the station: the frequent social assemblages of members of the leisure class; the 'throngs of newcomers' trying to gain entry into society; the 'crowds' of excluded

---

53 For an overview, see Donald Pizer, ed., *The Cambridge Companion to American Realism and Naturalism: Howells to London*. Cambridge: Cambridge University Press, 1995.
54 Kaplan, *The Social Construction of American Realism*, pp. 88–9.

onlookers and the threatening 'gaping mob' who peer into the gilded society 'cage'. Using the example of socialite Judy Trenor who, Wharton's narrative tells us, 'seemed to exist only as a hostess, not from any exaggerated instinct of hospitality as because she could not sustain life except in a crowd', Kaplan suggests that reality and identity for the elite is dependent on turning the 'rest of society into an audience.' In *The House of Mirth*, realism, for Kaplan, is not 'natural', but socially constructed in the relationship and exchange between spectacle and spectatorship, performance and audience.

In 1990 and 1991 a number of significant studies opened new approaches to Wharton. Janet Beer Goodwyn's *Edith Wharton: Traveller in the Land of Letters* pays particular attention to the landscapes which inform and enhance Wharton's fiction. Beer Goodwyn places *The House of Mirth* in Wharton's 'native context', juxtaposing the author's explorations of American society through its women with those which she undertakes in writings 'which are distinguished by their concern with French civilization':

> Wharton's writing is concerned with relatedness – with human relations, transatlantic relations, relations between past and present, present and future, relations between human and landscape and between art and society. Lily Bart is dying of isolation; she is defeated by the absence of a 'centre of early pieties' [II: xiii, 359], a constant to which she could refer, comparing and measuring experience through her relation to it – whether a literal house or a familial structure – and, most crucially, taking refuge in it in times of crisis. Wharton gives voice here to her feelings about the absence of a female role in America and the sexual isolation which results from it. The 'solidarity' and 'continuity' [II: xiii, 359] which she is driven, in the emblematic manner of the soap-opera, to locate in the poorest home [Nettie Struther's], are features of a society which has cross-cultural foundations, real relations between men and women such as those which she later locates in the French social structure.[55]

Also published at this time, Susan Goodman's readings of Wharton's work in *Edith Wharton's Women: Friends and Rivals* considers the author's relationships and interactions with female friends and relatives, and Penelope Vita-Finzi's *Edith Wharton and the Art of Fiction* explores the significance of art and the artist in Wharton's writing. The year 1991 also saw the publication of Lev Raphael's study, *Edith Wharton's Prisoners of Shame*, which applied the concepts of the psychology of shame to Wharton's fiction, and Candace Waid's *Edith Wharton's Letters from the Underworld: Fictions of Women and Writing* included an analysis of the novel which took account of Wharton's ideas about the woman writer in America. In the same year Katherine Joslin's *Edith Wharton* provided a useful introduction to the major novels and offered a detailed feminist reading of *The House of Mirth*. Joslin, who has contributed a new essay to this volume on gender and female identity in the novel (see Critical readings, **pp. 96–105**), was the first

---

55 Beer Goodwyn, *Edith Wharton: Traveller in the Land of Letters*, pp. 66–7.

critic to bring an overtly feminist approach to Wharton's writing and, in 1991, her exploration of *The House of Mirth*'s engagement with the 'Woman Question' forced a serious re-evaluation of the work.

Here, Joslin notes that, in 1912, Wharton was asked to write an essay on the 'Woman Question' for the *Yale Review*. While she declined the request, this was a subject, Joslin argues, that Wharton had already addressed in her fiction: 'The central issue in her first novel about American society, *The House of Mirth* (1905), is the Woman Question.'[56] Among the key questions Joslin believes Wharton is posing in her exploration of the conditions of existence for women at the turn of the century are: 'If a woman chooses to discard the usual plot of marriage and her subsequent economic dependence on a man, then what? Exactly who is she? In more practical terms, how is she to earn her own way?'[57] The tension between Lily's intended trajectory – a socially and economically advantageous marriage – and the path she actually takes is examined here in the context of her relationship with Laurence Selden:

> The heroine Lily Bart, a woman of rare sensibility, discernment and beauty, travels a course that should lead her to marriage, a union with male money and power, and yet she tarries along the way, escaping into the woods with the would-be romantic hero Lawrence Selden, whose chivalric impulse is to save her from the materialism of her society by guiding her to what he, having read and absorbed Emerson, calls 'the republic of the spirit' [I: vi, 104]. We know that even before Lily encounters Selden's utopia, she has fancied an escape from the prosaic imperative to marry. She is twenty-nine as the novel opens, uncomfortably close to the barrier of thirty, when a man may begin to think about marriage, but beyond the time a woman may. We also know that Lily seals her letters – epistolary contacts with the world around her – with the image of '*Beyond!* beneath a flying ship' [I: xiv, 191], a clear symbol of the romantic urge to 'light out' for the territory or to take to the sea. Selden imagines a role for himself in her romantic quest: 'Ah, he would take her beyond – beyond the ugliness, the pettiness, the attrition and corrosion of the soul—' [I: xiv, 191]. He seems indeed not to understand the ambivalent nature of the quest. If he succeeds in taking her 'beyond' to the realm of personal freedom and autonomous selfhood, what are they to do once they arrive? To marry places them back in the social structure with the mundane questions of where and how to live on his income?[58]

Specialist studies

Following on from this burgeoning of critical activity, scholars have started to take more issue-specific approaches to Wharton's work. Gloria Erlich published

---

56 Katherine Joslin, *Women Writers: Edith Wharton*, Basingstoke: Macmillan, 1991, p. 49.
57 Joslin, *Edith Wharton*, p. 50.
58 Joslin, *Edith Wharton*, p. 50.

The Sexual Education of Edith Wharton in 1992, a book which looks at the fiction through the prism of Wharton's filial and sexual relationships; Carol Singley's *Edith Wharton: Matters of Mind and Spirit* (1995) considers Wharton's religious and philosophical roots; Kathy Fedorko's *Gender and Gothic in the Fiction of Edith* Wharton (1995) looks at the short stories as well as the novels, placing the fiction in relation to feminist archetypal theory and female Gothic; and, in 1996, Alan Price published *The End of the Age of Innocence: Edith Wharton and the First World War*, which examines the influence of Wharton's war work in France.

Critics including Donald Pizer have discussed Wharton's writing in terms of literary naturalism. Naturalism is a form of realism which also involves the accumulation and documentation of minute details but which distinguishes itself from realism through its application of the principles of biology and social science, pioneered by Darwin and Spencer, to the depiction of individuals. Like realism, naturalism is a contested term and continues to be the subject of vigorous debate but, in broad terms, naturalistic texts typically present characters, often in an urban setting, who are incapable of exercising free will, whose lives, like those of insects or animals, are directed by external forces and whose fates are determined by heredity, environment and economics. An example of naturalist fiction is Upton Sinclair's *The Jungle* (1906) which employs a deterministic framework and evokes the notion of 'survival of the fittest' in its relentless and graphic portrayal of the grim experience of an East European immigrant in the brutal slums and slaughterhouses of Chicago. While very different in style, Wharton's writing reveals the distinct influence of social science and evolutionary theory. In his radical book *The Gold Standard and the Logic of Naturalism* (1987), influenced by the French philosopher and historian Michel Foucault (1926–84), Walter Benn Michaels dissociated naturalism from biology; his argument includes discussion of Lily Bart within complex reconfigurations of economics, speculation and power. Taking a different turn, Carol Singley, in *Edith Wharton: Matters of Mind and Spirit*, considers Wharton's complex engagement with Darwinism, suggesting that, while the author subscribed to the 'principles of natural selection, competition, and survival of the fittest' and 'explored the notion of chance occurrence in her fiction', in *The House of Mirth*, she dramatizes 'the conflict between religion and science'.[59] Singley draws comparisons between Wharton's writing and that of naturalist writers Stephen Crane and Frank Norris, 'champions of the poor', whose fictions explored the notion that 'humans, subject to biological and environmental forces, were in a losing battle for survival'.[60] Examining what she posits as Wharton's more complex and sophisticated exploration of evolutionary theories, she notes:

> Although Wharton's characters may fail just as miserably as any naturalists', her fiction never loses its spiritual or moral dimensions. For Edith Wharton, material and social considerations do not outweigh moral or spiritual ones. It became fashionable among the upper classes to

---

59 Carol Singley, *Edith Wharton: Matters of Mind and Spirit*, Cambridge: Cambridge University Press, 1995, p. 67.
60 Singley, *Matters of Mind and Spirit*, p. 68.

dispense cheerfully with God altogether and among the lower to curse his absence, but Wharton's response was somewhere between these two extremes. She criticized the privileged – who were capable of acting responsibly – for using their advantage indiscriminately and selfishly, and she sympathized with the weak, who by all measures deserved better than they received.[61]

Singley's reading of the novel acknowledges Darwinian influences in the portrait of Lily Bart who 'must outdo other contenders and strengthen her position in fashionable New York by finding a wealthy husband',[62] but she points out that *The House of Mirth* complicates this 'deterministic outlook' by combining it with a more idealistic one. The 'idealism' Singley describes is derived from 'the Christian doctrines that are under assault by science', and she argues that Wharton embeds 'ironic allegories about the fragility of spiritual values in a materialistic culture',[63] allegories which draw upon Christianity. Lily's 'homelessness and eighteen-month wanderings', for example, are interpreted as an 'inverted spiritual pilgrimage'; her search for a husband is likened to the 'idealized quest for perfect love' found in the biblical text, Song of Songs; and Lily's failure to use Bertha's letters and thus save her own reputation is said to evoke Christ's sacrifice:

> *The House of Mirth* disseminates meaning through contrasts – between the future that the reader expects Lily to have and that which occurs; between her society's material abundance and its spiritual depletion; between ostensible gentility and the actual viciousness with which individuals manipulate events and each other. Wharton contrasts Darwinian theories of chance, change without growth, and relativity with the Christian belief in a divine pattern of existence leading to salvation by God. These material and secular discourses compete for voice and position in the text and ultimately overwhelm the discourses of the spirit. Wharton is thus sceptical, and ruthlessly ironic, about the viability of spiritual values in turn-of-the-century society. The novel fails to affirm the redemption that is so painfully needed and concludes not in marriage but in pointless death in a dilapidated rooming house, a conclusion that, while showing Lily's failure to transcend her society, still demonstrates the need for such transcendence.[64]

While discussion of *The House of Mirth* in terms of literary realism and naturalism has been, and continues to be, a major critical strand (see Critical readings, **pp. 106–15**), alternative non-realist or symbolic interpretations of the novel have also been offered. Notable among these is Kathy Fedorko's work on Gothic elements in *The House of Mirth*, which places the novel in a completely different literary tradition. Specially commissioned for this volume is Fedorko's latest Gothic reading of the text (see Critical readings, **pp. 116–26**); in her earlier,

61 Singley, *Matters of Mind and Spirit*, p. 68.
62 Singley, *Matters of Mind and Spirit*, pp. 68–9.
63 Singley, *Matters of Mind and Spirit*, p. 69.
64 Singley, *Matters of Mind and Spirit*, p. 70.

ground-breaking study, *Gender and the Gothic in the Fiction of Edith Wharton* (1995), she considers the novel in relation to several of Wharton's short stories, figuring Lily's narrative as a revision of those of Wharton's earlier Gothic heroines.

In recent years, critical attention has been directed towards the significance of race in Wharton's writing; in particular, the depiction of Jewish character Simon Rosedale in *The House of Mirth* has generated robust debate. In 'The *"Perfect* Jew" and *The House of Mirth*' (1993), Irene C. Goldman-Price examines Wharton's complex treatment of Jewishness. She suggests that, on one level, Rosedale evokes racial stereotypes of the era; he is tainted by 'the traits of avarice [. . .] and social vulgarity [which] were seen as inherent to Jews'. And yet Goldman-Price recognises a 'complicated irony surrounding his characterization'.[65] She points out the good qualities Wharton affords her 'distasteful', Jewish character – honesty, a liking for children and compassion for Lily – virtues absent in the members of her fictional social elite. It is Goldman-Price's contention that Rosedale's 'position in society is a key indicator of what Wharton is trying to say about society'[66] – in other words, he exposes the hypocrisy of New York society.

In 2004, Jennie A. Kassanoff published the first book-length study of Wharton and race, taking as her starting point the critical 'neutralisation' of Edith Wharton's conservative politics and her 'protection' by certain scholars from suggestions of racist or anti-Semitic attitudes. In *Edith Wharton and the Politics of Race*, Kassanoff examines several pre-war fictions, including the 1905 novel, which, she suggests, articulate profound anxieties about the overwhelming of the American elite by the poor, the foreign and the generalised 'other'. Identifying *The House of Mirth*'s Lily Bart as an 'emblem of her race', Kassanoff reads her death as both the 'annihilation of a rare, endangered species and a stylised act of preservation'.[67] The eugenically 'superior' Lily, she suggests, is presented as vulnerable and in need of protection from the vulgarity of modern, democratic America, a vulgarity which includes the romantic attentions of Jewish character Simon Rosedale. Kassanoff disputes readings of the novel which identify Rosedale and his interactions with a young child as a sympathetic presentation of Jewishness, instead suggesting that the scene reveals Wharton's anxieties concerning Rosedale as father and her fears of Jewish reproduction. In having Lily die from an overdose of chloral, she argues that 'Wharton captures and immobilizes her heroine at the moment of racial purity.'[68]

New directions: the uncollected works and the library catalogue

The feminist approach to the work of Edith Wharton, exemplified by the contributions of Joslin and Showalter as discussed above, has been the dominant strain

65 Irene C. Goldman-Price, 'The *"Perfect* Jew" and *The House of Mirth*: A Study in Point of View', *Modern Language Studies*, 23.2, spring 1993, pp. 25–36.
66 Goldman-Price, 'The *"Perfect* Jew"', pp. 25–36.
67 Jennie A. Kassanoff, *Edith Wharton and the Politics of Race*, Cambridge: Cambridge University Press, 2004, p. 5.
68 Kassanoff, *Edith Wharton and the Politics of Race*, p. 56.

since the late 1970s, replacing the critical discourse that constantly placed her in an inferior position to the work of Henry James. Within feminism, there are a variety of different approaches, from retrieval of 'forgotten' texts and authors to complex theorisations of women writers' narrative structures and language. Such approaches continue to reinvigorate readings of Wharton and are exemplified in the new essays in this guide: Edith Thornton's placing of Lily in the contexts of early twentieth-century magazine illustrations (see Critical readings, pp. 84–95), and Pamela Knights's account of some recent reappropriations of Wharton's narrative (see Critical readings, pp. 127–41). Context – literary, social and intellectual – continues to fascinate and energise critics, and so too do questions of genre, as Wharton wrote in so many different modes: short story, novella, novel, autobiography, literary criticism, art history, travel book, interior design and cultural criticism. Elements of many of these genres enter *The House of Mirth*, offering scope for new readings and further destabilising attempts to categorise the novel under any single label (whether a moral tract or a realist text). Further contexts enter with new emphases on Wharton's own activities as a reader and thinker. Frederick Wegener's edition of *Edith Wharton: The Uncollected Critical Writings*, published in 1996, makes available Wharton's reviews, essays, tributes, eulogies, introductions and other writings, a collection which spans the whole of her career. The polyglot Wharton is now given credit for her capacious intelligence, and the publication in 1999 of the catalogue detailing her book collection presents further evidence of the extent and range of her reading. George Ramsden, the bookseller and publisher, gathered the surviving books from Edith Wharton's library into a collection which numbers approximately 2,600 volumes. The books bear witness to the extent of Wharton's appetite for philosophy, literature, religion, science and social science, an appetite which is visible in her writing. Such evidence lays new foundations for appreciating the design and detail of *The House of Mirth*, reviving debate about Wharton's treatment of her New York subject. More than 100 years after publication, the novel continues to inspire fresh approaches. The essays that follow demonstrate some directions for further exploration and invite readers of this guide to return to the novel and to think about it in new ways.

3

Critical readings

Introduction

The essays in this section are all newly commissioned for this volume and are designed to complement existing, often-anthologised, essays on *The House of Mirth*. All the contributors have established reputations in Wharton studies: Beer, Fedorko, Joslin and Knights belong to the first wave of feminist and cultural critics to engage with Wharton's work in the 1980s, following the opening of the Wharton archives at Yale University. Nolan and Thornton are the coming generation, bringing new insights from other media and cultural materialism to bear on Wharton's work. One of the distinctive features of all these essays is that they shape a new response to the novel: Fedorko refreshes and renews her original Gothic reading of the text; Joslin courts gender trouble in a problematisation of Lily's heterosexual identity; Beer, with Nolan, seeks to reposition *The House of Mirth* in its Whartonian context, pulling it away from the usual enforced contiguity with the other novels of New York; Thornton invites the reader to experience the text as it appeared in periodical form; and Knights traces the continuing life of Lily and her story in new best-selling fictions by American women today.

Edith Thornton, 'Beyond the Page: Visual Literacy and the Interpretation of Lily Bart'

Dominant critical approaches to *The House of Mirth* from the mid-twentieth century onwards have given precedence to the written word. Edith Thornton's essay, 'Beyond the Page: Visual Literacy and the Interpretation of Lily Bart', reclaims the visual dimension of the novel and re-places the text in the site of its original reception as a mass-audience magazine serial. In order to expand the critical boundaries of the text, this essay looks beyond Wharton's prose to the dominant images in popular culture in the early twentieth century. Thornton asks what original readers saw when they encountered the serialised *The House of Mirth* in 1905 and suggests how they might have used the illustrations to shape their understanding of Lily Bart's strengths and weaknesses. While literary critics of Wharton's era focused on the novel alone, readers wanted illustrations and combined both visual and textual literacy in their experience of Lily's story.[1]

Edith Thornton is one of a generation of scholars new in Wharton studies who brings a fresh eye to the cultural industry of image-making. She has published extensively on Wharton and visual culture, in particular the illustrative history of Wharton's works; she specialises in American women's self-expression in popular art forms, from magazines to television to film.

Consideration of the illustrations introduces further interpretative possibilities to the debates and discussions about *The House of Mirth*. Additionally, Thornton's analysis offers another way to explore Wharton's portrayal of Lily as a work of art.

---

1   For contemporary reviews, see Helen Killoran, *The Critical Reception of Edith Wharton*, Rochester, NY: Camden House, 2001.

From Edith Thornton, 'Beyond the Page: Visual Literacy and the Interpretation of Lily Bart'

'I sank to the depth of letting the illustrations be in the book—& oh, I wish I hadn't now' wrote Edith Wharton to William Cary Brownell on 5 August 1905.[2] Wharton may well have fretted, for the illustrations that accompanied the first appearance of *The House of Mirth* in *Scribner's Magazine* in January 1905 had catapulted her heroine, Lily Bart, into a thriving and expanding visual culture. Fuelled by new technologies for mass printing and distribution, illustration was in its 'Golden Age', with artists commanding huge fees and attaining celebrity status in a culture suddenly bombarded with images and new visual stimulations. A significant aspect of this visual explosion was a group of illustrators who focused on creating the 'look' of the American woman. These illustrators, including Howard Chandler Christy, Harrison Fisher, A. B. Wenzell and others, created images of the 'ideal woman' which were eagerly sought out by women readers who copied the clothing, hair and, more significantly, the implied attitudes of what a 'woman' should be. No illustrator was more influential in creating the idealised woman than the flamboyant and trend-setting Charles Dana Gibson.

Thus, the illustrations of Lily Bart propelled the character into a complex network of meanings associated with the abundance and popularity of the so-called 'American Beauty' illustrations. These associations altered the reading experience of *The House of Mirth* by linking Lily Bart to the many other visual representations of women and to the visual interpretations that readers had learned by examining the constant barrage of American Beauty images. While A. B. Wenzell, a well-known 'society' illustrator, drew the actual artwork, his images were necessarily in conversation with the most famous illustrator of the period, Gibson. As Terry Brown, curator and director of the Society for American Illustrators, noted: 'In illustration, a style becomes the mode and everyone goes with it.' In the early century, Brown continued, 'Gibson was the lynchpin'.[3] His Gibson Girl was not only the standard for how a woman should look, but she also enjoyed a cult-like following as the model for a new and independent woman. The Gibson Girl was everywhere, and other illustrators were swept into the visual net of Gibson's style even if, as in the case of Wenzell, they struggled to create illustrations that demonstrated their own interpretation of the text at hand. It was impossible, in 1905, to view an illustration of a beautiful woman without detecting obvious nods to the Gibson Girl. Try as he might to depict the emotional subtleties of Wharton's text, Wenzell was locked within visual coordinates that drove him to vacillate between the powerful ideal of the Gibson Girl and the increasingly fragile Lily Bart.

The Gibson Girl was omnipresent in what Donald Lowe has called 'the perceptual revolution' between the years 1905 and 1915.[4] This revolution called upon viewers to make connections between one visual text and the many others it echoed or quoted. As Norman Bryson describes:

2   Edith Wharton, Letter to William Cary Brownell, 5 August 1905, Scribner Collection, Firestone Library, Princeton University, Princeton, New Jersey.
3   Terry Brown, personal interview, 24 October 2002.
4   Walker and Chapman, eds, *Visual Culture: An Introduction*, Manchester and New York: Manchester University Press, 1997, p. 20.

For human beings collectively to orchestrate their visual experience together it is required that each submit his or her retinal experience to the socially agreed descriptions of an intelligible world . . . when I learn to see socially, that is, . . . to articulate my retinal experience with codes of recognition that come to me from my social milieu, I am inserted into systems of visual discourse that saw the world before I did, and will go on seeing it after I no longer see.[5]

This mediated vision, dependent as it is on certain commonly held understandings of how to interpret what is being seen, is shaped by many factors. Perhaps the most insistent factor is repetition, and when the serialised *House of Mirth* appeared in 1905, no image of a woman could approach the familiarity of the Gibson Girl. According to illustration historian Susan Meyer:

her lovely countenance was displayed in reproductions hung on living room walls and in copies of Gibson albums on parlor tables. She was seen on ashtrays, teacups and saucers, spoons and tiles. Wallpaper patterns suitable for bachelor apartments were hung everywhere [see Figure 6] [. . . her image was] inscribed on wooden and leather surfaces throughout the home [. . . on] pillow covers, shields, chair backs, table tops, whiskbroom holders, matchboxes, umbrella stands, easels, and screens [. . .] 'Why Do They Call Me a Gibson Girl?' [was] a hit song of 1906. Waltzes, two-steps, and polkas were named in her honor. 'A Night with Gibson' was performed [first in amateur and later in professional theatres]. Shop windows and advertisements were filled with Gibson Girl corsets, Gibson Girl shirtwaists, skirts, shoes, hats, pompadours, and riding stocks.[6]

Publications such as *Life* and later *Colliers* magazines, for whom Gibson drew extensively, played the cultural role that television and the Internet occupy today, and 'no single creation was more expressive of its times than the Gibson Girl'.[7]

'Expressive' is the key word here, for the Gibson Girl's appeal emerged as much from her implied attitudes about life as it did from her trademark upswept hair, nipped waist and tall, athletic figure. Spirited and independent, the Gibson Girl combined an alluring femininity with a sometimes imperious, sometimes mischievous command of every situation, particularly in regard to men. She was poised and patrician yet could venture from parlour to athletic field with fashionable ease. In short, the Gibson Girl was American popular culture's first depiction of the active woman, distinct from her passive Victorian forerunners, never the victim, always the victor. Terry Brown goes so far as to label Gibson a 'feminist'.[8] Yet Gibson's sly humour kept his creation from being overpowering to viewers who would certainly be suspicious of such a relationship between women and power. The knowing wink at the viewer shaped the visual experience of the

5   Norman Bryson, quoted in Walker and Chapman, *Visual Culture: An Introduction*, p. 22.
6   Susan Meyer, *America's Great Illustrators*, New York: Harry N. Abrams, 1978, p. 212.
7   Meyer, *America's Great Illustrators*, p. 211.
8   Terry Brown, personal interview.

Gibson Girl and softened Gibson's real agenda, which was to critique the upper classes in all their activities; it was an agenda shared, to no small degree, with his contemporary Edith Wharton.

These were the obstacles that Albert Wenzell faced in creating the first visual representations of Lily Bart. Wenzell has not aged well in the history of American illustration. While his contemporaries Howard Chandler Christy, Harrison Fisher and James Montgomery Flagg are the subjects of at least a chapter in chronicles of American Beauty illustration, Wenzell is often dismissed in a paragraph as a skilled technician, and, as one historian sniffs: 'If his preoccupation with the rendering of the sheen of a silk dress or a starched shirt sometimes lessens the message of his pictures, he did, nevertheless, leave us an historic record of the settings and costumes of fashionable society at the turn of the century.'[9] Little wonder that Edith Wharton balked at such a superficial reputation assigned to the rendering of her increasingly complex character.

As the acknowledged 'reflector of drawing room episodes', Wenzell was considered the appropriate illustrator of *The House of Mirth* by Charles Scribner, although certainly not by Edith Wharton.[10] A close examination of his illustrations, however, shows that Wenzell had a more sensitive touch than he has been given credit for. He complicates Gibsonesque simplicity by emphasising subtlety over humour, losing over winning. Yet if humour is absent, so too is danger; eschewing conventional melodrama, Wenzell diminishes Gus Trenor's physical threats, and Lily emerges as strangely emotionless, a blank to be filled in by the viewer's mediated vision. It is the collision of the Gibson Girl myth, Wenzell's attempts to avoid this myth and Wharton's decidedly un-Gibsonesque character that made the first visual depictions of Lily Bart a peculiar mix of the powerful and the powerless, the independent and the dependent, the victor and the victim. Which, the viewer of 1905 might wonder, is what Gerty Farish calls 'the real Lily – the Lily we know?' (I: xii, 172). By comparing Wenzell's drawings with other illustrations of the same period by other artists, this multiplicity of possible interpretations of Lily becomes a case study in the confusions of modernity, a site where the visual literacies described above create a narrative that veers both toward and away from Wharton's verbal depictions of her character. There is, in fact, no 'real' Lily Bart.

Gender politics are at the heart of Wenzell's interpretation of Lily, and his analysis differs from Gibson's established view. Compare the Gibson drawing in Figure 7, with the man intent on the woman whose eyes are demurely cast down or closed, thus 'closing off' her expression to him, with another from the same period by Howard Chandler Christy in Figure 8. The *mise-en-scène*, expressions, hair and hand-holding are remarkably alike, showing the debt illustrators paid to Gibson, his humour and, more importantly, his views about the relations between the sexes. The woman in each 'game' is clearly winning. Susan Meyer calls the Gibson man 'a chivalrous suitor and squire, distinguished and debonair, yet always victim to the whim of his spirited woman'.[11] Other artists' versions of the

9 Walt and Roger Reed, *The Illustrator in America, 1880–1980*, New York: Society of American Illustrators, 2001, p. 46.
10 Eastern Art League, *Essays on American Art and Artists*, New York: Temple Court, 1896, p. 46.
11 Meyer, *America's Great Illustrators*, p. 217.

card-playing couple found elsewhere indicate that magazine readers responded very positively to the hapless man and clever woman, a joke that suggests that while men may think that they are in charge, women actually hold all the cards in the game of courtship.

In contrast, the first illustration of Lily is oddly lacking in spirit (Figure 9). With her significant glare, Mrs Haffen, the cleaning woman, is the more powerful figure in this scene. While the woman on the far right in Gibson's 'The Interruption' (Figure 10) displays the same body shape and size of Wenzell's work, these women are full of facial expression and are in control of the situation, clearly disdaining the man who has disturbed them. Wenzell's illustration of Lily on the stairs at Bellomont (Figure 11) repeats the size and dimensions of the Gibson Girl's dress and hair, but her expression is curiously vacant. This 'expressionless' aspect of Wenzell's work is the main factor separating him from Gibson, but it requires close scrutiny to discern these differences in the overwhelming similarities between Wenzell's work and other Gibson imitators such as Christy. As Figure 12 shows, Gibson was also completely capable of delineating the aloof expression found in many of the illustrations of Lily, further blurring the line between Wenzell's interpretation of Lily and the omnipresence of Gibson's images.

The illustration of Lily and Selden at Bellomont is similar in expression to the Gibson picture of the chess-playing couple: her eyes are closed; his expression on her is intense; their hands are interlocked (Figure 13). Read as a Gibson, this work should indicate that Lily is winning whatever game is at hand. However, her suppliant posture and Selden's head bent over her suggest another reading, namely, that Selden is in control of this moment and Lily is the fragile one. While oversimplifying Wharton's scene, Wenzell does capture Lily's pained face; she has just wept:

> It was for a moment only, however; for when he leaned nearer and drew down her hands with a gesture less passionate than grave, she turned on him a face softened but not disfigured by emotion, and he said to himself, somewhat cruelly, that even her weeping was an art.[12]

Powerful or powerless? Independent or desperate? The picture, read in context with others of the period, does not confirm either reading; both exist together, supporting Lily's (increasingly mistaken) notion of herself as powerful by depicting her in the Gibson style while simultaneously suggesting that she is powerless under Selden's gaze. Significantly, Wenzell's picture is one of three that did not appear in the first hardcover edition and has thus disappeared from the visual discourse of Lily Bart.

Gus Trenor's escalating anger at Lily over her perceived neglect of him should make for some uncomfortable images of Lily in danger. However, in the very Gibsonesque depiction of Lily being threatened by Gus at the opera, Wenzell uses Lily's lack of affect to deflate Gus's menace. (Figure 14). While a scowling Gus leans over a seated Lily, her upturned face and raised eyebrows belie only mild

---

12 Edith Wharton, *The House of Mirth, Scribner's Magazine*, March 1905, pp. 330–1.

trepidation. She is the Gibson Girl being annoyed by a bore, although in Wharton's text she is wracking her brains to find a way to conciliate Gus and is only saved from his wrath by the sudden appearance of George Dorset in the opera box.[13]

In the scene of near-rape as Gus demands his 'seat at the table' (I: xiii, 182), a euphemism for Lily's sexual favours, Wenzell lessens the physical threat implicit in the text by rendering Gus in a relaxed posture, his intensity signalled only by his lowered brow (Figure 15). His hand is resting on the door, his other in his pocket, while Lily retains her imperious expression and assumes a rigid attitude. Even though this is the very scene in which Lily begins to realise that she has overestimated her own powers over men and underestimated their power over her, this picture simply indicates an insult, a passing moment of an inconsequential quarrel. Other illustrators of the period often used melodrama in depicting such a moment, taking full advantage of high emotional content to add dramatic tension to their illustrations. Wenzell ignores these conventions, choosing instead to erase the threat of rape from Gus and Lily's encounter.

Of course, one could argue that Lily's defence mechanism is the very detached countenance that Wenzell has chosen for her. Wenzell seems to fluctuate back and forth between a Lily in need and a Lily detached, but in the visual world so dominated by Charles Dana Gibson, Lily emerges as aloof and refined, two adjectives often used to describe the Gibson Girl. Thus, the other attributes of the cult of Gibson remain with Lily: independence, spiritedness and, most significantly, control over her situations with men. As Wharton's text amply shows, these are the very characteristics that Lily will slowly lose as the narrative unfolds.

Wenzell does attempt to insert at least some desperation into Lily's image. In Figure 16, the only picture to be printed in colour, Lily holds Gerty with an intimacy that cannot be ignored; their clasped hands, touching faces and the intermingled fabric of their dresses suggests real suffering and true attempts at comfort. Sadness haunts Wenzell's depictions of Lily as she begins her descent into squalor and eventual death. In Figure 17, the haughty gaze some might see in Lily's face as she is rudely evicted from the yacht *Sabrina* by a vicious Bertha Dorset is also filled with sorrow in the uplifted eyebrows, chin held just a shade too high and slight tilt of her head, as though it is heavy on her shoulders. While the absent look on Lily's face in Figure 18 as she contemplates her new life with the socially questionable Gormers might distract the viewer from her increasingly perilous position in the social world, her off-centred body, and, particularly, the helplessness of her open hands, suggest a growing sense of desperation that accedes Wharton's own words: 'It was indeed better [to be at the Gormers'] than a broiling day in town.'[14]

The image depicting Rosedale's horrified reaction to Lily's proposal of marriage is unusual for Wenzell in its impressionistic style and use of jungle as backdrop and metaphor (Figure 19). Rosedale is successfully emerging from the jungle of his otherness as a Jew, while Lily is hoping – in vain – to be rescued from her jungle of financial and social defeat. Interestingly, this illustration was also deleted from the book's first edition.

---

13 Wharton, *The House of Mirth, Scribner's*, March 1905, p. 485.
14 Wharton, *The House of Mirth, Scribner's*, August 1905, p. 216.

After these attempts to show Lily's complex inner state, Wenzell retreats in his delineation of Lily being reprimanded for her shoddy work at the milliner's where she has become an apprentice (Figure 20). It is hard to tell from Lily's expression that she is about to lose her last financial hope by being fired, and the situation is downplayed by the activity of the surrounding figures. Is she still independent and spirited, the viewer might ask, like the Gibsonesque representations earlier? Only the high level of movement or upset in her co-workers indicate the massive implications of this moment in Wharton's text.

In the final illustration, also deleted from the first hardcover edition, Lily kisses Selden goodbye before she retreats back to her boarding house to overdose on choral (Figure 21). The tenderness here is palpable, and while Lily is clearly in control of this moment, there is no Gibsonesque humour, no hint of her 'winning' at anything. While her dress does not reflect her wretched circumstances, Selden's sagging shoulders foreshadow the tragedy to come. His hand suggests helplessness, while hers is firmly planted on his shoulder; it is the moment where the missing word that should pass between them is represented to the viewer. The word, Wenzell's picture strongly implies, is love – a love that is lost to the characters, due, the picture indicates, to Selden's emotional impotence.

The three illustrations that did not appear in the final hardcover edition are the three that depict emotional moments when Lily is rejected by an inadequate or inappropriate man: two with Selden, one with Rosedale. The illustrations chosen for the first edition opt for a Lily who is, by turns, Gibsonesque and independent or sad but surviving. The only truly tender illustration that remains in the book is of Lily and Gerty. Was a helpless Lily confronted by a man's rejection too sentimental? Too conventional? Inaccurate? Too unlike the Gibson Girl?

An examination of the correspondence between Wharton and Charles Scribner over the first-edition illustrations reveals how the manipulation of visual images encourages certain textual interpretations over others. It also demonstrates how, by 1905, the visual was critical to selling any piece of literature to a mass audience now familiar with drawing connections between images, text, characters and interpretations. Wharton herself wanted all of Wenzell's illustrations out of the hardcover. While her other works of non-fiction contain photographs of places as illustrations, she resisted fictional representations. In responding to her, Scribner wrote:

> [The] $1.50 novel [. . . achieving] a wide sale has taken rather a conventional form and any departure from it is viewed with suspicion by the average bookseller or department store. Illustrations are expected and their absence may be unfavorably noticed [. . . I] do not wish to importune you but it seems only right to . . . ask you to decide. It might be added that the illustrations are useful for sales purposes.[15]

Reluctantly, Wharton responded: 'As for reproducing the illustrations in the volume, my personal taste is against it, but I am quite ready to waive that, if you

---

15 Charles Scribner, letter to Edith Wharton, 14 June 1905, Scribner Collection, Firestone Library.

consider it would be to our advantage to keep the pictures in.'[16] Scribner himself soon admitted that several of the illustrations were 'poor', and that he struggled with himself about removing all of them, but in the end omitted 'the worst' to avoid 'too great discouragement in the selling department.' So it was Charles Scribner himself who chose the illustrations and had twelve illustration-free copies bound for Wharton's own use.[17]

Through Scribner's decisions, Wharton's Lily Bart plunged into the noisy visual world of clashing images, sales figures, mass production and competing visual literacies that characterised modernity. As for Scribner's choice of omitted illustrations, his serious dislike of Selden's character can explain why he appears only twice in the first edition: 'In the next book you must give us a strong man, for I am getting tired of the [apparently negative] comments on Selden.'[18] The Rosedale illustration is an obvious choice because it does not match the others in style.

However, taking a broader perspective, we can surmise that Lily Bart emerged at a critical moment in the representation of women. The associations that accompanied her depictions in Scribner's introduced unique ways of reading Wharton's work. By examining Wharton's descriptions of Lily Bart beside the assumptions and 'common knowledge' of the Gibson Girl, a period reader's understanding of the character, and, thus, the novel itself, were significantly influenced by the mania for the Gibson Girl. Scribner's choices indicate his belief that readers would rather not see Lily losing the 'game' of heterosexual marriage quite so vividly; as I have argued, the Gibson Girl was a 'winner' and that quality would draw readers to the text. The personality traits of the Gibson Girl point to a visual culture outside the bounds of the novel and compete for understanding of Wharton's most famous heroine. In this light, Lily's signature seal of a ship with the word *Beyond!* underneath it takes on new meanings. Her image spills out of the pages of Scribner's into a visual world over which no one, not even Wenzell himself, had control.

On a final note, it is somewhat ironic to realise that Gibson, Wharton and, to a limited extent, Wenzell were all striving for a similar agenda. In his attempts to complicate Lily beyond the sunny aspect of the Gibson Girl, Wenzell tries to show Wharton's critique of a society capable of destroying the very products it creates. Gibson, for all his humour, travelled in high society but 'never hesitated to mock the more unsavory aspects of what he witnessed'.[19] Their combined efforts, whether intentional or not, underline how visual images exist in a complex discourse that is, as Lily's seal suggests, beyond the confines of the page on which it is printed.

16 Edith Wharton, letter to Charles Scribner, 16 June 1905, Scribner Collection, Firestone Library.
17 Charles Scribner, letter to Edith Wharton, 28 September 1905, Scribner Collection, Firestone Library.
18 Charles Scribner, letter to Edith Wharton, 20 November 1905, Scribner Collection, Firestone Library.
19 Meyer, *America's Great Illustrators*, p. 222.

Figure 6 'Gibson Girl' wallpaper pattern. (Gillon, Edmund Vincent, (ed.), *The Gibson Girl and Her America*. (New York: Dover Publications Inc., 1969), p. 114.)

Figure 7 'The Greatest Game in the World' by Charles Dana Gibson. (*The Gibson Girl and Her America*, p. 117.)

Figure 8 'A Winning Hand' by Howard Chandler Christy. (Moffat, H. C. C. *Drawings in Black and White*. (New York: Yard and Co., 1905), unpaginated.)

Figure 9 The woman continued to stare as Miss Bart swept by. (*Scribner's Magazine*, January 1905, Frontspiece.)

Figure 10 'The Interruption' by Charles Dana Gibson. (Courtesy of the Society of Illustrators.)

Figure 11 She lingered on the broad stairway, looking down into the hall below. (*Scribner's Magazine*, February 1905, p. 144.)

Figure 12 Gibson's aloof expression. (Courtesy of the Society of Illustrators.)

Figure 13 She turned on him a face softened but not disfigured by emotion. (*Scribner's Magazine*, March 1905, p. 320.)

Figure 14 'You don't seem to remember my existence nowadays.' (Source: *Scribner's Magazine*, April 1905, p. 468.)

Figure 15 'I mean to make you hear me out.' (*Scribner's Magazine*, May 1905, p. 548.)

Figure 16 'Oh, Gerty, the Furies ... you know the noise of their wings?' (*Scribner's Magazine*, June 1905, Frontspiece in colour, p. 640.)

Figure 17 'Dear Mr. Selden,' she said, 'you promised to see me to my cab.' (*Scribner's Magazine*, July 1905, p. 80.)

Figure 18 It was a good deal better than a broiling Sunday in town. (*Scribner's Magazine*, August 1905, p. 221.)

Figure 19 'I am ready to marry you whenever you wish.' (*Scribner's Magazine*, September 1905, p. 332.)

Figure 20 'Look at those spangles, Miss Bart – every one of 'em sewed on crooked.' (*Scribner's Magazine*, October 1905, p. 461.)

Figure 21 'Goodbye,' she said. (*Scribner's Magazine*, November 1905, p. 604.)

Katherine Joslin, 'Is Lily Gay?'

As Lily Bart shocked her first readers with her careless and apparently loose behaviour, so in the twenty-first century she continues to arouse speculation. Katherine Joslin's provocatively posed question, 'Is Lily Gay?' brings the insights of gender and performance theories to bear on questions of female sexuality and identity. Joslin reads the text through the lens of Judith Butler, feminist theorist, who questions, in her second book, *Gender Trouble: Feminism and the Subversion of Identity* (1989), the idea of an essential gender beyond the series of public performances we make every day. Butler's edgy insistence on a culturally constructed self that is always in flux (a series of iterations she calls 'performativity') contributed to the development of what is known as 'queer theory'. Butler is, thus, a provocative theorist for considering the construction of Lily Bart, a heroine who longs to move beyond the performances of New York society and yearns to discover an essential identity.

Katherine Joslin is a leading critic of women's culture in the early twentieth century: her literary biography, *Jane Addams, A Writer's Life,* was published by the University of Illinois Press in 2004. She has written extensively on Edith Wharton, including *Edith Wharton* (1990), the coedited volume, *Wretched Exotic: Essays on Edith Wharton in Europe* (1993), the coedited four-volume collection, *American Feminism: Key Source Documents, 1848–1920* (2003). She has also written essays on Willa Cather, Kate Chopin, Theodore Dreiser, Charlotte Perkins Gilman, Virginia Woolf and Émile Zola. Now, in this essay, Joslin, as one of Wharton's first feminist critics, reinvigorates the discussion of the dynamics of sexual politics within *The House of Mirth.*

From Katherine Joslin, 'Is Lily Gay?'

> 'A girl is only a sketch; a married woman is the finished picture.'[1]

Lily Bart would make a rich man a good wife. At twenty-nine, she is savvy about the rich interweavings of tone, nuance, gesture and ritual that express gender and social class in the United States. And she is lovely to look at with vivid hair, a shapely body, trim ankles and graceful hands, polished like ivory. She arrives on opera night tingling under the gaze of adoring men. 'Ah, it was good to be young, to be radiant, to glow with the sense of slenderness, strength and elasticity, of well-posed lines and happy tints, to feel one's self lifted to a height apart by that incommunicable grace which is the bodily counterpoint of genius!' (I: x, 152). Here, at the start, there seems every reason for gaiety in *The House of Mirth*.

Remarkably, Lily remains a virgin at twenty-nine, her flesh-and-blood loveliness an enticement to suitors. Make no mistake about it, the heroine is old enough and smart enough to know that marriage for her is transacted in the marketplace. Not until the end of the novel, and then *only* among the working class, does marriage offer companionship, camaraderie or intimacy, with its delights of sexual expression. Another thing that the novel makes clear is that any movement towards marriage, indeed any male touch, frightens Lily Bart. When the putative hero Lawrence Selden finally kisses her, she draws back: 'Ah, love me, love me— but don't tell me so!' (I: xii, 175). Only in the arms of Gerty Farish does the heroine feel secure. ' "Hold me, Gerty, hold me, or I shall think of things," she moaned; and Gerty silently slipped an arm under her, pillowing her head in its hollow as a mother makes a nest for a tossing child' (I: xiv, 205). What does this ritual cuddling suggest about our heroine?

It may be that Lily – now past her centenary year, when she turned 129 – continues to intrigue readers because she is not a full portrait of a lady. The faintness of the lines and the tentative use of shade and shape and meaning all puzzle the reader because the image of the heroine remains elusive. The novel tells the tale of a young woman, no longer quite young, who steps seductively into the narrative only to side-step marriage, a step that would finish the picture, as Wharton later put it in *French Ways and Their Meaning* (1919): 'A girl is only a sketch; a married woman is the finished picture.'[2]

Lily Bart occasions titters and tattles. After reading about her in *Town Talk*, Ned Van Alstyne snickers and strokes his moustache: 'When a girl's as good-looking as that she'd better marry; then no questions are asked. In our imperfectly organized society there is no provision as yet for the young woman who claims the privileges of marriage without assuming its obligations' (I: xiv, 195). The action of the novel springs from this tension. Lily Bart resists the heterosexual performances exacted by members of her social class.

There is trouble in the novel, all right, class trouble and gender trouble. In her ground-breaking book, *Gender Trouble: Feminism and the Subversion of Identity*

1 Edith Wharton, *French Ways and Their Meaning*, New York: D. Appleton, 1919, pp. 114–15.
2 Wharton, *French Ways and Their Meaning*, pp. 114–15.

(1989), Judith Butler explores the kind of trouble she believes we all encounter. A famously obscure stylist, here Butler delivers her argument straightforwardly: 'My argument is that there need not be a "doer behind the deed," but that the "doer" is variably constructed in and through the deed.'[3] A person comes to us culturally mired, so much so that there seems no escape from a constructed sense of self. In this early work, Butler helped to define what is known as 'queer theory', based on the notion that identity is always in flux.[4]

Gender, for Butler, is not essence but action, a series that she calls performativity. What we see and think of as a coherent pattern of gender is just that, a pattern repeated before our eyes. 'In this sense, gender is always a doing, though not a doing by a subject who might be said to preexist the deed,' Butler insists. 'The challenge for rethinking gender categories outside of the metaphysics of substance will have to consider the relevance of Nietzsche's claim in *On the Genealogy of Morals* that 'there is no "being" behind doing, effecting, becoming; "the doer" is merely a fiction added to the deed—the deed is everything.'[5]

Butler's crusade is a distinctly American one: to open rifts in feminist dialogue. 'The point was not to prescribe a new gendered way of life that might then serve as a model for readers of the text. Rather, the aim of the text was to open up the field of possibility for gender without dictating which kinds of possibilities ought to be realized', she writes in her Preface to the 1999 edition.[6] As provocateur, Butler uses parodies of gender performances to stimulate debate on the socially constructed patterns of gender. 'Instead, the text asks, how do non-normative sexual practices call into question the stability of gender as a category of analysis? How do certain sexual practices compel the question: what is a woman, what is a man?'[7]

Butler's rifting has called out critics. Martha Nussbaum has, in recent years, widened the rift, revealing her irritation with Butler's linguistic obfuscation and smarty tone. Considering the consequences of rhetoric in 'The Professor of Parody', Nussbaum takes Butler to task for thumbing her nose at practical politics. 'Something more insidious than provincialism has come to prominence in the American academy. It is the virtually complete turning from the material side of life, toward a type of verbal and symbolic politics that makes only the flimsiest of connections with the real situation of real women,' she warns.[8] She credits Butler with leading the charge away from a feminism that informs public discourse and, thus, stimulates social change.

Indeed, Butler distrusts the very idea of human agency and posits a theory of rebellion that takes the form of parody, a mocking pose that calls into question the stability of entities like gender or ethnicity or class. 'We are doomed to repetition of the power structures into which we are born, but we can at least make fun of them; and some ways of making fun are subversive assaults on the original

3 Judith Butler, *Gender Trouble: Feminism and the Subversion of Identity*, 1989; New York: Routledge, new edition, 1999, p. 181.
4 For a discussion of how the term 'queer' functions in the novel, see Lori Harrison-Kahan, 'The House of Mirth and the Fictions of Lily's Whiteness,' *Legacy*, 21.1, 2004, pp. 34–49.
5 Butler, *Gender Trouble*, p. 33.
6 Butler, *Gender Trouble*, p. viii.
7 Butler, *Gender Trouble*, p. xi.
8 Martha Nussbaum, 'The Professor of Parody', *The New Republic*, 22.8, 22 February 1999, pp. 37–45.

norms,'[9] she urges. Thus, in *Excitable Speech*, Butler offers her readers, not social change, but what she calls ironic hopefulness.

Edith Wharton had a keen sense of irony and very little hopefulness. She and Judith Butler would have agreed that desire for a utopian beyond is a fool's game. Lily Bart seals her letters with the word 'Beyond!' printed below an image of a flying ship. The central question for Wharton is where such a flight might lead one. 'Oh, my dear—where is that country?', Ellen Olenska famously asks Newland Archer in the later novel *The Age of Innocence*.[10] Can it be that in her longing for escape from ritual, Lily Bart loses her sense of place in gender and social class? If Lily ceases to perform, what is she?

Lily Bart may be the perfect heroine for performative theory. As a character, she is mired and in flux. She is 'manacled to her fate' (I: i, 49) and 'malleable as wax' (I: v, 88–9), hardly an agent in her destiny. Butler's ideas are familiar to any Wharton scholar. Edith Wharton had a heightened sense of performative acts involving taste, gesture, nuance and tone. It is also true that Wharton's sketch of Lily Bart delineates Butler's point that gender intersects with racial, class, ethnic, sexual and regional modalities. The heroine struggles to define herself – to move from sketch to finished picture – in terms of gender, but, perhaps more so, in terms of social class, ethnicity and sexuality.

Edith Wharton may well have had rifts in feminist thinking on her mind as she wrote *The House of Mirth*. We know that her review of three plays about Francesca da Rimini appeared in *The North American Review* in July 1902 next to a review of Charlotte Perkins Gilman's *Women and Economics* (1898).[11] Gilman's sociological study of female performance was reviewed by Vernon Lee, a woman Wharton knew and admired. In the review, Lee considers Gilman's analysis of the 'Woman Question': '[T]he present condition of women—their state of dependence, tutelage, and semi-idleness; their sequestration from the discipline of competition and social selection, in fact their economic parasitism—is in itself a most important factor in the wrongness of all our economic arrangements.'[12] Lee and Gilman accept the socio-biological argument that women act as parasites, attaching themselves to men, in order to store energy for mothering and, as a result, become the property of men, whose power and money provide for a woman's idleness. Ironically, the richer the woman, the more likely she is to be a slave in her marriage.

At the heart of Vernon Lee's analysis is an idea very much at the heart of Judith Butler's thinking about gender and performance. 'We do not really know what women *are*,' Lee insists. What she hoped she saw coming was a society that would allow male and female traits to blend Apollo and Athena into a single androgynous figure, an image very like her own. Butler and Lee, no doubt, would have enjoyed each other's company, both of them eager to turn gender on its head.

9 Butler, *Gender Trouble*, pp. 11–12.
10 Edith Wharton, *The Age of Innocence*, 1920; New York: Scribner's, 1968, p. 290.
11 See Katherine Joslin, '*The House of Mirth* and the Question of Women,' *Edith Wharton*, London: Macmillan, 1991 and 1993; and New York: St Martin's Press, 1991 and 1993, pp. 49–69, for a longer discussion of how Gilman's ideas may have reached Wharton as she began thinking about Lily Bart.
12 Vernon Lee, *The North American Review*, July 1902.

After writing *The House of Mirth*, a decade passed before Edith Wharton straightforwardly articulated her ideas about gender and class. It is under the grave pressure of the First World War – as she put it, 'The world since 1914 has been like a house on fire' – that Wharton wrote *French Ways and Their Meaning*, perhaps her most revealing analysis of American ways and their meaning.[13] She wrote the book to welcome the arrival of US troops into Europe, a movement that she hoped would end the First World War and preserve French culture. It is a desultory book, an impressionistic account of observations and assumptions. Differences between ethnic cultures, what she calls 'race-differences', are hard to plumb, and she seeks them in light of contrasts.[14]

As Wharton puts it: 'Most things in man's view of life depend on how many thousand years ago his land was deforested.'[15] In America, Europeans plunged into a fresh wilderness and, in the experience, broke away from Mediterranean culture and lost sight of the civic lessons of Rome. The value of culture for her comes in 'the preciousness of long accumulations of experience', precisely because 'whatever survives the close filtering of time is likely to answer to some deep racial need, moral or aesthetic'.[16] Wharton embraces what Butler would later define as 'performativity', the iterations of ritual, manners, movement and tone. Over time, performances are filtered and refined into cultural patterns that, for good and ill, define a people.

Wharton laments the fate of her American compatriots – 'a people which is still, intellectually and artistically, in search of itself'.[17] To get to Wharton's point of view, of course, we have to see her as a person very much of her time who believed 'the English and Dutch colonists found only a wilderness peopled by savages, who had kept no link of memory with those vanished societies'.[18] This idea of fragmentation is at the heart of her analysis of the culture in the United States. The French are superior in the culmination of their long 'homogenous and uninterrupted culture',[19] or so she believes. What is the cost of getting beyond established culture? For Wharton, there is much to lose in 'the sudden uprooting of our American ancestors and their violent cutting off from all their past, when they set out to create a new state, in a new hemisphere, in a new climate, and out of new materials'.[20]

Culture, Wharton argues, measures '*taste, reverence, continuity,* and *intellectual honesty*' and can be seen in 'the way the women put on their hats, and the upholsterers drape their curtains'.[21] A sense of scale, proportion, suitability, symmetry, harmony, order and fitness comes from 'the most complex assemblage of associations, visual and mental'.[22] Wharton's gripe with American women is not merely that they do not have French taste in hats and curtains – although that

13 Wharton, *French Ways and Their Meaning*, p. v.
14 Wharton, *French Ways and Their Meaning*, pp. vii–viii.
15 Wharton, *French Ways and Their Meaning*, p ix.
16 Wharton, *French Ways and Their Meaning*, p. 31.
17 Wharton, *French Ways and Their Meaning*, p. xi.
18 Wharton, *French Ways and Their Meaning*, p. 79.
19 Wharton, *French Ways and Their Meaning*, p. 80.
20 Wharton, *French Ways and Their Meaning*, p. 82.
21 Wharton, *French Ways and Their Meaning*, pp. 18, 39.
22 Wharton, *French Ways and Their Meaning*, p. 54.

is pointedly a gripe – but that their lack of taste is a sign of immaturity, cultural as well as individual. She cautions that '[i]ntellectual honesty, the courage to look at things as they are, is the first test of mental maturity and laments 'the intellectual laziness which rapid material prosperity is too apt to develop'.[23]

The chapter in *French Ways and Their Meaning* that is most useful in a discussion of Lily Bart is 'The New Frenchwoman', an essay Wharton first published in the *Ladies' Home Journal*. Edward Bok, the editor of *Ladies' Home Journal*, could be a bully and must have been pleased with the way Wharton took his readers to task, charging that intellectual laziness imprisons a woman 'in a perpetual immaturity'.[24] Wharton likens American women to Montessori children and complains that the separation of genders 'has done more than anything else to retard real civilization in America'.[25]

It is here that she observes: 'A girl is only a sketch; a married woman is the finished picture. And it is only the married woman who counts as a social factor.'[26] Lily Bart is one such sketch. The heroine eyes her world with a keen sense of irony and searches for a place beyond her New York society.

With Judith Butler's theory in mind, we read Edith Wharton's novel as a study of performances that mark gender, class, ethnicity and sexuality. *The House of Mirth* tells the story of Lily Bart through a series of such performances, beginning with what may well be the best scene in the novel. Lily's irresolute pose amid the rush of Grand Central Station – a throng of shallow-faced girls and flat-chested women – catches our attention as it does the eye of Lawrence Selden. Lily and Selden retreat from the hot afternoon into the cool recesses of a bachelor flat in the Benedick Hotel. In the privacy of male company, Lily saunters around the room, 'examining the bookshelves between the puffs of her cigarette-smoke', with her eyes lingering on old morocco bindings with 'agreeable tones and textures' (I: i, 44). She talks with Lawrence Selden, man to man, about the limits on personal freedom in the United States. As for marriage, she turns her eyes on him, 'Ah, there's the difference—a girl must, a man may if he chooses' (I: i, 46).

And it is here that gender trouble sets the plot into motion. Women must use sex to snare a man and, as Lee noted about Gilman's assessment, make a living in the world. 'If I were shabby no one would have me; a woman is asked out as much for her clothes as for herself. The clothes are the background, the frame, if you like: they don't make success, but they are a part of it. Who wants a dingy woman?' (I: i, 46). That is precisely what will happen to the heroine over the course of the novel as she moves out of the frame, shedding her clothes and losing her socially constructed self in a vain search to find an essential identity.

The 'streak of sylvan freedom' (I: ii, 47) that Lawrence Selden admires resurfaces at Bellomont, as Lily wanders onto the wooded path beyond the company of her peers. 'She hardly knew what she had been seeking, or why the failure to find it had so blotted the light from her sky; she was only aware of a vague sense of failure, of an inner isolation deeper than the loneliness about her'

---

23 Wharton, *French Ways and Their Meaning*, pp. 58, 95.
24 For a discussion of Edward Bok and his attitude toward his female audience, see Katherine Joslin, *Jane Addams, A Writer's Life*, Urbana, Ill.: University of Illinois Press, 2004.
25 Wharton, *French Ways and Their Meaning*, p. 112.
26 Wharton, *French Ways and Their Meaning*, pp. 114–15.

(I: v, 97). Who is she, after all, outside the gaze of others? If not in performance, what is her essence?

Nothing is more American in its national literature (think of Henry David Thoreau's walks around Walden Pond) than a walk in the autumn woods to ponder the essence of the self. 'Higher up, the lane showed thickening tufts of ferns and of the creeping glossy verdure of shaded slopes; trees began to over-hang it, and the shade deepened to the checkered dusk of a beech-grove' (I: vi, 99), Wharton sets the scene. Even in nature, of course, Lily is 'keenly sensitive to a scene which was the fitting background of her own sensations' (I: vi, 99). As she turns her mind to Selden, Lily imagines a 'chain that was drawing them together' (I: vi, 100). That chain in any comedy of manners, of course, is the very sign of sexual attraction, and readers might well ready themselves for a romantic inter-lude. Edith Wharton gives us a very different encounter as Selden assesses the nature of Lily's performance. 'You are an artist,' Selden confides, 'and I happened to be the bit of colour you are using today' (I: vi, 101). He credits her with being an artist, even a genius, of performance.

Lily Bart, however, longs to play his role, a man's performance of authenticity, in what Selden calls 'the republic of the spirit' (I; vi, 103). It is in the natural world that a man, according to American Transcendentalists, creates a republic of one and, in that act, frees himself from social convention. Selden asks the enticing question: 'Are you going to become one of us?' (I: vi, 104). And she admits that in proximity to him she finds herself 'spelling out a letter of the sign' (I: vi, 104). How much of a man does Lily dare to be?

As she rejects his offer of a cigarette, a gesture that would place her more clearly in male dress, he lectures her on membership in his manly republic. A *jeune fille à marier* in search of a moneyed man, the ritual at the heart of female identity in the United States, has little hope of cross-dressing by gender or by class. 'Whereas, in reality, you think I can never even get my foot across the threshold?' Lily responds to his question with one of her own (I: vi, 106). Even as Lily sheds layers of convention, she fails to convince Selden: 'She turned on him a face softened but not disfigured by emotion, and he said to himself, somewhat cruelly, that even her weeping was an art' (I: vi, 108).

The putative lovers work hard in the scene to avoid the obligatory marriage proposal, the performance they might be expected to play in New York society and, certainly, in a novel of manners. Distain holds the hero back, leaving the heroine free to parody the mating ritual. 'Do you want to marry me?' Lily asks, her 'face sparkling with derision'. And Selden picks up on her tone, responding playfully, 'No, I don't want to—but perhaps I should if you did!' (I: vi, 108). They clasp hands as she adds mockingly: 'I shall look hideous in dowdy clothes; but I can trim my own hats' (I: vi, 109), a line that reveals more to the reader about her ultimate fate than the reader may want to know. And they continue playing with the possibility 'like adventurous children', until a black car intrudes, and the hero seeks some 'habitual gesture' or performance that will place them back into their social reality. Wonderfully, they light cigarettes with heads together, trembling in a post-coital pose that has left out coitus altogether (I: vi, 109–10).

Judith Butler would know how to read the woodland scene but more so the evening of *tableaux vivants*, the staging of artistic masterpieces, designed to call into question the nature of art as well as the art of socially constructed notions of gender and class. Through 'the happy disposal of lights and the delusive interposition of layers of gauze' the *tableaux* come to life as parodies that 'may give magic glimpses of the boundary world between fact and imagination' (I; xii, 170). The 'splendid frieze' includes works by Botticelli, Goya, Titian, Vandyck, Kauffmann, Veronese and Watteau.

In the final *tableau*, the virginal heroine becomes Joshua Reynolds' *Mrs Lloyd*, 'a picture which was simply and undisguisedly the portrait of Miss Bart' (I: xii, 171). The effect of her flesh-and-blood loveliness overwhelms the painter's brushstrokes, leading Selden to observe: 'She had shown her artistic intelligence in selecting a type so like her own that she could embody the person represented without ceasing to be herself' (I: xii, 171). The sketch of the unmarried girl appears as the finished picture of the married and thereby fully matured woman, and, in that moment, the hero senses 'the whole tragedy of her life' (I: xii, 172). As Butler points out about gender, performance becomes reality, there is no distance between the doer and the deed.

The parody of the sexually awakened woman brings every man in the room to his senses or, rather, to one sense, 'an overmastering longing to be with her again' (I: xii, 172). As her performance ends, the men begin to hunt her, one by one. Selden pursues her through emerald caverns of hanging lights and past a fountain falling among lilies, stagecraft that parodies 'the creeping glossy verdure' (I: vi, 99) of their earlier woodland meeting. As Lily turns her face to him with 'the soft motion of a flower', their lips touch (I: xii, 175). That's the kiss readers have been waiting for, but, alas, only the faintest brush of lips. Lawrence Selden, a fully fleshed heterosexual who has had a long affair with the married Bertha Dorset, pulls back from even the merest touch of Lily Bart's lips. What are we to make of his reticence and hers?

Selden's backing away allows for Gus Trenor's pursuit of Lily in a scene of ritual rape. As the seduction sours, she is horrified by his words perhaps more than his touch: 'Her heart was beating all over her body—in her throat, her limbs, her helpless useless hands' (I: xiii, 184). For a heroine used to having precise control of her throat, her limbs and, especially, her hands, the power of performance nearly fails her. Wharton would have us believe that as the scene 'loomed black and naked', even Gus Trenor loses his nerve: 'Old habits, old restraints, the hand of inherited order, plucked back the bewildered mind which passion had jolted from its ruts' (I: xiii, 184). The ruts of habit, what Butler would call performativity, rescue the heroine.

At that very moment, when heterosexual contact comes closest, Lily Bart turns decidedly to Gerty Farish and the long night in her arms. The desire to escape a rapist, of course, tells us nothing about sexual preference. The evening with Gerty, however, does hint at Lily's desire. As that scene opens, we see Gerty in bed: 'And in her conscious impotence, she lay shivering, and hated her friend—' (I: xiv, 200). As Lily arrives shivering herself, Gerty performs as social worker: 'all personal feeling was merged in the sense of ministry.' She invites Lily to bed: 'Come and lie on my bed. Your hands are frozen—you must undress and be made warm' (I: xiv, 201). Gerty unlaces Lily's bodice as Lily pours out her misery and sinks into sleep in shelter of Gerty's arms.

The morning-after scene has the look and feel of parody. Lily awakens alone on the bed, bewildered by how she got there and puzzled about exactly where she is.

As she recalls the night before, she shivers again. Wharton describes 'a cold slant of light' and 'a tawdry heap on the chair' of unappetizing finery (I: xv, 205). After the long night of cramped sleeping – both women in fear of closer sexual touch – Lily has an acute sense of fatigue and stiffness. There is no call to Lesbos in the morning, whatever may have been the call in the night.

In truth, the night of sisterhood has the effect of ending Lily's virginal youth. Selden sees her in a carriage in Nice and notes 'the warm fluidity of youth is chilled into its final shape', a shape that seemed ' "perfect" to every one' (II: i, 230). Selden notes her skill as a performer with a subtle sense of fine shades of manner that put her in harmony with her social milieu. Yet, he perceives a distance between the doer and the deed, a rift in her performance and sees her 'poised on the brink of a chasm' (II: i, 231). Their earlier sense of play in the woods, the casual exchange of gender roles, falls away as Lawrence Selden observes Lily's performance – and possibly concludes with Silverton that there is 'nothing grimmer than the tragedy that wears a comic mask' (II: i, 231).

Lily's performances define her movement away from her social class and the performances expected of her gender. Bertha casts her out from the yacht 'like some deposed princess moving tranquilly to exile' (II: iii, 258). She performs, perhaps, most nobly after the reading of Aunt Peniston's will decides her financial destiny, leaving her 'feeling herself for the first time utterly alone' (II: iv, 265). And at the very moment of defeat, she holds out her hand to the triumphant Grace Stepney and completes the performance, ' "Dear Grace, I am so glad" ' (II: iv, 262). There is irony here but little hopefulness.

In the following scene with Gerty Farish, Lily's derision surfaces: 'Did you notice the women? They were afraid to snub me while they thought I was going to get the money—afterward they scuttled off as if I had the plague' (II: iv, 263). In a playful reprise of their midnight intimacy, she kisses Gerty whimsically. 'You'd never let it make any difference—but then you're fond of criminals, Gerty! How about the irreclaimable ones, though? For I'm absolutely impenitent, you know' (II: iv, 263). We see Lily Bart as a 'dark angel of defiance' as she drolly sums up what constitutes 'truth': '[W]ell, the truth about any girl is that once she's talked about she's done for' (II: iv, 263). We read the scene with Judith Butler in mind: Lily's scepticism about the absolute nature of truth and her witty acceptance of language as truth sound a good deal like performative theory.

The novel probes gender and class and also ethnicity. Mrs Haffen, a working-class German American, is capable of blackmail, for example, but Lily Bart, a leisure-class British American, is not. The workers in Madame Regina's millinery shop giggle and gossip unselfconsciously in a way that Lily, for all her attempts to join their ranks, cannot replicate, even as she reports sardonically to Rosedale, 'I have joined the working classes' (II: x, 329). Simon Rosedale, a Jewish business-man, looks at Lily with 'stock-taking eyes' (II: vii, 294) as a piece of merchandise and talks to her man to man. What is refreshing about Rosedale is that because he stands outside Christian Old New York, he sees identity as performance. When Lily proposes to him – 'I am ready to marry you whenever you wish' (II: vii, 292) – he reminds her that the gossip about her character *is* her character, a point that the heroine knows all too keenly. To have it any other way is fiction not truth. 'I believe it does in novels; but I'm certain it don't in real life' (II: vii, 294), Rosedale tells Lily, reminding us that this is, after all, a novel.

Lily Bart's final sexual performance begins as she slips Bertha's letters into her bosom, an act that relinquishes her claim on the female body. Readers might expect her return to Selden's apartment in the Benedick Hotel to culminate in their sexual union. The two intervening years have left both the heroine and the hero chastened and sober, ready in any domestic novel or novel of manners to kiss and seal their sexual fate. The hero offers a version of the vow, 'You have something to tell me—do you mean to marry?' (II: xii, 348). Oddly, as their hands touch, Lily feels the 'presence of death' and the promise of sexual fruition: 'But something lived between them also, and leaped up in her like an imperishable flame: it was the love his love had kindled, the passion of her soul for his' (II: xii, 349). Yet as Lily kneels on the hearthrug, she unbosoms herself of Bertha's letters, leaving her body shapeless and unsexed.

> He saw, too, under the loose lines of her dress, how the curves of her figure had shrunk to angularity; he remembered long afterward how the red play of the flame sharpened the depression of her nostrils, and intensified the blackness of the shadows which struck up from her cheekbones to her eyes.
>
> (II: xii, 350)

The final scene on the next morning, mild and bright in the promise of summer, parodies the heroic rescue as Gerty opens Lily's door and offers Selden a trembling hand. The lovely heroine has escaped sexual performance altogether, no longer palpable in the embrace of the female or the male body.

In the penultimate scene, Lily relives her identity through her clothes, the very markers of sex and gender as well as ethnicity and class. Her dresses measure 'the sweep and amplitude of the great artist's stroke', the length and breath of performative life. Lily caresses each fabric: 'An association lurked in every fold: each fall of lace and gleam of embroidery was like a letter in the record of her past' (II: xiii, 356–7). As she repacks the gowns, she relinquishes her identity: 'She put back the dresses one by one, laying away with each some gleam of light, some note of laughter, some stray waft from the rosy shores of pleasure' (II: xiii, 357). Without the very dresses that define her performances, Lily is indeed 'rootless and ephemeral, mere spin-drift of the whirling surface of existence' (II: xiii, 359).

The question about Lily Bart is finally not whether she is gay, a lesbian character of Wharton's conjuring. The question, as Vernon Lee put it, is what women *are*. Over the course of the novel, Wharton sketches possibilities but never completes the portrait of Lily as either straight or gay. Even her acts of parodic rebellion that call gender, class, ethnicity and sexuality into question cannot alter her fate. Her final rebellious act is delicious as she takes off her clothes and 'waits with sensuous pleasure for the first effects of the soporific' (II: xiii, 362). Without another performance to give, Lily Bart slips away from us altogether.

Janet Beer and Elizabeth Nolan, 'The House of Mirth: Genred Locations'

Familiar approaches to Wharton's writing juxtapose *The House of Mirth* with her other New York society novels: *The Custom of the Country* (1913) and *The Age of Innocence* (1920). In this essay, Beer and Nolan argue that the distinctiveness of Wharton's voice in *The House of Mirth* can only be fully accessed through the contrast with the novels to which it is adjacent. *The Valley of Decision*, published in 1902 but set in the Italian eighteenth century, represents Wharton's engagement with the historical novel genre. Informed by meticulous research of the period, the novel is loaded with local detail, paying minute attention to the arrangement of society and to contemporary art, architecture, landscape, religion, customs, costumes and language. In tracing the story of minor aristocrat Odo Valsecca through the era of the French Revolution to the point of the Napoleonic invasion, Wharton explores the choices faced at a moment of radical change to the social order. Odo's relationship with the educated Fulvia Vivaldi introduces the tension between freethinking, intellectual inquiry and established power structures based on religious tradition and rigid class distinction. In terms of genre, *The Fruit of the Tree* can be classified as a Victorian social-problem novel. The romance plot involving New England mill-owner Bessy Westmore, her reform-minded manager John Amherst and nurse Justine Brent is played out against a background of class conflict. The novel deals directly with the problems of industrial conditions and the ethical issue of euthanasia. In both the historical and the social-problem novel, Wharton's adherence to generic convention – her concern with moral questions and her obvious pedagogic intent – intrude into the narrative. Between these two, however, lies *The House of Mirth*, a distinctly naturalistic novel (see Critical history, **pp. 77–8**). While *The Valley of Decision* and *The Fruit of the Tree* remain firmly rooted in the nineteenth century, *The House of Mirth* shows Wharton manipulating genre in order to speak directly out of the modern world.

Janet Beer has written extensively on Edith Wharton, from *Edith Wharton: Traveller in the Land of Letters* (1990), through *Studies in Short Fiction: Kate Chopin,*

Edith Wharton and Charlotte Perkins Gilman (1997) to *Edith Wharton* (2002). Elizabeth Nolan has edited, with Janet Beer, *The Awakening: A Sourcebook* (2004), the Broadview Press edition of *The House of Mirth* (2005), and the *Lives of Victorian Literary Figures IV: Edith Wharton* (2006); she also works on women's periodicals of the early twentieth century.

From Janet Beer and Elizabeth Nolan, '*The House of Mirth*: Genred Locations'

The most compelling reason for undertaking a comparative reading of Wharton's second novel, *The House of Mirth* (1905) with her first, *The Valley of Decision* (1902) and her third, *The Fruit of the Tree* (1907) is to counter the first impression that these three novels do not have an aesthetic or developmental relationship. What they have most powerfully in common is that they are all written in genres – the historical novel, the naturalist novel and the social-problem novel – which express social change at moments of whole cultural upheaval. In their variety, the novels signal important shifts in Wharton's professional practice, but the movement she is making between genres is rarely looked at sequentially or in juxtaposition. Novels by Wharton which are considered to be superior – *The House of Mirth* being one – are usually plucked out from different moments in her career and placed in a variety of alliances – of setting, of theme or of genre – whereas the simple, incremental relationship between consecutive texts is neglected. So, in this essay, we intend to look at the potentially suggestive connections between Wharton's first three full-length novels, their similarities and differences and the distinctiveness of the range of reference which is established at the beginning of each text.

Placing *The House of Mirth* alongside her first and third full-length novels also permits a shift in perspective away from a determination of Wharton as simply a novelist of New York. Her first novel, *The Valley of Decision*, was set in eighteenth-century Italy and puts on display Wharton's keen and intelligent engagement with European culture – with art, architecture, landscape and tradition. Whilst she crafted her narrative very carefully and self-consciously with detail appropriate to the period – her 'Writer's Notebook' contains lists of features of daily life, from cosmetics to dog breeds – she was also aware that this very attention to detail could have an intrusive effect on the business of novel-writing. In a letter to her friend Sally Norton, she said: 'I imagine the real weakness of the book is that I haven't fused my facts sufficiently within the general atmosphere of the story, so that they stick out here & there, & bump into the reader.'[1] Wharton is probably overstating the case, but it is true that the historical novel can be slowed down by the necessity to periodise the plot and setting, a factor which did not, in any respect, apply to her construction of the contemporary setting of *The House of Mirth*. Similarly, when planning *The Fruit of the Tree*, Wharton took notes on

---

1 Letter to Sara Norton, 13 February 1902, included in R. W. B. Lewis and Nancy Lewis, eds, *The Letters of Edith Wharton*, p. 57.

factory conditions, on details of machinery and technical language – some of which she got wrong in the novel, giving her more pedantic readers the chance to write corrective letters – in order to portray the conditions of existence for those workers who provide the backdrop to a story featuring the leisure classes.

The details of life illustrated in the first and third of her novels by research into eighteenth-century Italy or industrialised New England provide some of the detail which goes to build up a picture of societies which are in transition. The revolutionary forces are visible here, as they are in *The House of Mirth*, and the conflict between old and new, past and future, is dramatised through the life of an individual caught in the eye of the storm of change. In experimenting with different genres, Wharton did not vary the fundamental themes of her writing or its indebtedness to literary traditions, which she could modulate to suit her own purposes as a writer. In all three of these texts, there is also a relationship, which can be clearly delineated, with one of the most dominant nineteenth-century realist novelists, George Eliot (1819–80). As has already been noted in the Critical History section of this volume, Wharton's writing was shaped significantly by the practices of a number European artists, and Eliot, in particular, was hugely influential in her career (see **pp. 61–2**). The two writers are often compared, not least for their late entry into careers as novelists. In addition, Wharton sustained a discursive relationship with her predecessor, commenting on and reacting to Eliot's work throughout her life. Our contention here is that although she was often intensely critical of Eliot, pointing out the failings as well as the successes of her fiction, Wharton followed the same developmental trajectory, making many of the same mistakes, reacting defensively to her critics and enacting her artistic uncertainties in a restless movement between genres. However, writing fifty years later than Eliot, Wharton not only had greater opportunities to free herself from the bonds of realism (see Critical history **pp. 74–5**), but she could also position herself differently in relation to that which she articulated as the greatest problem for her predecessor: 'If George Eliot had been what the parish calls "respectable," her books would have been a less continuous hymn to respectability.'[2] Wharton herself never ceased, in her fiction, to challenge the boundaries of the 'respectable'. She moved between what could be called imitation and innovation, between essentially nineteenth-century genres in the first and third of her novels to a genre closely aligned with American naturalism (see Critical history **pp. 77–8**) but nevertheless modified to express her purpose, which was 'how to extract from such a subject the typical human significance which is the story-teller's reason for telling one story rather than another'.[3] In reading *The Valley of Decision*, it would be fruitless to look for a straightforward portrait of late-nineteenth-/early twentieth-century American life, although, of course, the narrative is designed to instruct its US readership about eighteenth-century Italian visual arts, culture and politics. However, the same might actually be said of *The Fruit of the Tree*, the physical landscape here is simply what the plot requires. Set firmly in industrialised New England though it is, the novel deals with issues of class conflict and

2   Frederick Wegener, ed., *The Uncollected Critical Writings of Edith Wharton*, Princeton, NJ: Princeton University Press, 1998, p. 77; Eliot conducted an unconventional long-term relationship with a married man, George Henry Lewes.
3   Wharton, *A Backward Glance*, p. 207.

with the prescription of the limits of human agency and moral authority that are characteristic of the nineteenth-century English social-problem novel. The aesthetic choices which Wharton made in terms of the genred locations for her first and third fictions were enacted in order to achieve a balance between the demands of the nineteenth-century novel form and the particular *fin-de-siècle*[4] concerns which impelled her narratives. But in *The House of Mirth* Wharton found a form and a distinctively American rhetorical style which enabled her to portray late-nineteenth-century New York life through that 'little circle, secure behind its high stockade of convention',[5] in a manner which actually destabilized the familiarity of the home landscape. Lacing determinism with irony, she took her readers by surprise, confuting their expectations of the 'society novel' by constructing a narrative not so visibly concerned with the grand moral questions which fuelled *The Valley of Decision* and which would complicate *The Fruit of the Tree*. Instead she focused on a small, insignificant, 'very useless person' (II: xii, 348) to dramatize the most profound moral of all: that 'a frivolous society can acquire dramatic significance only through what its frivolity destroys.'[6]

The Valley of Decision is a careful, studied piece of work. It is an historical novel which hits all the right generic buttons, treating as it does, a significant, irrevocable moment of change in a society which has seen little disturbance to an essentially feudal social order in its previous history. Although the Italian states are poised, at the end of the novel, for the invasion of Napoleon, the subject of the novel is the prior civilisation, that which is about to be swept aside, just as it is in *The House of Mirth* and in *The Fruit of the Tree*, the latter a novel which locates itself if not literally then ideologically in the nineteenth century. The instruments of change are present in all three narratives, but they are background characters, used to flesh out the forces soon to be dominant in society. In *The Valley of Decision* the poet Alfieri is a revolutionary thinker (although a reactionary individual), and his public work signals the demise of the old ruling class; in *The House of Mirth*, Bertha Dorset is the amoral, parasitic embodiment of the decadence that will seal the decline of the *noblesse oblige* that would have previously characterised the relationship between the leisure class and wider society; and in *The Fruit of the Tree*, factory reformers like John Amherst, although distant geographically, are important harbingers of a new, more egalitarian social order.

The Fruit of the Tree, like *The Valley of Decision*, with its clear indebtedness to George Eliot's *Romola* and the *Waverley* novels of Sir Walter Scott, has European generic roots and has been much discussed as an artistic failure by critics like Katherine Joslin.[7] Whilst not dissenting from Joslin's view, a different perspective on the text and the reasons for some of its contradictions may be reached if the genealogy of the novel is located within the social-problem tradition.

4   End of the (nineteenth) century; literature treating this period is often characterised by the expression of anxieties relating to social and cultural change.
5   Wharton, Introduction to *The House of Mirth*, p. ix.
6   Wharton, *A Backward Glance*, p. 207.
7   Katherine Joslin, 'Architectonic or Episodic?: Edith Wharton, Gender, and *The Fruit of the Tree*', in Clare Colquitt, Susan Goodman, and Candace Waid, eds, *A Forward Glance: New Essays on Edith Wharton*, Newark, Del.: University of Delaware Press, 1999; London: Associated University Presses, 1999, p. 68.

The term, social-problem novel, is most usually applied to a group of texts written between the 1840s and 1860s in England – Charles Dickens's *Hard Times*, Elizabeth Gaskell's *Mary Barton* and *North and South*, Charles Kingsley's *Alton Locke*, Benjamin Disraeli's *Sybil* and George Eliot's *Felix Holt*. The writer of *The Fruit of the Tree* answers to the description given here by Josephine M. Guy:

> Social-problem novelists are commonly credited with the intention of trying to educate, and therefore by implication to change, the opinions and prejudices of their readers. In so doing, they are seen to be implying that the novel can, and should, have an important role to play in social and political life. As a consequence the moral authority often associated with Victorian fiction and the didactic function which proceeds from that authority are given a new dimension in the social-problem novel.[8]

Wharton's pronouncements on the moral imperatives of her art are well known. In an oft-quoted 1905 letter to Dr Morgan Dix she responds to his comments about *The House of Mirth* by saying: 'No novel worth anything can be anything but a novel "with a purpose," & if anyone who cared for the moral issue did not see in my work that *I* care for it, I should have no-one to blame but myself—or at least my inadequate means of rendering my effects.'[9] Wharton started her novel-writing career in a genre which deals with a seminal moment in the history of a culture; the pedagogic intent of *The Valley of Decision* is evident throughout, from the descriptions of the architecture, paintings and sculpture of the period to the processes of social reform; Wharton is intent on educating her readership. Here, and in the later *The Fruit of the Tree*, the message is clear and moral issues are foregrounded; the writing labours to deliver its lessons. Having gained in confidence from the writing of the historical novel, however, Wharton moved confidently onto 'the material nearest to hand, and most familiarly my own' in *The House of Mirth*, also a deeply – and purposefully – moral book but one in which the morality is woven into the texture of the writing.[10] The public response to *The House of Mirth* dwelt in some measure on what was perceived to be immorality in the text; but the response could not be said to be univocal, *The House of Mirth* did not provoke the same critical reaction as Kate Chopin's *The Awakening*, published six years earlier. However, even where the critic is conceding that the book is 'A Notable Novel' – as in the *Outlook* review of October 1905 – the concentration is upon the respectability – or not – of Lily Bart: 'The young woman, whatever her training or standing, who drinks cocktails, smokes, plays cards for money, and indulges in the occasional oath, may not go to the bad, but she cannot escape becoming coarse and vulgar.'[11] The *Nation* went further: 'If this is American society, the American House of Mirth, it is utterly unsuitable for conversion into literature' (see Critical history, **pp. 60–3**).[12] Criticism of this

8 Josephine M. Guy, *The Victorian Social Problem Novel*, Basingstoke: Macmillan, 1996, p. 4.
9 Quoted in R. W. B. Lewis and Nancy Lewis, eds, *The Letters of Edith Wharton*, p. 99.
10 Wharton, *A Backward Glance*, p. 206.
11 Tuttleton, James W., Kristin O. Lauer and Margaret P. Murray, eds, *Edith Wharton: The Contemporary Reviews*, New York: Cambridge University Press, 1992, p. 112.
12 'The House of Mirth and Other Novels', *Nation*, 81, 30 November 1905, pp. 447–8.

kind is not usually considered to have had a deleterious effect on Wharton either professionally or personally, since her productivity was unaffected, but it may just have been influential in her decision to turn to another genre, and an explicitly moral genre, as she received a significant enough check to her artistic confidence to seek refuge in a different class, geography and form for her third book. The responses Wharton made, whether to generally discriminating readers like Dr Dix or Charles Eliot Norton or to outraged members of the public, are defensive but are rarely read as such by contemporary critics because her career was not, apparently, materially affected. *The House of Mirth* was a best-seller and brought all kinds of acclaim as well as criticism. However, the criticism, as she says, 'from the very group among whom I had lived my life and situated my story',[13] which is still being vividly recalled in the introduction she wrote to the 1936 'World's Classics' edition of the novel, led her, in her next book, *The Fruit of the Tree*, to an archaic genre, explicitly moral and intrinsically issue – rather than character-driven.

In *The Valley of Decision* and in *The Fruit of the Tree* there is very little subtlety, and in both novels this is a problem which is linked to the freighting of the central protagonist with too many different narratorial burdens to carry. Odo, like all good heroes in historical novels, is located in the 'middle of the road' in Georg Lukács' terms: always able to see both sides of every question – being drawn to the hedonism of the Duchess whilst simultaneously being seduced by the high moral tone of Fulvia Vivaldi. Justine Brent, in becoming involved with the conditions in the factory and in executing a mercy killing, is given the burden of plot to carry whilst also having to maintain a sophisticated moral vision and the love interest. As already mentioned, *The Valley of Decision* bears close relationship with George Eliot's *Romola*, although Wharton was very critical of the novel in her review of Leslie Stephens's book, *George Eliot* (1902). However, Wharton's criticism of Eliot can also be seen to offer some insight into what might be considered to be the failings of *The Fruit of the Tree*:

> To [George Eliot] [life] was a drama of the soul, a battle of spiritual forces; and the endeavour to reconcile this study of moral crises with the popular demand for a plot, resulted as grotesquely as might the attempt of a portrait painter to reproduce the inner economy as well as the physical exterior of his sitters. The world of incidents and the world of emotions do, indeed, overlap and react on each other; but only to some myriad minded seer is it given to behold and report life "in the round," as it were: the greatest among the less great can seize but one angle of the complex vision.[14]

If Wharton had applied these critical strictures to her own work in *The Fruit of the Tree*, she might have realised that in the novel she makes too ambitious an attempt to achieve that 'complex' or comprehensive vision, relating the demands of an abstract morality too literally to the plot. It may be the case that the demands of her post-*House of Mirth* audience – as she perceived them through her editor's

---

13 Wharton, Introduction to *The House of Mirth*, p. ix.
14 Wegener, *The Uncollected Critical Writings of Edith Wharton*, p. 75.

letters and the reactions of friends and reviewers – led her astray. R. W. B. Lewis cites Charles Scribner's letter to Wharton: 'In your next book you must give us a strong man, for I am getting tired of the comments on Selden.'[15] She tries, and fails, to make Amherst, for all his posturing as a freethinker, anything other than finally inadequate to meeting the challenge of the exceptional woman. *The Fruit of the Tree* ultimately suffers because Wharton is simply afraid to leave anything out and the fact that this failure of omission was picked up by Henry James as demonstrating a likeness to George Eliot is further evidence of a pattern of relationship between Wharton and Eliot which is revelatory about her writing. James writes, from the Adelphi Hotel in Liverpool in November 1907:

> I have read *The Fruit* meanwhile with acute appreciation—the liveliest admiration & sympathy. I find it a thing of the highest & finest ability & lucidity & of a great deal of (though not perhaps of a completely) superior art. Where my qualifications would come in would be as to the terrible question of the composition & conduct of the thing—as to which you will think I'm always boring [. . .] The element of good writing in it is enormous—I perpetually catch you at writing admirably (though I do think here, somehow, of George Eliotizing a little more frankly than ever yet; I mean a little more *directly* and avowedly. However, I don't "mind" that—I like it; & you do things which are not in dear old Mary Ann's chords at all.) However, there are many more things to say than I can go into now—& I only attempt to note that you have to my mind produced a remarkably rich & accomplished & distinguished book—of more *kinds* of interest than anyone now going can pretend to achieve.[16]

James's comment about the 'more *kinds* of interest' in the novel is not meant as a compliment. For '*kinds*' read confusion, or, in Wharton's words about Eliot, the 'study of moral crises' in conflict with 'the popular demand for a plot'. Wharton was as susceptible, at this stage of her career, to public opinion as George Eliot, although Wharton was not quite as painfully and morbidly sensitive to criticism as her predecessor. The true sign of what is on James's mind – the placing of the really telling point in parenthesis – is the tendency to 'Eliotize'; this is more than a reference to an echo of *Middlemarch* in the hierarchy of moral positions between three main characters – where Lydgate, Rosamund Vincy and Dorothea Brooke are mirrored by Amherst, Bessy Westmore and Justine Brent – it is a comment upon the structure of the novel and its failure to connect the moral and the aesthetic. Wharton herself was all too aware of the pitfalls of the nineteenth-century predilection for multiple narratives. As she says in *The Writing of Fiction*:

> The English novelists of the early nineteenth century were [. . .] enslaved by the purely artificial necessity of the double plot [. . .] Throughout the novels of Dickens, George Eliot, Trollope and the majority of

---

15 Quoted in R. W. B. Lewis and Nancy Lewis, eds, *The Letters of Edith Wharton*, p. 159.
16 Henry James, letter written from the Adelphi Hotel, Liverpool, England, 24 November 1907, from *Henry James and Edith Wharton: Letters: 1900–1915*, p. 78.

their contemporaries, this tedious and senseless convention persists, checking the progress of each series of events and distracting the reader's attention.[17]

This did not stop her from falling into the same trap when writing her most nine-teenth-century novel, *The Fruit of the Tree*; indeed, the generic properties of the social-problem novel sucked her into full complicity. In *The House of Mirth*, however, there is only one relentless naturalist narrative. This narrative is centred upon change, but the external forces driving such change are enacted upon the person of Lily Bart, the representative of the species approaching extinction, upon whom all eyes are focused. Whilst the novel is often compared to Eliot's *Daniel Deronda* – the resonances between the two texts demonstrating a continuity of theme in their treatment of the conditions of existence for the clever, beautiful, fastidious, even reckless, dowry-less woman in upper-middle-class British or American society – the novels occupy different positions on the spectrum between realism and naturalism, between the Victorian and the modern novel. They share an essential focus on the heroine, in whom the conflicts of the age are played out, but Wharton freed herself here from the exigencies of the 'double plot', for instance, integrating her Jewish protagonist into the main narrative, unlike Eliot, whose Jewish plot is often a distraction from the central thrust of the novel.[18]

At the opening of *The House of Mirth*, Lawrence Selden makes the comment that Lily Bart 'must have cost a great deal to make, that a great many dull and ugly people must, in some mysterious way, have been sacrificed to produce her' (I: i, 39). Wharton thus announces both her genre and her mode of narrative progression. Lily has already been described as 'specialized' (I: i, 39); Darwin dominates here; the figurative language takes us deep into American naturalism and the survival of the fittest. At the beginning of the story of Odo Valsecca in *The Valley of Decision*, the narrator tells us: 'There was nothing unusual in Odo's lot. It was that of many children in the eighteenth century, especially those whose parents were cadets of noble houses, with an apanage barely sufficient to keep their wives and themselves in court finery, much less to pay their debts and clothe and educate their children.'[19] The time, the place, the class – all are communicated through direct telling, through scholarship and use of archaisms; there are not many Americans likely to be familiar with the concept of 'apanage', the provision made for the maintenance of the younger children of royalty. The genre is recog-nisably that of the historical novel. In *The Fruit of the Tree*, we are introduced to two of the main characters at the sickbed of an operative from the Westmore Mills. In a genre where politics and, in particular, class hierarchies, must be fore-grounded, the first dialogue between Justine Brent and John Amherst is a crucial one in establishing the context:

'Well, I won't try to put the general situation before you, though Dillon's accident is really the result of it. He works in the carding room, and on the day of the accident his "card" stopped suddenly, and he put his

---

17 Edith Wharton, *The Writing of Fiction*, 1925; reprinted, New York: Touchstone, 1997, pp. 60–1.
18 Wharton, *The Writing of Fiction*, p. 61.
19 Edith Wharton, *The Valley of Decision*, New York: Scribner's, 1902, p. 7.

hand behind him to get a tool he needed out of his trouser-pocket. He reached back a little too far, and the card behind him caught his hand in its million of diamond-pointed wires. Truscomb and the overseer of the room maintain that the accident was due to his own carelessness; but the hands say that it was caused by the fact of the cards being too near together, and that just such an accident was bound to happen sooner or later [. . .]

'But why do they crowd the rooms in that way?'

'To get the maximum of profit out of the minimum of floor-space. It costs more to increase the floor-space than to maim an operative now and then.'[20]

All we need to know about the political position of John Amherst, the intelligent compassion of Justine Brent, the oppressive regime in the mill, the supremacy of profit, the brutality of the working environment and its terrible human consequences is laid before us. The scene is one that would not be out of place in a Dickens or Gaskell novel. Both *The Fruit of the Tree* and *The Valley of Decision* are show-and-tell novels; their generic affinities make this inevitable. In *The House of Mirth*, the effects are deliberately muted. Its generic properties – as a naturalist novel – would seem to militate against subtlety; no one could call those standard texts of American naturalism, Frank Norris's *McTeague* (1899) or Upton Sinclair's *The Jungle* (1906) subtle in their effects – the first depicting the domestic life of a husband who bites his wife's fingers for pleasure and brutally murders her for her lottery winnings, and the second factory workers who regularly fall into steaming vats and end up as sausages. However, Wharton's intellectual engagement with and empowerment by the work of the social and natural scientists, when combined with her familiarity with the social scene of leisure-class New York, means that a refracting irony plays throughout the very texture of the novel. Freed, albeit temporarily, from the artificialities imposed upon her work by the strictures of essentially nineteenth-century forms, she found her own voice in the intimate tale of an insignificant individual, rather than in the public narratives of Italian unification or factory reform. In *A Backward Glance*, Wharton noted:

> My last page is always latent in my first; but the intervening windings of the way become clear only as I write, and now I was asked to gallop over them before I had even traced them out! I had expected to devote another year or eighteen months to the task, instead of which I was asked to be ready within six months.[21]

If we believe the claims about the hurried way in which she was forced to write the novel, then it may be the case that the absence of preparation, research, deliberation, elaborate plotting but, above all else, self-conscious reference to mid-nineteenth-century genres, that makes *The House of Mirth* the most compelling of narratives.

20 Edith Wharton, *The Fruit of the Tree*, New York: Scribner's, 1907, pp. 10–11.
21 Wharton, *A Backward Glance*, p. 208.

There are many structural similarities between the three novels discussed here, for instance, in their triangle of two women and one man and in the heroine's sacrifice of herself or her reputation for the sake of the man's future. The unnatural death of a beautiful woman also features in each: Fulvia is assassinated; Lily and Bessy both die of an overdose, although Bessy's is a mercy killing following a riding accident. There is, as mentioned at the outset, social upheaval imminent in each narrative; huge social change hovers just beyond the horizon of the text. In his book, *Genres in Discourse*, Tzvetan Todorov says: 'A society chooses and codifies the acts that correspond most closely to its ideology; that is why the existence of certain genres in one society, their absence in another, are revelatory of that ideology.'[22] The social-problem novel grew, entirely predictably, from a set of conditions, both intrinsic and extrinsic to the realist novel. Wharton found what she needed in realism and its variations, George Eliot being both model and anti-model for her work. *The House of Mirth* expresses ideologically Wharton's own New York, in Todorov's terms; harnessing the visceral power of naturalism behind the reins of a contained and restrained irony, she communicated an original vision of a society that had been, until then, as she puts it herself: 'unexploited by any novelist who had grown up in that little hot-house of traditions and conventions' and, furthermore, 'as yet, these traditions and conventions were unassailed, and tacitly regarded as unassailable'.[23] When she assailed them, she generated a new and distinct medium; in comparison with the novels which precede and follow *The House of Mirth*, its uniqueness can be clearly seen, but so can the intellectual enquiry – of purpose, mode and manner – which surrounded the conditions of its creation.

---

22 Tzvetan Todorov, *Genres in Discourse*, Cambridge: Cambridge University Press, 1990, p. 19.
23 Wharton, Introduction to *The House of Mirth*, p. vi.

Kathy Fedorko, ' "Seeing a Disfigurement": Reading the Gothic in *The House of Mirth*'

Kathy Fedorko's book, *Gender and the Gothic in the Fiction of Edith Wharton* (1995) looks at the writer's use of Gothic elements in exploring the limits of gender. Previous literary criticism had primarily concentrated on Wharton as a realistic analyst of upper-class American society. In a substantial body of work in this area, Fedorko has demonstrated that Wharton adapts Gothic mainstays such as haunted houses, ghosts, evil eyes, threatening darkness, sexually predatory men, and menaced young women to dramatise her exploration of gender identity beyond the social restraints that dominated her life.

Fedorko employs feminist and Jungian approaches, her work building on studies of female Gothic, a term first used by Ellen Moers in her book, *Literary Women: The Great Writers* (1977). In discussing Gothic fiction written by women, such as *Mysteries of Udolpho* (1794) and *The Italian* (1797), by Ann Radcliffe; *Frankenstein* (1818) by Mary Shelley; and *Wuthering Heights* (1847) by Emily Brontë, Moers locates her definition in female experiences of childbirth, childhood, sexuality and self-hatred. Implicitly, she distinguishes female Gothic from Gothic fiction written by men, such as *The Castle of Otranto* (1764), written by the initiator of the form, Horace Walpole; *The Monk* (1796) by Matthew Gregory Lewis; and *Vathek* (1786), by William Beckford, with its sadism, mutilation of women, incest and rape. The essay collection *The Female Gothic* (1983), edited by Julianne E. Fleenor, significantly expanded Moers' theory, as did Sandra M. Gilbert's and Susan Gubar's *The Madwoman in the Attic: The Woman Writer and the Nineteenth-Century Literary Imagination* (1979) and the work of psychoanalytic feminist critics such as Claire Kahane in her essay, 'The Gothic Mirror' (1985). As Fedorko demonstrates in this new essay, reading the Gothic text in *The House of Mirth* illustrates how Wharton deepens her story of Lily Bart by going beyond the conventions of realism.

From Kathy Fedorko, ' "Seeing a Disfigurement": Reading the Gothic in *The House of Mirth*'

Edith Wharton uses the language of Gothic eeriness, mysteriousness and uncanniness throughout her career in many of her short stories and novels, in her unpublished autobiography 'Life and I', and in her descriptions of her creative process to convey intense emotion, to describe intense experience and to say what otherwise might go unsaid.[1] Robert Heilman's article, 'Charlotte's Brontë's "New" Gothic' explains, in a way applicable to Wharton, how the Gothic performs this function for Brontë. Distinguishing 'new' Gothic from 'old' – with its ruined castle, rattling chains, and bloody portraits – Heilman explains that what he calls the 'new' Gothic functions more internally than externally, revealing passions below the 'rational surface of things' and, thus, serving as 'a great liberator of feeling'.[2] New Gothic functions to 'open horizons beyond social patterns, rational decisions, and institutionally approved emotions; in a word, to enlarge the sense of reality and its impact on the human being'.[3] Wharton, like Brontë, uses Gothic elements to go beyond conventions of realism into the darkness of human experience, while at the same time, unlike Brontë, she subverts the traditional Gothic plot.[4]

Gothic fiction exists in good part to inscribe fears. Anxieties about power, money, class and female sexuality, usually within a context of social upheaval, fuel the form. Wharton relies on a Gothic subtext in *The House of Mirth* to convey her struggle with cultural and personal anxieties about both class and female identity, anxieties that many critics have noted. R. W. B. Lewis, for instance, points out that 'Disintegration', an earlier version of *The House of Mirth*, focuses on the pressures of social change and the anxieties of possible 'social deterioration', and Jennie Kassanoff discusses how 'early-twentieth century patrician anxieties: that the ill-bred, the foreign, and the poor would overwhelm the native elite' play out in *The House of Mirth*.[5] Cynthia Griffin Wolff, for one, discusses the centrality of the 'woman problem' to Wharton's life and fiction, especially before and during her writing of *The House of Mirth*.[6]

When Wharton determined that she wanted to write a novel about something she knew best, 'fashionable New York', she was at first stymied by its 'flatness and

1 See Kathy A. Fedorko, *Gender and the Gothic in the Fiction of Edith Wharton*, Tuscaloosa, Ala.: University of Alabama Press, 1995, for an in-depth discussion of Wharton's use of the Gothic in her fiction and non-fiction.
2 Robert B. Heilman, 'Charlotte Brontë's "New" Gothic', in Robert Rathburn and Martin Steinmann, Jr., eds, *From Jane Austen to Joseph Conrad*, Minneapolis, Minn.: University of Minnesota Press, 1958, pp. 118–32, 127, 131.
3 Heilman, 'Charlotte Brontë's "New" Gothic', p. 131.
4 My references to traditional Gothic assume female Gothic. For discussions of the differences between female and male Gothic, see Ellen Moers, *Literary Women: The Great Writers*, Garden City, NY: Anchor Books, 1977; Juliann E. Fleenor, ed., *The Female Gothic*. Montreal: Eden Press, 1983; Kari J. Winter, 'Sexual/Textual Politics of Terror: Writing and Rewriting the Gothic Genre in the 1790s', in Katherine Anne Ackley, ed., *Misogyny in Literature: An Essay Collection*, New York: Garland Publishing, 1992, pp. 89–103; Anne Williams, *Art of Darkness: A Poetics of Gothic*, Chicago, Ill.: University of Chicago Press, 1995.
5 R. W. B. Lewis, *Edith Wharton: A Biography*, New York: Harper & Row, 1975; Jennie A. Kassanoff, 'Extinction, Taxidermy, Tableaux Vivants: Staging Race and Class in *The House of Mirth*', *PMLA*, 115.1, January 2000, pp. 60–74, 107, 61.
6 Griffin Wolff, *A Feast of Words*, pp. 1, 107.

futility'.[7] Then she imagined Lily Bart, the one destroyed by the 'frivolous society', and she knew she had the subject matter of a novel with humanity and moral substance.[8] Wolff posits that the 'brilliant success' of *The House of Mirth* derives from the way it captures Wharton's own experience, allowing her 'to speak with an undiluted intensity of expression that is rare in any novel', in particular about destructive restrictions on female identity.[9] Alan Lloyd-Smith, too, remarks that a 'deep gender-anxiety' permeates the Gothic. He elaborates by explaining that 'the perception of women's imperiled situation [. . .] created a further reach of Gothic, one written by women and conveying a sense of their own fears and oppression'.[10] The many Gothic elements in the novel – mirrors, claustrophobic rooms and houses, the orphaned heroine and her dangerous female double, secret letters, the paired hero and heroine – give Wharton the means for expressing these intense feelings that might otherwise have gone unspoken and help her negotiate her struggle to define adult womanhood.

Old New York society, the 'house of mirth' in which Lily Bart's story takes place, is haunted by greed, adultery, cruelty, suspicion and upper-class anxiety about interlopers. As a tentative resident in this house, Lily bears several key traits of the traditional Gothic heroine: she is orphaned, beautiful and penniless. Unlike the traditional heroine Emily St Aubert in Anne Radcliffe's classic Gothic novel *The Mysteries of Udolpho*, however, Lily has never been nurtured or morally educated, as Emily has been by her father. Having been raised in what Wharton calls 'the turbulent element called home' with a selfish, acquisitive, social-climbing mother and a meek, overworked father, Lily seems to have only received encouragement to be beautiful and to marry a rich husband (I: iii, 63). Lily's childhood, like Emily St Aubert's, ends not when her father dies, but when, like Mr St Aubert, Mr Bart loses his fortune. Ellen Moers observes that 'property seems to loom larger than love in *Udolpho*', and indeed money, and women's tenuous hold on it, functions as a key plot element in female Gothic fiction, just as it does in Wharton's novel.[11]

Wharton bluntly puts money above love when she describes that Mrs Bart's idea of emotional support for her dying husband is to assume that 'he no longer counted: he had become extinct when he ceased to fulfill his purpose (I: iii, 68). Lily's emotions during her father's dying, in turn, 'remained in a state of spectatorship, overshadowed by her mother's grim unflagging resentment' (I: iii, 68). Wharton's narrator tells us that Lily, 'Secretly ashamed of her mother's crude passion for money', would have preferred a life involving 'an English nobleman with political ambitions and vast estates; or, for second choice, an Italian prince with a castle in the Apennines and an hereditary office in the Vatican', not unlike the happy ending of a heroine in a Gothic novel by Anne Radcliffe that Lily won't have (I: iii, 70).

7 Wharton, *A Backward Glance*, p. 207.
8 Wharton, *A Backward Glance*, p. 207.
9 Wolff, *A Feast of Words*, p. 110.
10 Alan Lloyd-Smith, *American Gothic Fiction: An Introduction*, New York: Continuum, 2004, p. 58.
11 Moers, *Literary Women*, p. 207.

As occurs in many Gothic novels, an aunt becomes a surrogate mother for Lily. While Emily inherits her aunt's property, Lily's aunt disinherits her. Penurious monetarily, Aunt Julia doles out a sporadic allowance to Lily that keeps her financially dependent and insecure. Penurious emotionally, as well, Mrs Peniston provides Lily no guidance in navigating the social landscape: 'She had simply stood aside and let her take the field' (I: ii, 73). Lily *has* taken the field, at first confidently but now, at twenty-nine and unmarried, desperately; with a repetitiveness suggesting the uncanny, she has forfeited one chance after another to marry. (In his essay 'The Uncanny', Sigmund Freud discusses the 'compulsion to repeat, which proceeds from instinctual impulses'.[12] In Lily's case, the 'instinctual impulse' may be an act of self-preservation from the suffocating limitations of marriage for women in her society.)

Key to Gothic novels are claustrophobic, threatening spaces, acting as visual forms for the restrained, vulnerable lives of the heroines, the kind of spaces Lily feels repressed by.[13] Mrs Peniston's house, with its 'glacial neatness', feels 'as dreary as a tomb', and in it Lily feels herself 'buried alive' (I: iii, 72; I: ix, 136). Her room in the house, compared to the luxurious guestrooms in the elegant homes of her wealthy friends, seems 'as dreary as a prison' (I: ix, 146). Even her potential suitor, Percy Gryce, conveys suffocation not only in his dullness but also because his father's fortune, which he has just inherited, accrued from the invention of 'a patent device for excluding fresh air from hotels' (I: ii, 57). The Gryce home, 'an appalling house', the narrator tells us, has its valuable Americana book collection 'in a fire-proof annex that looked like a mausoleum' (I: ii, 56). When Lily goes to Gus Trenor's Fifth Avenue home, she enters the 'shrouded hall' and then the drawing room, about which Trenor comments, 'Doesn't this room look as if it was waiting for the body to be brought down?' (I: xiii, 178). The threatening creepiness of the house foregrounds Gus's attempt 'to bring Lily down' by raping her as 'payment' for the money he has loaned her.

Wharton extends the Gothic subtext in *The House of Mirth* most, however, at the end of the novel, in two spaces outside New York society: Nettie Struther's kitchen and Lily's narrow boarding-house room. In both of these places, Lily finally confronts what Claire Kahane, in her essay 'The Gothic Mirror', calls the 'awesome and powerful' maternal body.[14] The mother, Kahane writes, 'figuring the forces of life and death', is the one with whom the female child, unlike the male, 'remains locked in a . . . tenuous and fundamentally ambivalent struggle for a separate identity', because the mother is 'a mirror image who is both self and other'.[15] Female Gothic focuses on this struggle. For women, the mother's threatening female body represents the sexual self and 'to become the mother is to become the passive and perhaps unwilling victim of one's own body'.[16]

---

12 Sigmund Freud, 'The Uncanny', *The Uncanny*, trans. David Mclintock, New York, 2003, pp. 123–62, 145.
13 Lewis comments on Wharton's 'obsession with enclosed spaces': R. W. B. Lewis, *Edith Wharton*, p. 121.
14 Clair Kahane, 'The Gothic Mirror,' in Shirley Nelson Garner, Clair Kahane, Madelon Sprengnether, eds, *The (M)other Tongue: Essays in Feminist Psychoanalytical Interpretation*, Ithaca, NY: Cornell University Press, 1985, pp. 334–51, 336–7.
15 Kahane, 'The Gothic Mirror', p. 337.
16 Fleenor, ed., *The Female Gothic*, p. 16.

Lily Bart's fearful reactions to sexuality in *The House of Mirth* reflect Wharton's own early anxieties. In 'Life and I', Wharton tells us that as a child she was given a 'severe scolding', the 'penetrating sense of "not-niceness," ' and 'a vague sense of contamination' after asking her imperious mother questions about sex. When, as an adult about to marry, Wharton again asks her mother about the 'whole dark mystery' of sex, Lucretia Jones responds with frigid disgust and no information.[17] Leona Sherman, in 'Gothic Possibilities', her essay written with Norman Holland, explains that her own Gothic fear derives from the threat of 'nonseparation' and 'annihilation' posed by female sexuality. The mysteries of the maternal body, Sherman explains, 'are the issues of sex and birth and death and, too, the necessity of concealing them'.[18]

This fear of being annihilated by sexuality permeates Lily's reaction to it. Throughout *The House of Mirth*, up to the concluding scenes, Lily tries to keep the fantasy of marriage to a wealthy man alive at the same that that she tries to keep thoughts of sexuality repressed. Any contact with sexuality feels like physical harm to Lily. She experiences Bertha's love letters to Selden as 'the volcanic nether side of the surface over which conjecture and innuendo glide so lightly till the first fissure turns their whisper to a shriek', and she feels disgust and contamination in their presence (I: ix, 140). After George Dorset tells Lily about Bertha's most recent adultery, Lily leaves 'shrinking and seared, as though her lids had been scorched by its actual glare' (II: ii, 241).

Repressing sexuality is most difficult with Rosedale, who treats her most genuinely throughout the novel and, thus, most sexually. When Lily actually considers marrying Rosedale, being his wife is one of the 'midnight images that must at any cost be exorcised' (II: vi, 287). She shrinks 'in every nerve' from the sexuality his gaze and tone suggest and draws away 'instinctively from his touch' (II: vii, 292, 294).

Immediately before the scenes in Nettie Struther's kitchen and Lily's room, a quintessentially Gothic word repeats, 'dread'. Lily has 'dreadful things to think about', she 'dreaded' passing the chemist's, 'dreaded' returning to her narrow room, feels 'dread' that the chemist might refuse her the drug, 'a dread of returning to the solitude of her room', 'the secret dread' that she might get used to being indebted to Trenor, the 'old incurable dread of discomfort and poverty', and a 'dread of returning to a sleepless night' (II: viii, 305; II: x, 327, 327, 328, 333, 335, 335; II: xiii, 351).

Along with this dread comes new self-awareness for Lily, however: that her fear of poverty might cause her to not pay back Trenor, that she might be tempted to use Bertha's letters in order to marry Rosedale, that being fired from Mme Regina's hat shop was justified, given her ineptitude, although, 'It was bitter to acknowledge her inferiority even to herself' (II: xi, 337). No longer willing to rationalise her failures by the fact that 'she had been brought up to be ornamental', Lily now realises she cannot hide behind 'her consoling sense of universal efficiency' that used to fuel her sense of empowerment (II: xi, 337).

17 Wharton, 'Life and I', p. 1087.
18 Norman Holland and Leona F. Sherman, 'Gothic Possibilities,' *New Literary History*, 8, 1976–7, pp. 279–94: pp. 283, 286–7.

As she struggles to decide whether to pursue Rosedale's offer of help by blackmailing Bertha Dorset, Lily now knows, the narrator tells us, that 'she had neither the aptitude nor the moral constancy to remake her life on new lines' (II: xi, 341). Yet when she eventually decides to threaten Bertha with the letters, she goes instead to Selden's apartment and acts more authentically than she ever has up to this point.

While Selden remains silent, despite Lily's drenched presence at his door, Lily speaks spontaneously and directly to him about their encounter at Mrs Hatch's. Lily's 'strange state of extra-lucidity gives her the sense of being already at the heart of the situation' (II: xii, 345). Now she refuses to engage in coyness. Indeed, when Selden does, she feels incredulous that he should 'think it necessary to linger in the conventional outskirts of word-play and evasion', and his discomfort and reserve no longer disturb her (II: xii, 346).

Lily now believes that 'she had saved herself whole from the seeming ruin of her life', and she bravely insists that Selden see her wholly for once before they parted, that he be the true friend she tells him at the beginning of the novel she needs (II: xii, 347). Now she is bluntly honest with herself and with Selden that she is 'a very useless person' without 'an independent existence' (II: xii, 348). Yet when the time comes to, as she puts it, leave the Lily Bart that Selden knew with him, she reaches the crucial understanding that she *cannot* 'leave her old self with him' because that self 'must still continue to be hers' (III: xii, 349). Accepting herself as a moral individual able to feel love gives Lily the strength to burn Bertha's letters without Selden's knowledge.

Lily's encounter with Nettie Struther after leaving Selden's apartment has been called sentimental and clichéd, as well as socially progressive.[19] Recognising the Gothic in *The House of Mirth* allows us to read the ominousness of this ending. Nettie kindly recognises Lily's weakness and takes her home with her. Yet when Lily confesses, 'I have been unhappy—in great trouble,' Nettie negates the confession by gushing, '*You* in trouble? I've always thought of you as being so high up, where everything was just grand' (II: xiii, 352). Rather than asking Lily about her 'great trouble', Nettie talks about the fantasies she has had of Lily's life. Nettie can't hear Lily and so can't help her.

Nonetheless, despite her inability to empathise with Lily, Nettie has unconditional love from her husband and a sexual life, in contrast to Lily's lack of love and her fear of sexuality. This fear resonates when Lily holds Nettie's baby. At first, the baby feels 'as light as a pink cloud or a heap of down' (II: xiii, 355). Subsequently, however, 'the weight increased, sinking deeper, and penetrating her with a strange sense of weakness, as though the child entered into her and became a part of herself' (II: xiii, 355). The sinking weight, the phallic verb 'penetrating', the ensuing 'weakness' from the sense of the child entering her body all give this scene of metaphorical impregnation an ominous quality.

---

19 See, for instance, Joan Lidoff, 'Another Sleeping Beauty: Narcissism in *The House of Mirth*', *American Quarterly*, 32, 1980, pp. 519–39; and Frances L. Restuccia, 'The Name of the Lily: Edith Wharton's Feminism(s)', in Shari Benstock, ed., *Edith Wharton: The House of Mirth*, Boston, Mass.: Bedford Books of St Martin's Press, 1994, pp. 404–18. Lidoff and Restuccia disparage the scene in Nettie's kitchen as clichéd. See also Ammons, *Edith Wharton's Argument with America*, 1980 and Showalter, 'The Death of the Lady (Novelist)', pp. 133–49. Ammons and Showalter read the scene as socially progressive.

When Lily returns to her own lonely room, she realises with 'intense clearness' her separation from 'the solidarity of life', from true connection with others, and that she is 'mere spin-drift of the whirling surface of existence' (II: xiii, 359–60). The 'sweet vision' of her time with Selden gives her a 'sense of kinship with all the loving and foregoing in the world' she has never felt until now because she has never understood herself to be an individual, separate from her role as a beautiful commodity (II: xiii, 361). The truth Lily is facing about herself makes her feel as if 'a great blaze of electric light had been turned on in her head, and her poor little anguished self shrank and cowered in it, without knowing where to take refuge' (II: xiii, 361). Strong enough to face intense realisation about her individuality, yet exhausted by what she has been through, Lily shrinks from 'the glare of thought as instinctively as eyes contract in a blaze of light—darkness, darkness was what she must have at any cost' (II: xiii, 362).

Chloral brings Lilly passiveness and the 'delicious' willingness to 'lean over and look down into the dim abysses of unconsciousness' (II: xiii, 362). It dulls and then obliterates the truth she has reached about her separate identity and the mature connections with others she has never achieved. As a sense of 'complete subjugation' (II: xiii, 362) comes over her, Lily loses what Claire Kahane refers to as the 'tenuous and fundamentally ambivalent struggle for a separate identity', the struggle with the maternal self that figures 'the forces of life and death'.[20] Lily dies with a hallucinatory image of Nettie's baby lying on her arm, giving her 'a gentle penetrating thrill of warmth and pleasure' (II: xiii, 363). Becoming one with the infant as its 'warmth flowed through her', she 'yielded to it, sank into it, and slept' (II: xiii, 363). Too weak to live with the truth she has finally faced about her female selfhood, she succumbs to the 'annihilation' that Sherman identifies as her Gothic fear.[21] This moment calls to mind, too, Margaret Homans' discussion of literalisation in Gothic fiction: viewing this as an objectification of subjective states, Homans suggests, in particular, the danger of women returning figuratively to childhood, as Lily seems to as she holds Nettie's child. As Homans asserts: 'The threat that hides within all losses of identity, all self-duplications, all kinds of objectifications of the self' is that 'no longer to be oneself is to die'.[22]

At Lily's deathbed, the narrator has Selden appropriate a phrase from Lily's thoughts in his apartment, that 'she had saved herself whole from the seeming ruin of her life' (II: xii, 347). Selden, in turn, thinks that the 'moment of love' he had experienced with Lily 'had been saved whole out of the ruin of their lives' (II: xiv, 369). This eerie parallel is one of many they share, marking them as paired characters common in Gothic fiction. Like Lily, Selden comes from a family living beyond its means, run by a mother who relishes balancing good taste with limited funds. When Selden contrasts Lily to the working women around her, he wonders, 'Was it possible that she belonged to the same race? The dinginess, the crudity of this average section of womanhood made him feel how highly specialized she was' (I: i, 39). Likewise Selden stands out from the common crowd with his 'keenly-modelled dark features which, in a land of amorphous types,

---

20 Kahane, 'The Gothic Mirror,' pp. 336–7.
21 Holland and Sherman, 'Gothic Possibilities', p. 283.
22 Margaret Homans, 'Dreaming of Children: Literalization in *Jane Eyre and Wuthering Heights*', in Fleenor, ed., *The Female Gothic*, pp. 257–79: pp. 269, 278.

gave him the air of belonging to a more specialized race' (I: vi, 101). Both Lily and Selden feel repugnance for 'red and massive' Gus Trenor. First, Lily responds with disgust to Trenor's drink-induced 'dark flush on his face and the glistening dampness of his forehead' (I: x, 153), and then later Selden turns away sickened by the drink-induced 'dark flush on Trenor's face, the unpleasant moisture of his intensely white forehead' (I: xiv, 191). Wharton even has her narrator say that, like Lily, though in a different way, Selden is 'the victim of his environment' (I: xiv, 189).

The parallels between Lily and Selden extend to their connection with the same woman, Bertha Dorset, Selden's former lover who also serves as Lily's doppelgänger in the novel, the double living out Lily's rebellion.[23] Described as 'a disembodied spirit who took up a great deal of room', Bertha haunts Lily's life as the spectre of female sexuality who manages to manipulate the male-dominated system of exchange (I: ii, 58). Bertha is dangerous, sexually assertive and reckless about appearances, traits that Lily unsuccessfully flirts with. As Candace Waid puts it, when Lily buys Bertha's love letters from the charwoman Mrs Haffen, who mistakes her for being their author, it is 'as if she were accepting the role of Bertha's double rather than her rival'.[24]

Bertha's name, like Selden's, alludes to other Gothic-inspired texts. Bertha, especially when Carry Fisher describes her as 'behaving more than ever like a madwoman' (II: v, 277) suggests Bertha Rochester, who has been described as 'the libidinous, monstrous female' imprisoned in *Jane Eyre*'s Thornfield Hall and who serves as Jane's double.[25] Bertha is also the name of the beautiful, cruel heroine in the Gothic novella 'The Lifted Veil', written by George Eliot, one of Wharton's favorite authors. Selden shares the name of the escaped convict in *The Hound of the Baskervilles*, Sir Arthur Conan Doyle's immensely popular Gothic tale published in 1901 and reviewed in America in *The Bookman* in 1902.[26] Selden, 'the Notting Hill murderer' in the story, interests Sherlock Holmes because of 'the peculiar ferocity of the crime and the wanton brutality which had marked all the actions of the assassin'.[27] This seemingly unlikely allusion for the undemonstrative lawyer Lawrence Selden is supported, however, by Wharton's insistence on Selden's 'dark features', especially his 'dark skin' that suggests his racialised, dangerous 'otherness' (I: vi, 101; II: xii, 348). Although Selden assures Lily at the novel's beginning, 'Oh, I'm not dangerous', he ends up being quite dangerous to her well-being, by judging her, behaving intimately then distancing himself and interfering each time she is about to act to secure her future welfare (I: i, 40). Ultimately, if indirectly, Selden might be considered responsible for Lily's death.

23 Freud, 'The Uncanny', pp. 141–3.
24 Candace Waid, *Edith Wharton's Letters from the Underworld: Fictions of Women and Writing*, Chapel Hill, NC: University of North Carolina Press, 1991, p. 25.
25 Anne-Marie Ford, 'Gothic Legacies: Jane Eyre in Elizabeth Stoddard's New England', in Janet Beer and Bridget Bennett, ed., *Special Relationships: Anglo-American affinities and antagonisms 1854–1936*, New York: Manchester University Press, 2002, pp. 42–64: p. 45; Sandra M. Gilbert and Susan Gubar, *The Madwoman in the Attic: The Woman Writer and the Nineteenth-Century Imagination*, New Haven Conn.: Yale University Press, 1979, p. 360.
26 Martin Booth, *The Doctor and the Detective: A Biography of Sir Arthur Conan Doyle*, New York: St Martin's Press, 1997, p. 341.
27 Sir Arthur Conan Doyle, *The Hound of the Baskervilles*, 1902, reprinted New York: Puffin Books, 1994, p. 78.

The doubling and pairing Lily shares with Bertha and Selden, Lily experiences in her own psyche, as dramatised by another Gothic staple, mirrors. As Elizabeth MacAndrew writes, 'The devices of reflection, the mainstay of Gothic fiction from the beginning, tend to be its central feature. The heroes and heroines, the doubles, the house, portraits, statues, and mirrors continue to show images of the self'.[28] From the beginning of the novel, when Lily pauses in front of Selden's mantelpiece, 'studying herself in the mirror while she adjusted her veil', mirrors reflect Lily's inner self – her tenuous hold on her identity, her fears, her self-loathing, her maternally and culturally induced obsession with beauty (I: i, 47). When Lily arrives at the Trenors' home and sits before the mirror in her guestroom brushing her hair, 'her face looked hollow and pale, and she was frightened by two little lines near her mouth, faint flaws in the smooth curve of the cheek' (I: iii, 62). As she 'peered at herself between the candle-flames', her white face 'swam out waveringly from a background of shadows, the uncertain light blurring it like a haze; but the two lines about the mouth remained' (I: iii, 62). Lily's face is a ghostly blur except for the 'two lines', the inscription on her face of ageing and potential social demise.

After Gus Trenor's attempted rape, which Lily blames solely on herself, 'She seemed a stranger to herself, or rather there were two selves in her, the one she had always known and a new abhorrent being to which it found itself chained' (I: xii, 185). Lily attempts to explain her feelings to Gerty Farish with a mirror metaphor: 'Can you imagine looking into your glass some morning and seeing a disfigurement—some hideous change that has come to you while you slept? Well, I seem to myself like that—I can't bear myself in my own thoughts' (I: xiv, 202). In Ellen Moers' words, 'To give *visual* form to the fear of self, to hold anxiety up to the Gothic mirror of the imagination', as Lily does in 'seeing a disfigurement' in herself, defines the female Gothic.[29]

Lily tries to repress the abhorrent image of disfigurement, but 'the brightly-lit mirror above the mantelpiece' in her room shows the consequences of this struggle: 'The lines in her face came out terribly—she looked old' (I: xv, 217). Trying not to see 'horrors' in her dreams, Lily tries not to sleep; yet she is terrified when Gerty points out how tired she looks. Moving quickly to 'the little mirror above the writing-table', she asks, 'Do I look ill? Does my face show it?' (II: viii, 304). Before Lily leaves Gerty's apartment, she goes to the mirror again and, 'adjusting her hair with a light hand, drawing down her veil, and giving a dexterous touch to her furs', acts as if her life were proceeding as usual (II: viii, 306). The next mirrors in Lily's story, however, are 'the fragmentary and distorted image of the world she had lived in reflected in the mirror of the working-girls' minds' in Mme Regina's hat shop and then 'the blank surface of the toilet-mirror' near her deathbed (II: x, 325; II: xiv, 366).

Wharton's doubling of Lily and Bertha, pairing of Lily and Selden and doubling within Lily herself are in turn reflected by the novel's narrative structure. Dani Cavallaro, in *The Gothic Vision*, discusses the 'compound textuality' common to Gothic fiction, 'flouting the ethos of authorial omniscience'.[30] The many stories

28 Elizabeth MacAndrew, *The Gothic Tradition in Fiction*, New York: Columbia University Press, 1979, p. 155.
29 Moers, *Literary Women*, p. 163.
30 Dani Cavallaro, *The Gothic Vision: Three Centuries of Horror, Terror and Fear*, New York: Continuum, 2002, p. 113.

about Lily in *The House of Mirth* create an 'indeterminacy' that echoes her divided self.[31]

The novel begins with Selden's story about Lily Bart, his mistaken assumptions that her 'air of irresolution' is instead 'the mask of a very definite purpose' and that 'her simplest acts seemed the result of far-reaching intentions' (I: i, 37). As Linda Wagner-Martin explains, 'Rather than omniscient, and supposedly impartial, narration, here Wharton gives the reader the opinions of a man who is never objective about Lily;[32] a view reinforced in Elsa Nettels' theory that Wharton uses male narrators to model 'a male-dominated society which seeks to suppress or deny the truth' of women.[33]

Lily also attempts to tell her own story. After Gus's attempted rape, she asks Gerty if she should tell Selden her story of self-loathing so that he can become her restorative mirror:

> 'If I said: "I am bad through and through—I want admiration, I want excitement, I want money—" yes, *money*! That's my shame, Gerty—and it's known, it's said of me—it's what men think of me—If I said it all to him—told him the whole story—[. . .] if I told him everything would he loathe me? Or would he pity me, and understand me, and save me from loathing myself?'
>
> (I: xiv, 204)

Later, however, when Gerty asks Lily to tell her friends 'the whole truth' about being refused return to Bertha's yacht, Lily sardonically and incisively replies that she really *has* no story of her own:

> What is the truth? Where a woman is concerned, it's the story that's easiest to believe. In this case it's a great deal easier to believe Bertha Dorset's story than mine, because she has a big house and an opera box, and it's convenient to be on good terms with her.
>
> (II: iv, 264)

Bertha's stories have indeed dominated Lily's life, even though the reader never hears them. There is also, as Amy Kaplan points out, the letters plot authored by Rosedale, the only person in the novel 'who knows as much about Lily as do the narrator and the reader'.[34]

The House of Mirth ends with the self-serving story Selden tells himself, that 'at least he *had* loved her—had been willing to stake his future on his faith in her', despite once again expecting the worst of Lily when he sees the envelope on which she has written Gus Trenor's name (II: xiv, 369). Clearly, neither his perspective on

31 George E. Haggerty, *Gothic Fiction/Gothic Form*, University Park, Pa.: Pennsylvania State University Press, 1989, p. 8.

32 Linda Wagner-Martin, *The House of Mirth: A Novel of Admonition*, Boston, Mass.: Twayne Publishers, 1990, p. 16.

33 Elsa Nettels, 'Gender and First-Person Narration', in Albert Bendixen and Annette Zilversmit, eds, *Edith Wharton: New Critical Essays*, New York: Garland, 1992, pp. 245–60: p. 258.

34 Amy Kaplan, 'Crowded Spaces', in Carol J. Singley, ed., *Edith Wharton's The House of Mirth: A Casebook*, New York: Oxford University Press, 2003, pp. 85–105, 103.

Lily nor anyone else's in the novel explains her definitively. One hundred years of literary criticism about *The House of Mirth* also illustrate how 'resistant to interpretation' Lily is.[35] Gothic elements in the novel – Lily doubled with Bertha and paired with Selden, her terrifying confrontations with sexuality – serve Wharton well in conveying Lily's indeterminable female selfhood.

During her last minutes alive, Lily tells herself that 'there was something she must tell Selden, some word she had found that should make life clear between them' (II: xiii, 363). As she tries to repeat the word, it 'lingered vague and luminous on the far edge of thought' (II: xiii, 363). Selden, paired narratively with Lily to the end, also has 'found the word he meant to say to her' (II: xiv, 364). The novel's last line tells us that as Selden kneels by Lily's bed, 'in the silence there passed between them the word which made all clear' (II: xiv, 369). This is what Alan Lloyd-Smith, in *American Gothic Fiction*, calls a moment of 'almost-meaning'.[36] Like Lily herself, this word remains 'stubbornly resistant to interpretation, however persuasive,' as Lloyd-Smith writes about the kind of Gothic object this word has become, lingering ghostly, as it does, 'vague and luminous' on the edge of thought (II: xiii, 363). Lloyd-Smith notes that 'the figure of an enigmatic "something else," replete with meanings but not decipherable', haunts American Gothic writing.[37] Given Wharton's sense of the writing process itself as uncanny, how fitting that the word that lives beyond Lily should remain, like Lily herself, 'luminous' and indefinable.

---

35 Lloyd-Smith, *American Gothic Fiction*, p. 74
36 Lloyd-Smith, *American Gothic Fiction*, p. 123.
37 Lloyd-Smith, *American Gothic Fiction*, p. 72.

Pamela Knights, ' "Hypertexts" and the City: *The House of Mirth* at the Millennium'

In later life, Wharton herself was the first to suggest that her writing had dated; and, although she now enjoys unprecedented critical regard, her rank as a classic might imply that she has little to say about complex lives today. In this essay, Pamela Knights argues that Wharton's influence is undiminished. Taking up the discourses of money, the city and the 'Woman Question' from 'Text and contexts' (see, especially, **pp. 26–52**), she demonstrates that in her treatment of modernity, Wharton is a significant model for writers concerned with the contemporary scene; and that their fictions return us, to look again, with fresh emphases, at Wharton's text.

Knights' previous work includes the chapter on *The Age of Innocence* in *The Cambridge Companion to Edith Wharton*, editions of *Ethan Frome* and *The House of Mirth*, and, for Oxford World's Classics, of Kate Chopin's *The Awakening and Other Stories*. In her discussions of these and other writings of the period, she takes a broadly cultural materialist approach, in order to tease out the complex and often oblique dialogue of these narratives with their own societies. In this new essay, she turns to the cultural afterlife of *The House of Mirth*. Her study is stimulated by new approaches which argue that imaginative reworkings might offer insights as valuable as those presented in more conventional discursive critical accounts. As in the other new critical readings here, the essay encourages readers to think across boundaries: to consider what Wharton has to say to contemporary writers and to suggest how modern popular fiction is placing *The House of Mirth*, once again, at the centre of topical debate.

From Pamela Knights, ' "Hypertexts" and the City: *The House of Mirth* at the Millennium'

> 'Right. What's changed for women in a hundred years, since the time when Edith Wharton set her novels?'
>
> (Tama Janowitz, interview)[1]

> Charlie didn't understand that my life in New York would be ruined unless I found another fiancé. All anyone cared about in New York was who was married to whom, or was going to be. Didn't he know it was like the nineteenth century there? Didn't he know what had happened to poor Lily Bart?
>
> (Plum Sykes, *Bergdorf Blondes*)[2]

Introduction

Commenting on *The House of Mirth* in 1936, Wharton speculated with amusement as to whether 'the novelists of the present day, so put to it to find new horrors in the domestic circle, do not envy *me*—', and pictured their nostalgia for the days when 'the mere appearance of lapsing from conventional rules of conduct' gave material enough for a scandal.[3] At the turn into the twenty-first century, Wharton's novel (or, from 2000, Terence Davies' screen adaptation) has become a frequent reference point for writers exploring the contemporary American scene.

The House of Mirth enters later texts as a background presence (as in the social fiction of F. Scott Fitzgerald or Sinclair Lewis).[4] It also features as an important source of signification, living on, transformed and reshaped, in new and usually seemingly independent, literary narratives. The phenomenon of texts interpenetrating, acting as sources, or alluding to other texts, is now referred to, generally, as 'intertextuality', a term interpreted and theorised in widely different ways. At the centre of the idea of intertextual allusions, however, is the point that no text can be read in isolation, that all, to some degree, engage us in searching for meaning between texts, 'moving out from the independent text into a network of textual relations'.[5] In cases where one text, in particular, seems to exert a considerable shaping force on a later text, the narratological critic, Gérard Genette, provides a useful set of terms. Genette designates the earlier text (A) the 'hypotext', and the later text (B), the 'hypertext': B derives or draws on A in ways 'more or less officially stated'.[6] (The more explicit version of such a relationship would be what

1 Laura L. Buchwald, interview with Tama Janowitz, 'My Lunch with Tama', available online at <www.randomhouse.com/boldtype/0899/janowitz/interview.html> (accessed 15 March 2005).
2 Plum Sykes, *Bergdorf Blondes*, London: Penguin, 2004, p. 140.
3 Wharton, Introduction to *The House of Mirth*, p. xi (see Critical history, **p. 59**).
4 See, for example, F. Scott Fitzgerald, *The Beautiful and Damned*, 1922, and *The Great Gatsby*, 1925; Sinclair Lewis, *Main Street*, 1920.
5 Graham Allen, *Intertextuality*, London and New York: Routledge, 2000, p. 1.
6 Gérard Genette, *Palimpsests: Literature in the Second Degree*, trans. Channa Newman, Claude Doubinsky, Lincoln, Nebr.: University of Nebraska Press, 1997, pp. 5, 9.

is more popularly called a 'spin-off', a catch-all term which glosses over shades of difference in individual sets of textual transformations.) Every instance of a hyper-textual transformation prompts inquiry about how far the secondary work still needs its hypotext to give it meaning. Do we need to have read A in order to read B; or, more radically, can reading B enrich our understanding of the earlier text A, the hypotext? Such questions are intensified when the reworking is in a different genre or medium, or when it occupies a separate cultural sphere. In the case of *The House of Mirth*, for example, the novel has generated dance-drama and screen adaptation (see Performance/adaptation, **pp. 148–54**); and, as in the 'gossip lit' below, fictions which seem to sit on the opposite side of a 'high'/'popular' aesthetic divide.

As the critical history of *The House of Mirth* makes clear (see Critical history **pp. 59–80**), the discussions of literary scholars have powerfully reshaped the text for each generation of readers. However, tracing *The House of Mirth*'s persistent cultural afterlife suggests that it might be artificial to separate the 'creative' and the 'critical'. For those encountering any imaginative reworkings with Wharton's novel fresh in mind, all function, to some degree, as a critical reinterpretation. Many responses, however labelled formally, seem generated along a continuum of reading, as an extension of the discussions, hypotheses and questions staged within the text itself. Other characters, and even the novel's narrator, are always asking questions about Lily: 'But what *is* your story, Lily? I don't believe any one knows it yet' (II: iv, 264); 'And it's the difficulty of deciding that makes her such an interesting study' (II: i, 227). Such questions come from many directions – whether aroused by Gerty's sympathy, Carry's probing of motive, Selden's intrigued frustration, or the clubmen's destructive innuendo. Receiving few answers in the text itself, the conjectures reverberate in the debates which followed publication as reviewers argued (see Critical history, **pp. 60–3**). We hear them, for example, in the Massachusetts' short-story writer, Olivia Howard Dunbar's anxieties about 'the girl's unlovely history'; her troubled suspicions as to what 'Mrs. Wharton has suppressed'; and her conviction that the 'real' Lily is inaccessible: 'The reader is not allowed to know her with real intimacy, to get behind the scenes. One thinks of her, after all, as gloved, veiled, smiling, erectly on her guard.' And they resonate again in Alice May Boutell's fierce disagreement: 'If I ever felt on terms of "real intimacy" with anyone in a book it is with Lily Bart.'[7]

Such passionate, first-person engagements foreshadow some of the representations in later reworkings. They also clearly bring out what is often understated in seemingly more objective critical discourses: the way readers respond to writers' invitations to fill in what Wolfgang Iser described as the 'gaps' and 'blanks' in the text. Iser is one of a generation of theorists who began to redirect attention from the literary text as a self-contained object, to the activities of readers. For Iser and other reader-oriented critics, the text does not hold meanings in itself, but needs a reader, in effect, to bring it to life in the very act of meaning.[8] (A broad analogy

---

7   Reviews by Massachussetts short-story writer, Olivia Howard Dunbar, *Critic*, 47, December 1905, pp. 509–10; and by Alice May Boutell, *Critic*, 48, January 1906, pp. 87–8; both reprinted in James W. Tuttleton, Kristin O. Lauer and Margaret P. Murray, eds, *Edith Wharton: The Contemporary Reviews*, Cambridge: Cambridge University Press, 1992, pp. 121–2, 129.
8   For an introduction to reader-oriented theories, see Elizabeth Freund, *The Return of the Reader: Reader-Response Criticism*, London: Methuen, 1987; and Andrew Bennett, *Readers and Reading*, London: Longman, 1995.

would be a musical score, where the music is produced in performance and is different with each interpretation.) Projecting their own stories into the spaces, readers thus become, in Iser's view, co-creators of the work of art. They 'concretise' the possibilities of the narrative, as active agents who draw meanings out of the text and feed their responses back to 'complete' it.[9] Reframing the text through critical discussion can suggest new narratives – a Marxist or Gothic novel (see **pp. 72–80**), or a gay Lily (see Critical readings, **pp. 96–105**). However, whereas academic criticism must acknowledge other viewpoints, and justify its argument, creative responses are at liberty to select even a single shade of meaning and use it to colour an entire new work of art. Further, today, with the rise of creative writing as a legitimate area in university-degree studies, creative inflections are entering critical discourse: alongside conventional discussions, literature students may also gain insights by, for example, trying out considering Wharton's text from an alternative viewpoint, or narrative mode.[10]

For those who value the original text, the kind of reworkings described below might seem to close down its subtle indeterminacies. *The House of Mirth*, after all, sustains its tension between the sharply delineated surfaces and the sense of blanks and shadows – Lily's veil and the story behind it. Wharton makes it impossible for readers to share Selden's faith that Lily's 'real self' can be distinguished from her 'semblance' (II: xiv, 365). If there exists any 'word which made all clear' (II: xiv, 365), readers never know it. Wharton herself loathed the novel's first reworking, in illustration (see Critical readings, **p. 85**); and she excised every plate from her copy.[11] Years later, she reflected on the 'curious, and sometimes [. . .] painful, revelation' experienced by novelists, seeing 'through the medium of reviews or dramatizations of their work [. . .] their books as they have taken shape in other minds'.[12] But, at best, new works may refresh response to the 'original': bringing, as Wharton remarked of the staging of *Ethan Frome*, 'a new lease of life', an inexpressibly moving 'discovery'.[13]

Reworking Wharton

An important precursor for a range of contemporary fictions, *The House of Mirth* has been entering a wide variety of genres, from murder mystery to 'chick lit'. In some texts, Wharton's work acts as a touchstone. In Lev Raphael's *The Edith Wharton Murders* (1997), the second of his satirical 'Nick Hoffman' campus mysteries, it is part of a set of Wharton-centred allusions, which extend

9 Wolfgang Iser, *The Act of Reading: A Theory of Aesthetic Response*, 1976; reprinted Baltimore, Md. and London: Johns Hopkins University Press, 1978.

10 For an account of these practices, see Rob Pope, *Textual Intervention: Critical and Creative Strategies for Literary Studies*, London: Routledge, 1995; and Ben Knights and Chris Thurgar-Dawson, *Active Reading: Transformative Writing in Literary Studies*, London: Continuum, 2006.

11 *Edith Wharton's Library: A Catalogue*, compiled George Ramsden; Introduction, Hermione Lee, Settington: Stone Trough Books, 1999, p. 137.

12 Edith Wharton, 'Foreword to *Ethan Frome: A Dramatization of Edith Wharton's Novel*', in Wegener, ed., *The Uncollected Critical Writings*, p. 263.

13 Wegener, *The Uncollected Critical Writings*, p. 263.

throughout the series to date.[14] Here, Raphael, who is himself a Wharton scholar and who deploys a Wharton expert as his narrator, draws readers into a tangle of references, parading and withdrawing possible connections. Is the Penguin edition of the novel, discovered beside the corpse, a clue or a distraction? ('Chloe—chloral. It sort of sounds the same. Maybe it's some kind of pun'.)[15] Is *The House of Mirth* a hypotext, which, for those who know it, will unlock the plot, or is it merely part of a postmodern collage of literary reference, where meanings are endlessly deferred? – 'Can you explain how this book might be significant?'[16] as Detective Valley asks.

In Raphael's revisionary game with the detective story, he foregrounds generic conventions. Nick is a bibliographer who prides himself on 'having read more about Wharton than anyone in the galaxy'.[17] His own desire, as narrator, amateur investigator and scholar, is to stabilise truth, to stick to facts; and he despises the competing schools of Wharton critics (presented as eccentrics and egotists all), who try to appropriate her texts to advance their own professional ambitions. Yet, in trying to sum up and explain the novel to a non-scholarly listener, Nick finds himself engaged in the difficult act of interpretation:

> I put my hand down, sat up straighter, crossed my legs, breathed in deeply a few times. 'Okay. *The House of Mirth*, it's set in turn-of-the-century New York, and it's about a society woman who's really beautiful, but even though she doesn't have any money of her own and she's growing older and needs to be married to be financially secure, she keeps screwing up her chances to nab eligible men.' I took a breath.[18]

Any retelling of a text, whether in a specialist academic article, a student guide or a blurb on a book cover (which Nick's synopsis somewhat resembles), foregrounds some aspects and occludes others, creating, for different audiences, a different fiction. Here, Nick tries to simplify and update the novel for a man he clearly views as an unsophisticated, inexperienced reader; but Valley's response surprises him. He anticipates the plot, repositioning the text as a sentimental 'Silhouette' romance ('like the kind of book my wife reads') and, thus, suggests the predictability of all fictions: 'She probably loves somebody who's poor like she is, huh?'[19] But, as Nick undercuts Valley's own next piece of gap-filling, so his own narrative teases reader expectations:

> 'This one doesn't have a happy ending.'
> 'No?'
> 'Not at all. Lily Bart—that's the woman—keeps moving down the social ladder, falling, really, until—'
> 'Until she's a hooker?'

14 Beginning with *Let's Get Criminal* (1996), Raphael has written six books in the series, and a seventh, *Hot Rocks*, is announced for publication in 2007.
15 Lev Raphael, *The Edith Wharton Murders*, New York: St. Martin's Press, 1997, p. 21.
16 Raphael, *The Edith Wharton Murders*, p. 120.
17 Raphael, *The Edith Wharton Murders*, p. 120.
18 Raphael, *The Edith Wharton Murders*, p. 120.
19 Raphael, *The Edith Wharton Murders*, p. 120.

'Jesus, no! This was published in 1905. She commits suicide.'
Valley frowned. 'Suicide? Chloe DeVore didn't commit suicide.'
'Right.'
'How's she do it in the book?'[20]

Raphael leaves his own readers space to accept both men's versions: Lily's story as Valley (or his wife) would understand it is perhaps no cruder than Nick's arrogantly assured sense of ownership. Though brief, the episode is part of the series' broader inquiry, as Raphael goes beyond campus intrigue to explore gay, Jewish and gender identities and the relative modes of creative, critical and scholarly knowledge. In this flux of experience, Nick clings to his bibliographical records, to preserve Wharton's work as a touchstone of value, a place of certainty, untarnished by the vagaries of its many interpreters.

The House of Mirth serves a similar function for a very different narrator in Jennifer Donnelly's *A Gathering Light* (2003), published for a young-adult audience. This feminist story moves (unbeknownst to its narrator) into the gendered gaps of Theodore Dreiser's real-life murder story, *An American Tragedy* (1925). (Where Dreiser follows the viewpoint of the male murderer, Donnelly seeks to open up the history of his pregnant female victim.) Wharton, too, is a pervasive presence, evoked in names from her own tragedies of remote, rural life ('Mattie', from *Ethan Frome*, and 'Royal[l]', from *Summer*), which many readers place with *The House of Mirth* as the bleakest of her stories. The heroine of *A Gathering Light*, growing up at the turn of the century, is trapped by many of the cultural forces Wharton so clearly identifies; but she gains an agency (through a dawning feminist consciousness) that, to many readers' sadness, remains unavailable to Wharton's characters. Whereas Lily and the rest fail to escape, Donnelly's Mattie recounts her journey out of domestic oppression, and intellectual darkness, towards college and a career as a writer. Wharton is a landmark on her journey. In the remote North Woods in 1906, a library book ('Brand-new. Just come in. By a Mrs. Wharton. *House of Mirth* it's called')[21] excites and inspires Mattie. But, before she has even opened it, the librarian, in another homely summary, tells us something of Mattie's own dilemma: 'What's it about?' 'Can't hardly say. Some flighty city girl who can't decide if she wants to fish or cut bait. Don't know why it's called *House of Mirth*. It ain't funny in the least.'[22]

But it is the reaction of Royal, Mattie's would-be lover, which warns of what might destroy her: ' "Words and stories," he said [. . .]. "I don't know what you see in them. Waste of time, if you ask me." '[23] The episode's final image, in the wake of his reckless driving, leaves Mattie torn, 'between excitement and terror', wanting to defend her reading but spellbound by Royal, the horseman: 'Heedless. Fearless. Perfect and beautiful'; Wharton's novel, injured in the chase, 'a smudge on the cover [. . .] and the spine [. . .] dented' is forgotten. '*Can a girl be unmanned?* I wondered. *By a boy? Can she be unbrained?*'[24]

20 Raphael, *The Edith Wharton Murders*, p. 120.
21 Jennifer Donnelly, *A Gathering Light*, 2003; London: Bloomsbury, 2004, p. 68.
22 Donnelly, *A Gathering Light*, p. 68.
23 Donnelly, *A Gathering Light*, p. 76.
24 Donnelly, *A Gathering Light*, p. 78.

In *A Gathering Light*, 'Words and stories' (Lily Bart's among them) are empowering, illuminating Mattie's options. In a move which allows readers to hope that one young twentieth-century woman's journey will have a different ending, Donnelly leaves her heroine on the point of departure: 'To New York City. To my future. My life.'[25] In other recent women's writings, largely set in the new New York City, *The House of Mirth* serves to open up bleaker visions of contemporary women's fortunes. In a tonal range that varies from dark satire to light 'gossip lit', two novels stand out as sustained and serious reworkings: Tama Janowitz's *A Certain Age* (1999) and Candace Bushnell's *Trading Up* (2003).[26] Each writer's earlier publications included short-story cycles for which they became well known: Janowitz's *Slaves of New York* (1986) and Bushnell's *Sex and the City* (1996; assembled from her *New York Observer* columns) and a novella cycle, *Four Blondes* (2000). This versatile form, according to James Nagel 'one of the most important' in twentieth-century American literature,[27] seems particularly fitted to representing the shifting connections of the contemporary city. With gaps between stories, continually revised links and repetitions, partial disclosures, half-revealed overlaps, these narratives present urban subjectivity in fragments. Readers, inside and outside the text, work for meaning, a sense of completion, which may or may not be there: 'Then the gradual bafflement on the realization that not only wasn't there going to be any connection, there wasn't even going to be a punch-line.'[28]

In revising an early twentieth-century author, Janowitz and Bushnell take this process further. Each recognises the affinity of Wharton's classic realist work with the provisional forms of the postmodern era. Moving into Wharton's own textual spaces, their reworkings involve readers in making new connections across the gap of a century. Wharton's novel becomes part of an extended narrative cycle, gaining as well as generating fresh meanings, when reread through the later texts. Although Janowitz has asserted that she has little interest in 'post-modern fiction', or in language if 'at the expense of a story and characters',[29] she also echoes the post-structuralist sense of intertextuality, that no text can ever be entirely 'consumed' – be brought to an entire close.[30] In taking Wharton's novel as her starting point, she remarks: 'Sometimes I think that *The House of Mirth*, which ends with Lily Bart's suicide, ends too soon. It was a bit . . . easy.' Allowing 'that was common then', Janowitz gestures at her own (and Wharton's) hesitancy: 'Now something will end not with a finality. At least with *The House of Mirth*, at the end you never quite know whether it was an accident or whether she was murdered [*sic*].'[31]

25 Donelly, *A Gathering Light*, p. 380.
26 Tama Janowitz, *A Certain Age*, 1999; London: Bloomsbury, 2000; Candace Bushnell, *Trading Up*, London: Little, Brown, 2003.
27 James Nagel, 'The American Short Story Cycle', in Blanche Gelfant, ed., *The Columbia Companion to the Twentieth-Century American Short Story*, New York: Columbia University Press, 2000, p. 9. I thank Rachel Lister for helpful discussions of this form; Lister explores its gendered dimensions in 'Open Destinies: Modern American Women and the Short-Story Cycle', Ph.D. thesis: Durham University, 2005.
28 Tama Janowitz, *Slaves of New York*, 1986; London: Bloomsbury, 2004, p. 77.
29 Buchwald, 'Lunch with Tama'.
30 Allen, *Intertextuality*, p. 205.
31 Buchwald, 'Lunch with Tama'.

Bushnell, too, resists closed endings. She revised the ending of *Sex and the City* after publication. In the first edition, she acceded to a tentatively conventional closure, with her final sentence affirming the continuing relationship of her central couple ('Carrie and Mr. Big are still together').[32] Subsequently, she added two further 'stories' – inserting before the final chapter, vignettes of the disintegrating relationship and finishing her book with the ex-lovers apart, separated in individual closing sentences ('Mr. Big is happily married. Carrie is happily single').[33] She supplements *Four Blondes* with characters' further stories. It is Janey Wilcox from 'Nice N'Easy', the first novella, who moves to the centre of *Trading Up*. Resenting comparison with Janowitz, Bushnell frequently emphasises instead her affinities with Wharton: 'Don't these people read the classics? If anything, Janey [. . .] is like Lily Bart from *The House of Mirth*.'[34] In *Sex and the City*, too, she sets the scene with a backward glance: 'Welcome to the Age of Un-innocence. The glittering lights of Manhattan that served as backdrops for Edith Wharton's bodice-heaving trysts are still glowing—but the stage is empty.'[35]

Bushnell describes her attempts 'to get rid of Janey' – for her to die in a plane crash or go crazy. In an anecdote echoing early readers' hopes for Lily, she attributes her survival to her publisher, who 'felt sorry for her and said, "No, we can't do that to Janey" '; and finally, turns to the character herself: 'She is the kind of woman where you've just had it with her drama, then, at the last minute, somebody comes along and buys her story and saves her. So, in a way, Selden— who is her husband—says to her, "You know, you're like a virus." She is kind of like a virus.'[36]

In this extraordinary image of infection and replication, stories and affinities fuse and multiply; at the end of the interview, Selden is promised his own novel. Meanwhile, in a smaller role, he reappears in a new novel, saddened by his experience: another character 'recalled hearing vague rumors about some crazy woman Selden Rose had been married to, but Selden never talked about her'.[37]

In these palimpsests and revisions, where does the story happen? In New York in 1905, or at the millennium? Most reviewers noticed *A Certain Age* as an update of 'the brittle social jockeying in *The House of Mirth*';[38] and many, though by no means all, remarked its presence in *Trading Up*. Virginia Heffernan, for example, celebrated Bushnell's 'inspired iconoclasm', challenging those who dismissed the novel as 'cake for social aspirants': 'She refuses to preserve him [Selden] as the chaste man of honor that Wharton invented. Instead, she of matter-of-factly fixes up Selden and Janey in the second chapter [. . .] In spite of

32 Bushnell, *Sex and the City*, 1996; reprinted London: Abacus, 2003, p. 228.
33 Bushnell, *Sex and the City*, revised edition, 2004; reprinted London: Abacus, 2005, p. 245.
34 Alex Richmond, 'Candace Bushnell', 21–8 September 2000, available online at <http://citypaper .net/articles/092100/ae.books.shtml> (accessed 4 April, 2004).
35 Candace Bushnell, *Sex and the City*, 1996; London: Abacus, 2003, p. 2.
36 C. McDonald, 'The Candace Bushnell Interview: *Trading Up*', 2004, available online at <www.modestyarbor.com/candace_bushnell1.html> (accessed 4 April 2005).
37 Candace Bushnell, *Lipstick Jungle*, 2005, London: Abacus, 2006 (published as this guide was in process), pp. 32, 189.
38 Kristin Keith, 'Money, Marriage, and Mirth', 22–9 July 1999, available online at <http:// citypaper.net/browse/072299.shtml> (accessed 15 March 2005). For a more hostile critique ('Edith Wharton it is not'), see Rob Stout, 'Bad Manners', CityBeat, 5.46, 7–13 October, 1999, available online at <www.citybeat.com/1999–10–07/books.shtml> (accessed 15 March 2005).

early promise, Selden goes on to be more of a killjoy than a saint.'[39] Although many might argue with this interpretation (is Wharton's Selden a 'saint'?), for Heffernan, *The House of Mirth* is clearly integral to her reading.

It is possible to take both Bushnell's and Janowitz's texts as self-sufficient; each, however, also acts as commentary on Wharton's novel. In teasing out strands of her narrative, they gloss their own contemporary scene. Readers of *The House of Mirth* will instantly recognise the dynamics of these texts and be struck by the way Wharton anticipates them. These topical fictions remind us of the acuteness of Wharton's analysis. Here, again, in their sexual and social economies, are themes which persist across the century: the validation of women through wealthy marriages; failures of education and useful work; female competitiveness (and maternal indifference) in the patriarchal family structures; dubious deals; the weaponry of the weak, where women must be 'cunning supplicants'.[40] Wharton, like these modern writers, was aware that, in a culture of commercial exchange, a woman's 'façade was her property'.[41] She, too, surrounds the heroine with male admirers and female rivals who measure her beauty against the passage of time – for example, as Selden registers in Lily, 'that moment of pause and arrest when the warm fluidity of youth is chilled into its final shape (II: i, 230). In Wharton's text, as in those of her successors, we too become witnesses: we view the heroines' distress in a sequence of scenes in front of mirrors, and, although methods differ, their efforts of self-maintenance: Miss Bart's hair is perhaps 'ever so slightly brightened by art' (I: i, 39), heroines at the millennium deploy surgical remodelling. Where the body is thus objectified, feelings become dissociated from consciousness. Lily obscures from herself the thought of her suitors' sexual demands: 'Even [. . .] letting Trenor [. . .] lean a little nearer and rest his hand reassuringly on hers, cost her only a momentary shiver of reluctance' (I: vii, 121). Janowitz and Bushnell take their cue from Wharton, making explicit in each text the central character's emotional dysfunction, her sexual coldness. Although Lily's successors go further, they share her detachment: 'It wasn't until she was in the front lobby of the building, staring out at the rain, that she realized the gravity of what had occurred, that Claudia was dead, that her tears were connected to an emotion';[42] 'Everyone else seemed to have some essential piece except her, and that piece was the part that connected actions to an emotional core.'[43] In all these texts, even in the anonymous city, the private becomes public; women are surveyed and punished in the screaming headlines: the centre of 'Town Talk' (I: xiv, 195), the 'blond home-wrecker',[44] 'MODEL PROSTITUTE'.[45]

With *A Certain Age*, Janowitz attempts the closer transposition. Transmuting Lily into Florence – another thirty-year-old fading bloom, her narrative refers closely back to its source: 'Now a hat designer—with her own shop on Madison Avenue—was a rich girl [. . .]. There were no jobs for poor women as milliners

39 Virginia Heffernan, 'Cosmopolitan Girl', *New York Times*, 13 July 2003, available online at <www.nytimes.com> (accessed 4 April 2005).
40 Janowitz, *A Certain Age*, p. 91.
41 Janowitz, *A Certain Age*, p. 120.
42 Janowitz, *A Certain Age*, p. 254.
43 Bushnell, *Trading Up*, p. 135.
44 Janowitz, *A Certain Age*, p. 296.
45 Bushnell, *Trading Up*, p. 411.

now.'[46] The city becomes a chronotope, a time/space where both textual worlds can meet. In this darkest of reworkings, one of the reading-pleasures may be identifying such equivalences – which elements the text condenses, which it sentimentally 'improves'. In spite of her earlier 'Generation X' tag, as one of a group without hope, trust or illusions,[47] Janowitz cannot resist some of life's old-fashioned little ironies. Darryl Lever (an unmaterialistic 'Selden' figure) harbours few illusions about Florence, but is unequivocally in love. Finally, too late for Florence, who rejects his proposal, the plot unveils him as the biggest catch of all: the son of 'Old Money', heir to a family mansion, dating from the years of Wharton's novel.

More often, Janowitz intensifies detail: cocaine, not tea, is the drug of choice; sex is instant; the text makes explicit the dark secrets of the rich ('New Money' in modern Manhattan comes from drug-running, using children). As Wharton predicted, the modern novelist has to ratchet up the indiscretions, and the pitch of the denunciations: 'You come to my house for a weekend, murder my daughter, seduce my husband, completely destroy the place [. . .], and for what reason? [. . .] Because you've slept your way through New York and didn't make it?'[48]

Notably, Janowitz concentrates on the 'dingy', the 'rubbish heap' (II. xii, 348) of *The House of Mirth*. Piling up the detritus of the city, her text, like Wharton's, sweeps its individual's story into larger *fin-de-siècle* narratives. One strand, again, is historical, giving a view of aristocratic decadence, in the hints of collapsed empires, with affinities with Wharton's extravagant Brys, or Henry George's 'Princes of Privilege' (see Text and contexts, p. 36) – the decor of a bar, 'like a miniature Roman bath';[49] the Birdman's crumbling mansion, its Venetian chandelier riddled with pigeon-droppings, its Aubusson carpet 'rimmed with furry mold'.[50] In such a society, nature, a traditional source of restoration, is, as Wharton presents it, distant, owned and controlled – viewed from the 'tutored' landscape of Bellomont (I: iv, 84) or the luxury 'camp' in the Adirondacks, from which Lily returns rejuvenated (I: x, 149). In Janowitz's narrative, too, the older, pastoral America of Florence's grandparents in Maine exists merely in memory;[51] 'the old New York of culture' becomes 'a movie set designed to soothe'.[52]

Janowitz presents a view of the world of late capitalism, consonant with Wharton's observations of its early stages in the post-Civil War Gilded Age (see Text and contexts, pp. 33–41). Here, too, money denatures; the rich preserve perfect surfaces. Florence wants to be a character in a poem: a golden doll 'glazed with perfection / her eyelids on gold hinges / swinging open and shut / at intervals marked by the sun'.[53] The lines echo those Wharton originally quoted beneath her working title for *The House of Mirth*, 'The Year of the Rose': 'A brittle glory

46 Janowitz, *A Certain Age*, p. 151.
47 Expressed most famously in Douglas Coupland's novel, *Generation X: Tales for an Accelerated Culture*, 1991.
48 Janowitz, *A Certain Age*, p. 254.
49 Janowitz, *A Certain Age*, p. 232.
50 Janowitz, *A Certain Age*, p. 314.
51 Janowitz, *A Certain Age*, p. 76.
52 Janowitz, *A Certain Age*, p. 184.
53 Janowitz, *A Certain Age*, p. 36.

shineth in this face—/ As brittle as the glory is the face.'[54] Taken from Shakespeare's *Richard II* (IV.i), they are followed there by the King's dramatic shattering of the mirror into which he gazes at the moment of his deposition: 'For there it is, crack'd in a hundred shivers.' Janowitz, like Wharton, is interested in what ruins beautiful images, the signs of flaws in the mirror. Her narrative, too, is obsessed with graininess, grit, cracks – abrading the smoothness. As Lily in decline is agitated by the dirt, noise and odours of the street, so here repeated motifs configure New York in terms of assault, physical and olfactory – violent sex, coke snortings, synthetic, invasive, glutinous smells. Lily tries to cut herself off from what the novel calls, in sum, the 'promiscuities' (II: xi, 341) of the dingy: through physical distance, emotional guards, narcotics. One of Florence's impulses is towards complete artifice, to defensive numbness. Another is to rediscover sensation: touch, pain, sharpness (the edges of a hard muffin) are the only way she feels that she is 'proving she was alive'.[55]

Taking up another narrative strand from Wharton, one of degeneration, Janowitz too infuses social commentary with the more scientific notes of naturalism. Within such passages, she plays on one of Wharton's key motifs: the image of Lily as a 'water-plant in the flux of the tides' (I: v, 89); 'an organism as helpless out of its narrow range as the sea-anemone torn from the rock' (II: xi, 341). In Janowitz's variations, from the dead fish in the first chapter to Florence's final drift towards the river, smells, again, transform the city into primeval pond. What is left of natural – even instinctual – behaviour resurfaces in images of unthinking creatures, in Florence's moments of humiliation and defeat. Caught by sexual impulse, Florence splits in two, her 'top half' protesting, her torso meeting the man's like 'organisms on the seafloor—blind, brainless—starfish or squid or sea cucumbers'.[56] Binging on ice cream, 'She ate blindly, unable to stop herself, no different from a butterfly repetitively plunging its proboscis, or a leopard tearing at a carcass.'[57]

More extensively, outside the charmed circle of money, the city seethes like a world of lesser organisms, from which Florence seeks to separate herself. Paralleling Lily's horror of the 'promiscuous', Janowitz presents a vision of gross physicality. Towards the end, the narrative moves into the crowded subway, to the underworld of the dingy, viewed in close-up: slurping drinks, clipping nails, combing hair. Taking its cue from Wharton's first chapter, at this station, the text presents 'a whole carful of a species scarcely less evolved, just as ill-mannered, as chimpanzees'.[58] In this trope, a nightmare of melting or merging, readers might ask, as critics have of Wharton, about the cultural moment of the novel; about the intensity of Florence's disgust. Does the text hint at any alternative beyond her vision? The narrative as a whole avoids resolution, drifting backwards, out of history: 'It was one of those days when the whole city smelled of fish and fishy water, a primordial fragrance churned from the limnetic source. This was how it

54 Viewable at Edith Wharton *The House of Mirth*, Typescript. Image ID 1027020. <http://beinecke .library.yale.edu/dl_crosscollex/> (accessed 7 July 2005).
55 Janowitz, *A Certain Age*, p. 73.
56 Janowitz, *A Certain Age*, p. 237.
57 Janowitz, *A Certain Age*, p. 70.
58 Janowitz, *A Certain Age*, pp. 301–2.

must have smelled a million years ago on earth, the odor of something straining to become something else'.[59]

Ending 'not with a finality', Janowitz leaves all questions open: is Florence heading towards the Hudson or the Statue of Liberty? Will she sell the jewels and save herself (like Wharton's Undine Spragg)? Or disappear into the water (like Kate Chopin's Edna Pontellier)?[60] For New York, at the millennium, is the primordial soup an end or beginning? In which direction is it evolving? Perhaps *The House of Mirth* lies behind not ahead. In a text that is itself always 'straining to become something else', can any metamorphosis lie beyond?

After *A Certain Age*, Candace Bushnell's *Trading Up* might seem, at first reading, less gritty and interrogative; and was, indeed, treated by some reviewers as true-life gossip. Its sources, however, lie in literary texts – including two of Wharton's own sharpest society novels. The additional presence of Wharton's later novel, *The Custom of the Country*, as a further major hypotext, complicates direct comparisons either with *A Certain Age* or with *The House of Mirth* itself. By merging two of Wharton's society beauties – the refined, somewhat passive Lily Bart and the vulgar, hard-nosed Undine Spragg – in her own Janey Wilcox, Bushnell (despite her stated intentions) reinterprets Lily as a survivor. Opening in summer 2000, with the World Trade Center's twin towers visible from Selden Rose's office window, *Trading Up* directs readers' attention to a global history hidden from the characters. With this *aide-memoire* at the margins, Bushnell focuses on Janey's ruthlessly self-centred vision. Echoing Miss Bart's 'faculty for renewing herself in new scenes' (I: ii, 234), the narrative captures the society of the makeover. Looking back to Wharton, and to Bushnell's own *Four Blondes*, it produces a sequence of multiple renewals out of the gaps in Janey's previous stories.

Reading Bushnell's text raises anew questions about the author's perspective on women's lives framed by Wharton's feminist critics in the wake of second-wave feminism (see Critical history, **pp. 72–4** and **75–6**). The text presents readers with a vision of women's behaviour which might seem remote from the overtly feminist constructions of sisterhood, self-awareness and political purpose in many women's narratives of the late 1960s–1970s.[61] Yet, in this society of bitches and rivals, it is possible, as it is in Lily Bart's similar terrain, to read a critique of power-structures damaging to women. In a life of poses (Janey, like Lily, knows the charm of self-arrangement on a balustrade), Janey identifies herself as a feminist – in her terms, a woman who uses men. Readers discover what Janey's self-definition represses: the sordid abuses in the depths of her history. *The House of Mirth* reserves Lily's worst experience for the present: the encounter with Trenor in the silent room. In the (now controversial) plot sequence, of a possible marriage to the Jewish Simon Rosedale, some critics (though by no means all) see Wharton hinting at further horrors (see Critical readings, **p. 79**). *Trading Up*, however, buries Janey's abuses in her past, in a racist, Orientalist nightmare: her hire as a

---

59 Janowitz, *A Certain Age*, p. 314.
60 Edith Wharton, *The Custom of the Country*, 1913, ed. Stephen Orgel, Oxford: Oxford University Press, 1995, p. 238; Kate Chopin, '*The Awakening*' 1899 *and Other Stories*, ed. Pamela Knights, Oxford: Oxford University Press, 2000, pp. 127–8.
61 For a helpful overview, see Imelda Whelehan, *The Feminist Bestseller: From* Sex and the Single Girl *to* Sex and the City, Basingstoke: Palgrave, 2005, especially pp. 93–118.

sex slave on Rasheed's Mediterranean yacht. Repeatedly, as Bushnell remarks, men 'rescue' Janey, in a spiralling narrative where victim and abuser become hard to distinguish. 'Selden Rose', like both Selden and Rosedale (fused in his name), regards himself as the heroine's saviour: he 'fervently believed that if he could only get her away from this world, the real Janey Wilcox would blossom'.[62] Bushnell exposes the dream as delusion. Janey marries him, but leaves him. Like Undine Spragg, in *The Custom of the Country*, she becomes her own rescuer, with each setback returning the stronger – in this trajectory, trading upwards. The novel concludes with Janey, like Undine, on the point of further conquest. In a self-reflexive moment, Janey urges a hostile ex-lover to produce *Custom*'s first screen adaptation; and, in her mythic movement westward, ends the novel poised, perhaps, to make the movie herself: 'From her vantage point high in the Hollywood Hills, the twinkling lights of Los Angeles lay spread out beneath her like a golden carpet, welcoming her.'[63]

At the (resonantly named) *Vanity Fair* party, Bushnell posits gendered readings of Janey: a new male admirer sees 'the sad eyes of a weary angel'; a powerful woman studio boss sees 'the perpetually turning wheels of ambition'.[64] As web sites witness, Janey provokes many readers (of both sexes) to nothing but dislike.[65] Others, as Janowitz too discovered, see a counter-story, of vulnerability, chagrin and ever-diminishing control. Here the text merges closely with *The House of Mirth*. Lily has a 'fatalistic sense of being drawn from one wrong turning to another, without ever perceiving the right road till it was too late to take it' (I: xii, 164). So Janey senses some missed direction, 'spawning a series of branches that had also become wrong paths, and yet she had trudged on, hoping that one of the paths would somehow lead her back to the right road'.[66] Like Lily, she takes 'the path of least resistance – the one she always took'.[67] Like Lily, too, she has grown up believing in 'sentimental crap'[68] as Bill Westacott, the novel's own actual Selden figure, insists on telling her: 'Where was this fantastic life her beauty was supposed to bring her?' as she first exclaims.[69] Janowitz's Florence drifts towards deliquescence, in a city where everything is 'being forced to meld, to merge'.[70] Janey's movement, from model to celebrity to studio dominatrix, is one of increasing disembodiment – from a body as 'art',[71] through a set of remakings, to the possible movie of her life. In her journey here, Lily becomes Undine; but Bushnell reprises the closing of *The House of Mirth*, as Westacott seems to absolve her: 'She reached out and touched his face, and he leaned his head into her

62 Bushnell, *Trading Up*, p. 84
63 Bushnell, *Trading Up*, p. 504.
64 Bushnell, *Trading Up*, p. 490.
65 Examples are numerous, and any search engine will lead to reviewers and readers in avid argument – see, for instance, the comments by readers at eNotalone <http://www.enotalone.com>; Juliet Waters, 'Bland Ambition', at Montreal Mirror Archives, 17–23 July 2003, available online at <http://www.montrealmirror.com/ARCHIVES/2003>; Mark Lindquist, Review, 'Bushnell Takes Another Stab at Skewering New York's Social Circles', 25 July 2003, available online at <http://www.marklindquist.net> (all accessed 15 April 2005).
66 Bushnell, *Trading Up*, p. 328.
67 Bushnell, *Trading Up*, p. 355.
68 Bushnell, *Trading Up*, p. 79.
69 Bushnell, *Four Blondes*, 2000; London, Abacus, 2003, p. 60.
70 Janowitz, *A Certain Age*, p. 302.
71 Bushnell, *Trading Up*, p. 266.

palm, holding her eyes with his. In that instant, all their knowledge of each other—all their rivalries and resentments, their desires and aspirations—seemed to pass silently between them, and all was forgiven.'[72]

Conclusion: going 'beyond'? Wharton in 'gossip lit'

> It was almost impossible to find our table because Muffy had bunches of white lilies and candles so densely packed in the room you could barely see a yard in front of you. (Flower-wise, the Lily Jungle is absolutely it right now in Manhattan despite the inherent navigational difficulties.)[73]

Bushnell's work is often marketed under the recent label, 'gossip lit' – a subgenre of the currently flourishing outpourings of 'chick lit' This further set of hypertexts, which can be only gestured at in concluding this essay, spread Wharton's influence further. Manhattan gossip lit, of which the British-born Plum Sykes's *Bergdorf Blondes* (2004) will serve as an example, is now producing its own Lily Jungle. Sykes herself, resenting labelling, insists: 'Honestly, if Edith Wharton published "The Custom of the Country" now, it would be considered chick lit.'[74] Wharton's name appears (with Jane Austen's) in increasing numbers of reviews and interviews, as the genre continues to appropriate classic texts, and critical studies are multiplying.[75] Harold Bloom identifies the 'anxiety of influence', as a generative struggle for 'high-art' male writers, locked in creative combat with their great predecessors.[76] In contemporary women's chick lit, empathy seems perhaps the stronger force. Such constructions of influence acquire New Age inflections, as younger authors suggest they are taking on the voice, even the presence of the earlier writer: 'trying to channel Edith Wharton', as one review remarked.[77] If Wharton is read as a feminist, such claims might seem slight – even a betrayal. For some, gossip lit might seem the essence of narcissism (Sykes's self-obsessed narrator is known only as '*moi*'). Others, however, might celebrate its post-feminism, reading the narratives as self-conscious critique. (Novels such as Lauren Weisberger's *The Devil Wears Prada* [2003] are clearly stretching the genre.)[78]

---

72 Bushnell, *Trading Up*, p. 502.
73 Sykes, *Bergdorf Blondes*, p. 41.
74 Interview. Deborah Solomons, 'Hazards of New Fortunes', *New York Times*, 30 May 2004, Note the allusion here to an earlier wave of nineteenth-century city fictions, in the echo of William Dean Howells' title (see Text and contexts, **p. 29**).
75 See, for example, the discussion of Wharton's fiction (including *The House of Mirth*), and that of Austen, Charlotte Brontë and others, by Juliette Wells, 'Mothers of Chick Lit? Women Writers, Readers, and Literary History', in Suzanne Ferriss and Mallory Young, eds, *Chick Lit: The New Woman's Fiction*, New York and London: Routledge, 2006, pp. 47–70 (this appeared as this guide was in process). Screen adaptations of Wharton's novels also feature in the listings in Jo Berry and Angie Errigo, *Chick Flicks: Movies Women Love*, London: Orien, 2004. Jane Austen receives special attention in Jennifer Crusie, ed., with Glenn Yeffeth, *Flirting with Pride and Prejudice: Fresh Perspectives on the Original Chick-Lit Masterpiece*, Dallas, Tex.: Benbella Books, 2005.
76 Harold Bloom, *The Anxiety of Influence: A Theory of Poetry*, 2nd edn, New York; Oxford: Oxford University Press, 1997.
77 Claire Dederer, editorial review: *Trading Up* <www.amazon.com> (accessed 15 April 2005).
78 The screen adaptation, dir. David Frankel, 2006, appeared too late to be discussed here; however, its reviews will offer readers scope for further investigation.

Unlike Bushnell's and Janowitz's narratives, chick lit, however, does not usually 'write beyond the ending' (to take the feminist critic Rachel Blau DuPlessis's phrase). DuPlessis suggests that 'Writing beyond the ending means the transgressive invention of narrative strategies, strategies that express critical dissent from dominant narrative.'[79] For the nineteenth-century novel tradition, this concept alerts us to the enduring force of the energies of the central narrative line, beyond the conventional ending. DuPlessis cites Lily Bart as an example: it is because she expends her energies outside the traditional marriage plot that she suffers the kind of punitive death meted out to transgressive nineteenth-century heroines.[80] On the contrary, in most chick lit, as in Plum Sykes's narrative, the romance plot, what DuPlessis terms the 'aura around the couple'[81] is paramount. Lily's aspirations, her gesture to the inexpressible, reappear throughout *Bergdorf Blondes*, but are explicated in the narrator's glossary: 'Manhattan Shorthand: A Translation': '3. Beyond – not somewhere far away. It's a substitute superlative replacing words like fabulous/stunning/gorgeous. E.g. "That eyebrow wax is beyond".'[82]

Some readers may regard such reworkings as a travesty of Wharton's complex and searching vision. But others may agree with Janowitz, Bushnell and Sykes: that Wharton and these new Manhattan writers are compatriots – translators of women's lives in the modern city.

79 Rachel Blau DuPlessis, *Writing Beyond the Ending: Narrative Strategies of Twentieth-Century Women Writers*, Bloomington, Ind.: Indiana University Press, 1985, p. 5.
80 DuPlessis, *Writing Beyond the Ending*, pp. 15–17.
81 DuPlessis, *Writing Beyond the Ending*, p. 5.
82 Sykes, *Bergdorf Blondes*, p. 32.

4

Performance/adaptation

'[. . .] in interpreting Miss Bart's state of mind, so many alternative readings were possible.'

(II: iii, 251)

Introduction

Raising ripples of guesswork and gossip throughout the narrative, Lily's story has continued to provoke readers to similarly endless speculation; and alongside its many critical reappraisals, *The House of Mirth*, with its rich interpretative possibilities, has inspired numerous imaginative responses. Sadly, some have been lost – the 1918 silent screen adaptation among them; but readers can revisit Wharton's plot and style, her heroine's life, her social and psychological vision, in novels (see Critical readings, **pp. 127–41**), drama, dance and film. For writers and directors, one recurring pressure has been to keep Lily alive, to let her marry Selden: to provide, in short, the 'tragedy with a happy ending' that, as William Dean Howells generalised after the failure of the first Broadway staging, is 'what the American public always wants'.[1] Whether they resist or explore such variants, to suggest the range of these reworkings and to look more closely at some examples will be the main business of this chapter. All have their own independent existence, but, whether in passing allusions or in sustained treatments, they can also offer fresh viewpoints on Wharton's writing.

Edith Wharton: transplanting Lily

It was as she had said to Selden—people were tired of her. They would welcome her in a new character, but as Miss Bart they knew her by heart. She knew herself by heart too, and was sick of the old story.

(I: ix, 136)

1   Wharton, *A Backward Glance*, p. 147.

Although her readers showed few signs of being tired of Lily, Wharton herself was the first to publish stories which supplemented or offered alternative visions of her narrative. There are elements of *The House of Mirth* in 'The Introducers' (1905–6), in its close relation, 'Les Metteurs en Scène' ['The Producers'], written in French, and published in September 1908 in the *Revue des Deux Mondes* (where the novel had been serialised); and in her novel, *The Glimpses of the Moon* (1922). (*Glimpses* itself was screened, in a silent version, by Paramount in 1923; this is now lost.) All these enable readers to revisit the novel's general social milieu, and, though never finding 'a happy ending', to test, to various degrees, a different resolution of some of its situations and central relationships.

'Les Metteurs en Scène' and *The Glimpses of the Moon*

Each text offers a version of Lily Bart: in 'Les Metteurs en Scène', Blanche Lambart (a name with a striking echo), who seems to be 'a casualty of New York society, too poor to resist the luxury that surrounded her, yet too proud and particular to tie herself down to a second-rate marriage';[2] in *The Glimpses of the Moon*, 'Susy Branch, pauper' who was 'fond of picturing' how her fancied double, 'Susy Branch, heiress', would imaginatively employ her millions.[3] Each is self-possessed, charming and fascinating, to a similarly situated man.

Miss Lambart, like Lily and Carry, helps the *nouveaux riches* to make their way in Parisian society. Attractive 'in a unique and undefinable way', she precariously manages a life 'at the expense of people she despised'.[4] The story allows her a qualified form of the freedom Lily craves: she maintains a tiny apartment, where she 'received callers with the independence of a married woman'[5] and preserves a friendship with Jean Le Fanois, her male equivalent. The narrative takes the friends beyond their customary collegiality, playing out the fantasy that the Lambart/Le Fanois pair will be able to adore each other in 'a fairy tale'.[6] Fortune bestows a gift of a million dollars, but metaphors of manipulation and string-pulling dominate the story, and Fate catches out its lovers in a punitive twist at the story's close. The story's final paragraphs, filled with discomfort and bitterness, could not be further from the silent tableau of *The House of Mirth*.

In a further step, *The Glimpses of the Moon* sees Susy married to Nick Lansing, her counterpart, in an experiment which gives a different turn to Lily and Selden's musings at the rock-ledge at Bellomont (I: vi): 'Why shouldn't they marry; belong to each other openly and honourably, if for ever so short a time, and with the definite understanding that whenever either of them got the chance to do better he or she should be immediately released?'[7]

2   'Les Metteurs en Scène' in *The Stories of Edith Wharton*, selected and introduced by Anita Brookner, Vol. II, London: Simon and Schuster, 1989, pp. 87–8.
3   Edith Wharton, *The Glimpses of the Moon*, 1922; London: Virago, 1995, p. 6.
4   Wharton, 'Les Metteurs en Scène', p. 87.
5   Wharton, 'Les Metteurs en Scène', p. 89.
6   Wharton'Les Metteurs en Scène', p. 97.
7   Wharton, *Glimpses of the Moon*, p. 21.

Wharton follows through this doomed bargain in a narrative which Hildegarde Hoeller suggests 'was written to disappoint those sentimental hopes that "the word not spoken" between Selden and Lily had left'.[8] Hoeller also cites, as 'another link in a chain of revisions and self-references' an undated synopsis Wharton composed under the title 'Love Among the Ruins' (after the poem by Robert Browning). This story remained unwritten, but Wharton left the draft in her papers, now held by the Beinecke Library and Rare Books archive at Yale University. (Hoeller helpfully reproduces the whole synopsis.) It suggests a dim future for the couple – a mismatched existence as 'a humdrum married pair'.[9]

'The Introducers'

Looking in detail at any of these narratives brings out more of the crosslights which Wharton casts on her textual hinterland. Take, for example, the earliest: 'The Introducers', which came out in *Ainslee's* magazine, in December 1905 and January 1906.[10] (With the cover-line, 'The Magazine That Entertains', *Ainslee's* had been an all-story magazine since 1902, and aimed at a wide general audience. The cover of the January issue featured an elegant Society lady, in scarlet, with black furs and a striking plumed hat.[11]) Appearing as sales of *The House of Mirth* continued to escalate, the story evokes, in particular, the episode with Mrs Hatch, one of Lily's most sordid entanglements and the occasion of Selden's harshest disapproval. In *The Custom of the Country* (1913), Wharton would invert the emphasis. There she brings to the centre Undine Spragg, who occupies Mrs Hatch's position as aspirant outsider, albeit one more destructive even than in Selden's direst implications. In 'The Introducers', however, her interest remains with those who help such newcomers navigate Society. Here, she implicates her hero and heroine in mirrored parts: both Miss Belle Grantham (Lily) and Mr Frederick Tilney (Selden) are cast as social secretaries to the new rich of Newport, paid to manoeuvre their clients into select gatherings and select marriages, and playing, in effect, the part of procurers. (A further literary intertext invites more speculation about Tilney/Selden's character: from the opening sentence, his name points back to *Northanger Abbey*, Jane Austen's reworking of the Gothic novel, where Captain Frederick Tilney, the hero's brother, is notorious as a shallow, mischief-making flirt.) The history of their lapsed ideals, their professional and private disappointments, is kept light. Nonetheless, the dishonour of their roles emerges plainly in Miss Grantham's succinct self-description as 'a circulating beauty',[12] and in the

8 Hoeller, *Edith Wharton's Dialogue with Realism and Sentimental Fiction*, p. 137.
9 Hoeller, *Edith Wharton's Dialogue with Realism and Sentimental Fiction*, pp. 137–8.
10 *Ainslee's* 16, December 1905, pp. 139–48; 16, January 1906, pp. 61–7. Wharton did not collect the story in book form; it is reprinted in Wharton, *Collected Stories 1891–1910*, pp. 548–77; and in Beer and Nolan, eds, *The House of Mirth*, Peterborough, Ontario: Broadview Press, 2005, pp. 453–80. It can also be accessed at the Edith Wharton Society web site (see Further reading and Web resources, **p. 160**).
11 This may be viewed on the 'Magazine Issues' pages of the 'Galactic Central' site at http:// www.philsp.com/data/images/a/ainslees_190601.jpg (accessed 13 July 2005).
12 Wharton, 'The Introducers', p. 552.

small hesitations and blushes that mark the dialogue, as each acknowledges their failures.

Wharton designs the story like a set for a one-act farce, with parallel entrances and exits, and characters watching each other from concealment, with mutterings and exclamations. The theatricality recalls images from *The House of Mirth*, that this world, with its 'whizzing social machinery' is 'all part of the stupid show—the expensive stage setting of a rottenly cheap play—to be folded up and packed away with the rest of the rubbish when the performance is over'.[13] Into this stylised spectacle, Wharton infuses different notes, bringing out the costs of 'the wreckage of many shattered illusions', the sense of moral miasma: 'I don't see anything more than if the fog were inside me!'[14]

The narrative keeps the new rich largely at a distance, viewed only through the eyes of their hirelings. Some readers might feel that the story is weighted too much on the side of the fastidious social insiders, a lament for 'old' gentility overpowered by invaders. Tilney, for example, describes his employer, an upstart millionaire, as a 'monster [. . .] the Minotaur'.[15] But Wharton keeps sympathies in balance. In a sequence of echoes of *The House of Mirth*, Tilney and Miss Grantham seek their version of a republic of the spirit, outside a society of 'fools'.[16] Finally, discovering even their private trysting place colonised by their employers, they have to look beyond. In Tilney's 'huge, world-defying laugh' (a gesture which readers wait in vain to hear from Selden), the story hints that they will find their space. But its final sentence is equivocal – hinting that once the monsters are loose, there might be nowhere 'Beyond!' for Old New York to go: 'Don't you see [. . .] nothing remains for you and me but to find a new seat for ourselves?'[17]

The House of Mirth on stage

Wharton and Clyde Fitch

The theatrical metaphors of *The House of Mirth* appear in the foreground of many critical interpretations, but presenting the novel's social spectacle on an actual stage posed problems. Wharton declared herself against any such project:

> Once 'The House of Mirth' had started on its prosperous career I was of course beseiged with applications for leave to dramatize it; but I refused them all, convinced that (apart from the intrinsic weakness of most plays drawn from books) there was nothing in this particular book out of which to make a play. Great was my surprise, therefore, when I heard that Clyde Fitch, then at the height of his career, was eager to undertake the task.[18]

13 Wharton, 'The Introducers', pp. 548, 549.
14 Wharton, 'The Introducers', pp. 562, 577.
15 Wharton, 'The Introducers', p. 571.
16 Wharton, 'The Introducers', p. 549.
17 Wharton, 'The Introducers', p. 577.
18 Wharton, *A Backward Glance*, pp. 160–1.

Though surprised, she was flattered into collaborating. Fitch was the most famous American playwright of his day ('earning from his plays alone upwards of $250,000.00 a year, in a time when a dollar a day was a working wage');[19] and his work, though now largely forgotten, seemed consonant with Wharton's. He was a realist, interested in the social scene, and it was said that his plays, 'would give "future generations a better idea of American life from 1890 to 1910 than newspapers or historical records." '[20] (*The Climbers*, [1905] for example, shares ingredients with *The House of Mirth*, including an interest in social ambition and decline, a father's death, the need for leisure-class women to seek work, and even a suicide through chloral.[21]) Although Wharton discovered later that Fitch himself had been manoeuvred into the project, through being told of Wharton's eagerness to work with him, they completed the adaptation. The drama was tried out in Detroit, on 17 September 1906, and reported a success: 'The play follows closely the outline of the book, the characters and situations being practically unchanged. It was received with approval by the audience. Miss Fay Davis appeared as Lily Bart, and gave an excellent performance. Mrs. Wharton and a party of friends saw the performance.'[22]

After the first night, however, it declined; and, despite some hurried rewriting, in its transfer to New York in October, it was a flop. The disaster roused a flurry of commentary and a fresh wave of publicity for the book. Headlines asked why a best-selling novel should fail as a play; rumours circulated (denied by both parties) about clashes between the collaborators; and readers had their say in the letter columns:

> Permit me, through the columns of your entertaining paper, to commend the good taste of the New York theatre-going folk for exhibiting so unmistakably their dislike for the dramatization of 'The House of Mirth,' that much overpraised and tedious tale. I wonder at any one tackling such a dolorous story with a view to producing an attractive play.[23]

Much of the commentary, however, was more reflective, and the circumstances unleashed heated discussion about the condition of American theatre, particularly in contrast with that of France. In Paris, it was said, audiences could attend to serious, quiet, drama; in New York, they demanded the obvious. Wharton's opinion was sought, and a high-profile article emphasised her admiration for Fitch's work. It reported that she had thought in Detroit 'the interpretation of Miss Fay Davis an almost perfect interpretation of Lily Bart'; but in New York, it had 'faded artistically'. The following extracts give a unique insight into how actively Wharton became involved in the actual production, and into the strength of her responses:

---

19 Wayne S. Turney, 'Clyde Fitch (1865–1909): Playwright, Regisseur', available online at www .wayneturney.20m.com/fitchclyde.htm (accessed 13 July 2005).
20 Walter Pritchard Eaton, quoted by Turney 'Clyde Fitch' . . .
21 Available online at http://www.gutenberg.org/etext/16635 (accessed 13 July 2005).
22 *New York Times*, 18 September 1906, p. 9.
23 Letter, *New York Times*, 30 October 1906, p. 8.

'The House of Mirth' on its return trip from the West to New York, underwent a rapid revision of such atmosphere as Mrs. Wharton had insisted upon, even to the point of instructing Miss Davis to interpret hysterics at the end of the third act—'to strengthen the play'. [. . .] A comparison of the characters as they live in the book and as they strutted upon the stage left Mrs. Wharton in a coma of amazement [. . .] Those who know the authoress of the novel, who are the sort of people who have standards of deportment and feeling that are without hysteria, or limelight effects, understand her surprise.[24]

The interviewer, too, takes up the debate about interpretation; and is particularly sensitive to the problems of representing interior drama – here termed, in a strikingly modern phrase, 'psychologic moments':

Ladies and gentlemen are not noisy, their restrictions of manner are standards of breeding, and there are psychologic moments in the human play of their emotions that they don't talk about, but that they show, nevertheless, and yet the authoress was asked to give them words, to make them talk, when the drama of the situation was in the proper proportion of silence.[25]

As is often the case with adaptations of novels today, many readers saw the adaptation as a betrayal of what they valued in the book. As the interviewer emphasises: 'The trouble, say Mrs. Wharton's friends and admirers, is that "The House of Mirth" was the real thing in its own field, and the theatre reduced it to a claptrap drama of unreality.'[26]

Fitch was interviewed, in turn, in a piece about the death of the play, presented in metaphors of an inquest. While recalling the 'vitality and excitement' of the first night in Detroit, he admitted to having made mistakes with casting, to problems in rehearsal and to loss of clarity in the outline, but he insisted on the intrinsic merits of both book and drama. His purpose had been firm:

It was either to transcribe the book intact to the stage, or not at all. Of course, usually, the book play is a version, or perversion, of its literary intention [. . .] 'The House of Mirth' was a negative story, however, and for that reason was particularly an innovation to rules of the stage.[27]

Above all, he praised Wharton's abilities ('Mrs. Wharton's dialogue was brilliant, there is no question about that') and her potential as a dramatist:

'Then what was the cause of the death of this play?' asked the jury of one.
    'The American theatregoer chiefly, and the unpopularity of purely literary plays. But I hope that Mrs. Wharton will not be discouraged; I

24 'Mrs. Wharton's Views on the Society Drama', New York Times, 28 October 1906, p. 2.
25 'Mrs. Wharton's Views on the Society Drama', p. 2.
26 'Mrs. Wharton's Views on the Society Drama', p. 2.
27 'Clyde Fitch Discusses "The House of Mirth" ', New York Times, 4 November 1906, p. 2.

hope she will write another play, for she has with the distinction of her dialogue true dramatic instinct. She does not need me or any one else to write a really fine play.'[28]

Modern revivals: drama and dance

Wharton's account of her work with Fitch, and their play's unfortunate history, has led many readers to assume that *The House of Mirth* in performance might hold little of interest. The script was never published in Wharton's lifetime, and, while there have been a number of subsequent adaptations,[29] the Wharton-Fitch version lay neglected until the end of the century. Its successful revival in 1998 at the Mint Theater in New York City, however, awakened critical interest in the drama itself and opened up new dimensions of the novel. Introducing his edition, the director Jonathan Bank explains that his interest lay initially in exploring Fitch's work, as 'the first millionaire dramatist in America'.[30] Drawn to seek out the play by the 'irresistible'[31] combination of Wharton and Fitch, Bank, who had not at that time read the novel, found Lily's story deeply moving.

Discussing performance disturbs traditional ideas of authorship – Bank's production, drawn from a collation of four typescripts, emerged from a collaboration between editor, actors and director, as well as between a novelist and a playwright. The audience themselves contribute: as Bank says of the staging, 'If the story is compelling enough, they won't miss the details.'[32] However, Bank himself emphasises Wharton's chief role: he suggests that working with Fitch gave her a 'second chance' to revisit her narrative and express some areas more fully.[33] (In the pressure of serial composition, she would have had no chance to return to earlier chapters.) His striking example offers an image of a reworking which allows Lily to fill in her own story. On the yacht, she explains to Selden:

> Some letters—no matter how—came into possession of a woman I know. They were written by another woman to the man my friend loves—and they tell a story he has never told her—the story of a love he grew tired of, just as he may grow tired of hers—and sometimes, my friend says, when she's alone, that writing comes out so plainly that it blackens the whole page of her happiness. But the moment she hears his voice and looks into his eyes the page is washed white again—she doesn't know who wrote on it before![34]

28 'Clyde Fitch Discusses "The House of Mirth" ', p. 2.
29 Among them, an adaptation by John Tillinger (USA, 1976); by the Wharton scholar, Louis Auchincloss (USA, 1977); by Annie Castledine and Dawn Keeler (UK, 1995).
30 Jonathan Bank, ed., *Worthy but Neglected: Plays of the Mint Theater Company*, New York: Granville Press, 2002, p. 49.
31 Bank, *Worthy but Neglected*, p. 3.
32 Bank, *Worthy but Neglected*, p. 51.
33 Jonathan Bank, Conference address, 'Celebrating the Centenary of Edith Wharton's *The House of Mirth*', Marist College, Poughkeepsie, NY, 25 June 2005.
34 Edith Wharton and Clyde Fitch, *The House of Mirth*, adapted by Jonathan Bank, *Worthy but Neglected*, p. 80.

While Bank wanted to bring out emotional nuance, he also kept in view the social drama (a strong feature of the dialogue, which specialises in the barbed retort, the snide undertone). A dominant metaphor in the Mint Theater's design was the cage, created by the use of a rolling gazebo, which characters entered, left or surrounded. What, on the page of the playscript, seems a conventional drawing-room drama, in performance becomes poetic, stylised. (A photograph in *Worthy But Neglected* captures such a moment.[35])

Another recent New York City production, *Innocents*, transformed the story into dance. Conceived, directed and adapted by Rachel Dickstein, with Emily Morse as dramaturge, this production opened at the Ohio Theater, in New York City, 8 January 2005. Cages, again, featured as a unifying image. Performers were viewed through screens and veils, the women's bodies gripped in visible corsets.[36] Here, Lily is a trapped creature, a butterfly, caught whirling in movement and music, swept along in a narrative of money and ambition. Created over eighteen months, in an ensemble production, *Innocents* stripped the novel down to rhythms of repeated dialogue, of obsessive movement. Wishing to convey the story, but not wanting to have Edith Wharton sitting by the side of the stage to narrate it, Dickstein and Morse sought ways of representing the 'prison of character', of asking what was going on in Lily's mind.[37] To 'reflect on' Lily, they doubled the actors, using the performer playing Gerty to embody her other self – a solution that dramatises the 'mirrors' of Gothic readings (see Critical readings, pp. 116–26).

The House of Mirth on screen

The House of Mirth was first adapted for screen in 1918, in a silent, six-reel production, directed by Albert Capellani, with Capellani and June Mathis's screenplay. This version remains lost. A television version (95 minutes long) was made in 1981, starring Geraldine Chaplin as Lily; this was directed by Adrian Hall, who created the screenplay with Richard Cumming.[38] A later screening, however, made more impact. Terence Davies, the British Film Director, chiefly renowned for his art-house, often autobiographical, low-budget but highly critically regarded films, wrote the screenplay and directed the film of *The House of Mirth*, released in 2000. This version, which has reached a wide audience, is the subject of discussion here.

The film, shot on location in Glasgow as well as in the south of France, is a less sumptuous representation of Wharton's New York than that which characterises the film of *The Age of Innocence* (1993) directed by Martin Scorsese. In Davies'

---

35 Photograph by Jonathan Bank, *Worthy but Neglected*, p. 3, and on cover.
36 For review and photographs from 'Innocents', see Ellen Carpenter, 'Bringing Down the House of Mirth', 9 January 2005, available online at www.offoffonline.com/index.html (accessed 13 July 2005).
37 Rachel Dickstein and Emily Morse. Conference address, 'Celebrating the Centenary of *The House of Mirth*', 25 June 2005.
38 See Scott Marshall, 'Edith Wharton on Film and Television: A Filmography', in Sarah Bird Wright, ed., *Edith Wharton A to Z: The Essential Guide to the Life and Work*, New York: Facts on File, 1998, pp. 287–95.

rendition, the New York of *The House of Mirth* is functional. Although aspects of Wharton's plot which treat the working classes are lost because of the absence of Gerty Farish, the life that Lily leads is filmed as being in proximity to the streets of the city and the precarious lives of New York's poorest citizens. From the outset, the locations where the drama is played out have the feel of public spaces, always susceptible to interruption or to being observed. Lily's precipitous hold on her place in society is reflected in the endless series of scenes where she is positioned either outdoors in the grounds of grand houses or in the street; she is often caught in liminal spaces – in halls, cafés, lobbies and the borrowed bedrooms into which others are seen to gain too easy an access. From the exposure of Lily in her new subservient role in the hotel lobby where she receives the amendments to Mrs Hatch's diary and has a public row with Selden, it is a seamless transition to the public glare of the workroom at Madame Regina's millinery establishment. She has no access to solitude and no dignity in either space, but what is clear is that the absence of any right to privacy has been true of her life among the leisured classes as well as in the working-class milieu of the workroom and the boarding house.

In laying bare the precipitous nature of Lily's life, Davies is faithful to the novel, which characterises its heroine as having 'the feeling of being something rootless and ephemeral, mere spindrift of the whirling surface of existence, without anything to which the poor little tentacles of self could cling before the awful flood submerged them' (II: xiii, 358–9). Those locations that are dignified with the name of home – Mrs Peniston's sepulchral town house and Carry Fisher's country cottage – speak either of an absence of human contact or of the fact that the proximity of human contact is too seldom experienced. It is clear in the film that it is beyond Lily's power to make anyone believe in Mrs Peniston's house as a dwelling which contains her. The scenes where the camera moves through the house as it is shrouded in dust sheets while its owner leaves the city for the summer reinforce the sense that it is a place that resists human occupation. Throughout the film – as in the novel – Lily asks, even implores, the men who want her company, to visit her in her aunt's house. Only the wrong man, Simon Rosedale, comes, unbidden, in Selden's stead, to ask what might be the right question in the right place. However, the fact of his offer – a business as well as a marriage proposal to join forces to take his conquest of New York society to a further stage – renders Lily's only home even more of a fiction as a place where intimacy could exist. Similarly, the appearance of Mrs Haffen, the blackmailing cleaner from the Benedick, in Mrs Peniston's drawing room, selling the incriminating letters to the wrong woman, reinforces the surreality of the setting. It is a place of darkness and gloom, of duplicity and misinformation, and Davies is clear that Lily is ill at ease here and vulnerable to both shame and dread. There is nowhere she can gain any respite.

The omission of the character of Gerty Farish from the film has the additional effect of heightening Lily's isolation. There is no woman whom Lily can trust – apart from Carry Fisher, and she makes no pretence that her relationship with Lily can be conducted in public since it would drive away her paying customers. The conflation in the film narrative of the characters of Gerty Farish and Grace Stepney was mentioned by Terence Davies in a press-conference question-and-answer session during the 2000 Toronto Film Festival, and reported by David Walsh.

The template is always the original material, which is the novel. And the novel is savage. I mean, these people are some of the cruelest [*sic*] you have ever come across. If there is a subversion going on, it's from the Edith Wharton. And so one simply tries to be true to that and the tone. But also, there are times when you have to alter it slightly. There are two separate characters in the film, for instance: Gertie [*sic*] Farish and Grace Stepney. Separate, they're not interesting; together, they are, because Gertie loves Lawrence. And in the book, Grace doesn't. So if they're together it makes them infinitely more powerful.[39]

The convergence of the sexual jealousy which Gerty feels towards Lily and the familial and financial jealousy Grace feels towards her allows Davies an economy of plot which also intensifies the sense of the whispering campaign being mounted against Lily and highlights her carelessness, her lack of attention to those agents who might wish her ill. Lily's haughty dismissal of Simon Rosedale in the lobby of the Benedick at the beginning of the film is the first political error we see her perform; many others follow. Davies decks Lily in the reddest of dresses to appear in the opera box with Gus Trenor and Simon Rosedale on opening night and has the dialogue in which Grace Stepney gives Mrs Peniston just sufficient information to allow her to think Lily has become Gus Trenor's mistress to take place while the women observe her on public display.

While the history of Lily's indiscretions and careless behaviour is laid before us in the film so, however, is the real sense of erotic attraction between Selden and Lily. Davies exploits the fact that it was still controversial for a woman to smoke by giving the lighting of Lily's cigarette from Selden's own an erotic charge that almost makes the kisses between them anticlimactic. One illicit, questionable act for a woman – the smoking of a cigarette – becomes a visible substitute for another. Davies' Selden is kinder than Wharton's, but he is no more satisfactory as a romantic lead. The film offers no hostages to sentimentality; Davies' gaze is no less unflinching than Wharton's, and his Lily Bart just as clearly a 'victim of the civilization which had produced her' (I: i, 41).

---

39 David Walsh, 'Terence Davies' *The House of Mirth*: a comment and a press conference with the director', 28 December 2000, available online at www.wsws.org/articles/2000/oct2000/tff5-o09.shtml (accessed 13 February 2005).

5

Further reading and web resources

Further reading

The majority of the following books are referred to in the text; many of them are commented on in 'Critical history'. As there is a wealth of criticism on *The House of Mirth*, and readers will wish to pursue and develop their own individual lines of interest, this section offers a wide-ranging selection. The section headings in 'Critical history' indicate starting points for different lines of bibliographic research, but here they are simply divided into 'Auto/Biography and letters' and 'Critical studies'.

Auto/biography and letters

Benstock, Shari. *No Gifts from Chance: A Biography of Edith Wharton*. New York: Scribner's, 1994. A solid biography from a critic whose special interest is American women writers in Europe.

Dwight, Eleanor. *Edith Wharton: An Extraordinary Life*. New York: Abrams, 1994. Contains a large number of good photographs of Wharton's houses, gardens, life and times.

Lewis, R. W. B. *Edith Wharton*. London: Constable, 1975. The foundation biography, the first major account of the writer's life to be published after the Wharton archive became accessible to scholars.

Lewis, R. W. B. and Nancy Lewis, eds. *The Letters of Edith Wharton*. New York: Scribner's, 1988.

Powers, Lyall H. *Henry James and Edith Wharton: Letters: 1900–1915*. New York: Scribner's, 1990. This volume contains letters between the two writers offering vivid insights into their craft and their friendship.

Wharton, Edith. *A Backward Glance*. New York: D. Appleton-Century, 1934. Wharton's own, very discrete, memoir, written when she was a public figure.

——'Life and I', in *Novellas and Other Writings*, selected Cynthia Griffin Wolff, New York: The Library of America, 1990. An autobiographical fragment, which is much more revealing about Wharton's family and upbringing.

Wolff, Cynthia Griffin. *A Feast of Words: The Triumph of Edith Wharton*. New York: Oxford University Press, 1977. A pioneering biography which offers psychoanalytical readings of the life and works.

Critical studies

Ammons, Elizabeth. *Edith Wharton's Argument with America*. Athens, Ga.: University of Georgia Press, 1980. A study focusing on Wharton's women characters within the particular conditions of American society.

Beer, Janet. *Edith Wharton*. Devon: Northcote House, 2002. A brief introductory volume to the life and works.

Beer Goodwyn, Janet. *Edith Wharton: Traveller in the Land of Letters*. Basingstoke: Macmillan. 1990. A book which reads the fiction and non-fiction through landscape and autobiographical writing.

Bell, Millicent, ed. *The Cambridge Companion to Edith Wharton*. New York: Cambridge University Press, 1995. A general essay collection, in which a number of contributors focus on *The House of Mirth*.

Bentley, Nancy. *The Ethnography of Manners: Hawthorne, James, Wharton*. New York: Cambridge University Press, 1995. An extended analysis of Wharton's work in terms of anthropological treatment of cultural groups.

Erlich, Gloria. *The Sexual Education of Edith Wharton*. Berkeley, Calif.: University of California Press, 1992. Speculates about the influence of familial and sexual relationships within a selection of Wharton's writing.

Esch, Deborah. *New Essays on The House of Mirth*. Cambridge: Cambridge University Press, 2001. Offers four contrasting perspectives on the text, from influence studies to discussions of identity.

Fedorko, Kathy. *Gender and the Gothic in the Fiction of Edith Wharton*. Tuscaloosa, Ala.: University of Alabama Press, 1995. A ground-breaking work which opened up the study of Wharton to non-realist readings.

Fryer, Judith. *Felicitous Space: The Imaginative Structures of Edith Wharton and Willa Cather*. Chapel Hill, NC: University of North Carolina Press, 1986. A treatment of Wharton which is particularly interesting for its investigation of the house and interiors in the work.

Goodman, Susan. *Edith Wharton's Women: Friends and Rivals*. Hanover, NH and London: University Press of New England, 1990. A re-evaluation of Wharton's writings alongside a consideration of her relationships with women friends and family members.

Hoeller, Hildegard. *Edith Wharton's Dialogue with Realism and Sentimental Fiction*. Gainesville, Fla.: University Press of Florida, 2000. Places Wharton's writing within an unfolding history of dominant fictional forms in the United States.

Joslin, Katherine. *Edith Wharton*. London: Macmillan, 1991. An introduction to the major novels which provides a good starting point to feminist readings of Wharton's work.

Kaplan, Amy. *The Social Construction of American Realism*. Chicago, Ill.: University of Chicago Press, 1988. A landmark intervention in the debates about the wider context and nature of realism.

Kassanoff, Jennie A. *Edith Wharton and the Politics of Race*, Cambridge: Cambridge University Press, 2004. Offers a reading of Wharton as a conservative, within American political and cultural debates of her period.

Michaels, Walter Benn. *The Gold Standard and the Logic of Naturalism*, Berkeley, Calif. and London: University of California Press, 1987. A complex and challenging book which contested conventional accounts of literary naturalism; has a section on Lily Bart.

Montgomery, Maureen E. *Displaying Women: Spectacles of Leisure in Edith Wharton's New York*. New York: Routledge, 1998. Offers historical and cultural information about middle-class mores, especially those affecting the lives of women.

Ramsden, George. *Edith Wharton's Library: A Catalogue*. York: Stone Trough Books, 1999. A catalogue of the surviving books from Wharton's extensive collection giving powerful insights into the depth and breadth of her reading.

Raphael, Lev. *Edith Wharton's Prisoners of Shame*. London and New York: Macmillan and St Martin's Press, 1991. A reading of Wharton's fiction using insights derived from the psychology of shame.

Singley, Carol J., *Edith Wharton's* The House of Mirth: *A Casebook*. Oxford: Oxford University Press, 2003. Contains a range of essays on the novel, old and new.

Singley, Carol J., *Edith Wharton: Matters of Mind and Spirit*. Cambridge: Cambridge University Press, 1995. A study which looks at Wharton's religious and philosophical debts and allegiances.

—— ed. *A Historical Guide to Edith Wharton*. New York: Oxford University Press, 2003. A useful range of essays contextualising Wharton's writing career.

Tuttleton, James W., Kristin O. Lauer and Margaret P. Murray, eds. *Edith Wharton: The Contemporary Reviews*. New York: Cambridge University Press, 1992. A volume which collects the majority of the most important reviews of Wharton's work.

Waid, Candace. *Edith Wharton's Letters from the Underworld: Fictions of Women and Writing*. Chapel Hill, NC: University of North Carolina Press, 1991. A critical analysis of six texts with reference to Wharton's ideas about the woman writer in America.

Wegener, Frederick, ed. *The Uncollected Critical Writings of Edith Wharton*. Princeton, NJ: Princeton University Press, 1998. Offers insights into Wharton's own reading and critical responses; it also reprints her introduction to the 1936 Oxford World's Classics edition of *The House of Mirth*.

Wershoven, Carol. *The Female Intruder in the Novels of Edith Wharton*. Rutherford, NJ: Farleigh Dickinson Press, 1982. This study considers the interventionist role played by women in Wharton's fiction.

Wright, Sarah Bird, ed. *Edith Wharton A to Z*. New York: Checkmark Books, 1998. The essential guide to Wharton's life and works.

Selected essays on *The House of Mirth*

The particular argument being pursued in these essays is generally evident from the titles; the selection represents different critical approaches to the novel, and the essays have been chosen for the significant influence they have had in Wharton studies. Readers new to the text will find that reading even two or three of these essays will offer a strong sense of differing perspectives.

Abbott, Reginald. ' "A Moment's Ornament": Wharton's Lily Bart and Art Nouveau'. *Mosaic* 24.2 (1991): 73–91.

Benert, Anette Larson. 'The Geography of Gender in *The House of Mirth*'. *Studies in the Novel* 22.1 (1990): 26–42.

Dimock, Wai-Chee. 'Debasing Exchange: Edith Wharton's *The House of Mirth*'. *Studies in American Fiction*, 13.1 (1985): 54–63. A pioneering Marxist treatment.

Fetterley, Judith. ' "The Temptation to a Beautiful Object": Double Standard and Double Bind in *The House of Mirth*'. *Studies in American Fiction* 5 (1977): 199–211.

Gibson, Mary Ellis. 'Edith Wharton and the Ethnography of Old New York'. *Studies in American Fiction* 13 (1985): 57–69.

Hochman, Barbara. '*The Awakening* and *The House of Mirth*: Plotting Experience and Experiencing Plot'. In Donald Pizer, ed., *The Cambridge Companion to American Realism and Naturalism: Howells to London*. New York: Cambridge University Press, 1995, pp. 211–35.

Hutchinson, Stuart. 'From *Daniel Deronda* to *The House of Mirth*'. *Essays in Criticism* 47.4 (1997): 315–42.

Pizer, Donald. 'The Naturalism of Edith Wharton's *The House of Mirth*'. *Twentieth Century Literature* 41.2 (1995): 241–8.

Riegel, Christian. 'Rosedale and Anti-Semitism in *The House of Mirth*'. *Studies in American Fiction* 20.2 (1992): 219–24.

Showalter, Elaine. 'The Death of the Lady (Novelist): Wharton's *The House of Mirth*'. *Representations* 9 (1985): 133–49.

Yeazell, Ruth Bernard. 'The Conspicuous Wasting of Lily Bart'. *English Literary History* 59 (1992): 713–34.

Web resources

Edith Wharton

For an invaluable starting point for online texts, selections of original reviews, bibliographies, queries, Wharton news and many interesting links: The Edith Wharton Society, <http://www.wsu.edu/~campbelld/wharton/index.html>.

A rich range of photographs of Wharton and her associates; and page images from Wharton's manuscripts and typescripts of *The House of Mirth*: Yale University Beinecke Rare Book and Manuscript Library, <http://beinecke.library.-yale.edu/dl_crosscollex/SearchExecXC.asp>.

'The Mount: Edith Wharton and the American Renaissance' (Kay Davis, 2001–3). This site explores Wharton's Lenox home as a model of American Renaissance estates and illuminates Wharton's architectural principles and philosophy of design (with images), <http://xroads.virginia.edu/~MA01/Davis/wharton/home/home.html>.

Other cultural and textual resources

For a range of textual and visual materials, visit the 'Xroads' site, American Studies at the University of Virginia. For example, follow the 'Hypertexts' link for Thorstein Veblen's *The Theory of the Leisure Class*; or 'The Astor Collection' to view a series of page images from *Scenes of Modern New York* (1905), <http://xroads.virginia.edu>.

For impressions of Lily Bart's New York, visit the American Memory site at the Library of Congress; go to Cities/Towns>New York City>'The Life of a City: Early Films of New York, 1898–1906': <http://memory.loc.gov/ammem>; forty-five short clips, including 'Bargain day on 14th Street' and 'The Elevated Railway'.

For a rich, searchable collection of nineteenth-century and early twentieth-century magazines and books, browse Cornell University Library's 'Making of America' site. While the extracts in 'Text and contexts' are drawn largely from rare archive sources, those interested in exploring the social aspects noted there will find rich rewards in searching this site. Read, for example, Louise Bolard More's study of the New York poor (see Text and contexts, p. 31); or look for 'A Day at a Country Home on the Hudson': <http://cdl.library.cornell.edu/moa>.

The 'Visual Arts' pages at the Victorian Web provide access to numerous images of nineteenth-century women in painting (for example, the Lady of Shalott in Pre-Raphaelite art, see Text and contexts, p. 24): <http://www.victorianweb.org/painting/prb/mariotti12.html>.

'The Gilded Age: Treasures from the Smithsonian American Art Museum', a touring exhibition, appears on a number of sites. This richly informative exhibition offers examples of leisure-class portraiture and of the decorative arts. Visit it at the Cleveland Museum of Art: <http://www.clevelandart.org/exhibcef/gilded-age/html>.

Many texts of the period are collected on the Project Gutenberg site – among them Charlotte Perkins Gilman's 'The Yellow Wallpaper' (see Text and contexts, p. 43) and her feminist journal, *The Forerunner* and *The Climbers*, a play by Clyde Fitch (see Performance/adaptation, p. 149): <http://www.gutenberg.org>.

Other contemporary texts may be found through University of Pennsylvania's 'A Celebration of Women Writers', including Charlotte Perkins Gilman, *Women and Economics* <http://digital.library.upenn.edu/women/writers.html>. This text is also available in a new scholarly edition by Michael Kimmell and Amy Aronson: <http://ark.cdlib.org/ark:/13030/ft896nb5rd>.

To see images of the Staatsburg Estate (formerly known as the Mills Mansion), believed to be the model for the Trenors' Bellomont, visit the 'Hudson Valley Network': <http://www.hvnet.com/alist/alist_dutchess_staatsburg.htm>.

Index

Index notes: Page numbers in italics refer to illustrations.

Printed in Great
Britain
by Amazon